The Best of *Jazz*

*To Steve and Jenny Voce,
under whose hospitable roof the best of jazz
constantly resounds.*

The Best of Jazz

Basin Street to Harlem

Jazz Masters and Masterpieces, 1917-1930

Humphrey Lyttelton

A CRESCENDO BOOK
TAPLINGER PUBLISHING COMPANY
New York

First published in the United States in 1979 by
TAPLINGER PUBLISHING CO., INC.
New York, New York

*Grateful acknowledgement is made to Jazz Music Books
for the photographs which appear in this book.*

LIBRARY OF CONGRESS CATALOGING IN PUBLICATION DATA

Lyttelton, Humphrey, 1921-
    The best in jazz.
    Basin Street to Harlem

    Bibliography: p.
    Discography: p.
    Includes index.
    1. Jazz music—History and criticism.   2. Jazz
musicians.   I. Title.
ML3561.J3L9   785.4′2′0922   [B]   79-13159
ISBN 0-8008-0727-8

9 8 7 6 5 4 3 2 1

Contents

Introduction

THIS BOOK sprang from a single thought. Over the ten or so years it has been running, the letters which my weekly BBC record programme 'The Best of Jazz' has attracted have complained of the difficulties that nowadays confront anyone wanting to build a sensible record collection. Albums come on to the market in great profusion bearing the names of those musicians whom, according to the pundits, every self-respecting record collection should include. Alas, there is no guarantee that, when the eager purchaser gets the record on to his turntable, it will offer up essential, important or even worthwhile examples of the artist's work. Louis Armstrong presents perhaps the most extreme example of this dilemma. An album bearing on the cover the familiar features either converging upon a trumpet mouthpiece or bisected in an inviting grin may well contain some of his greatest masterpieces. It could equally well turn out to be a collection of commercial performances bedecked with strings, a routine 'live' concert recording of no great distinction, some obscure pieces aimed primarily at collectors who know most of Louis' standard works by heart or, worst of all, a ragbag of 'airshots' in ultra-lo-fi taken down on home equipment years ago and with little to offer besides their well-deserved rarity. Fortunes can be spent on a collection of this material which, in the end, leaves the collector no better informed about Louis Armstrong's real contribution to jazz.

The thought that occurred to me was that those of us who cultivated an interest in jazz during the pre-microgroove era of 'seventy-eights' were particular lucky, though, heaven knows, we did not realise it at the time. In Britain, certainly, our monthly ration of jazz consisted of a handful of 'singles' in a special jazz-and-swing corner of the catalogues. How we grumbled at the fact that, out of maybe half-a-dozen records in this category, only two or three would conform to our rather strict notions of the 'real thing'! In the arbitrary listings, Louis Armstrong's Hot Fives would go hand in hand with Harry Parry's Sextet, Sidney Bechet's New Orleans Feetwarmers would rub shoulders with the latest from Benny Goodman and Artie Shaw. And as a result, the products of the very greatest recording sessions in jazz history were fed to us two at a time, like a sort of life-giving saline drip. In the musical papers and magazines, each of these couplings would be reviewed and dissected in about the same space as is now devoted to a complete album. What luxury! By the time we had amassed the full set of Muggsy Spanier Ragtimers, vintage '39, the first discs to reach us (they called them 'platters' then) had acquired that chalky pallor that signified retirement.

Pursuing the thought, I intended first of all to compile a handbook listing, with appropriate 'reviews', all those 'seventy-eight' recordings which I and my contemporaries have come to regard as 'classics'. All went well until I came to writing, and researching for, the required two or three thousand words on the Original Dixieland Band's 'Tiger Rag'. A great mass of material assembled—quotes, anecdotes, musical analogies and so on—and hung about on my desk defying me to abridge or discard it. Much of it was new to me, and I found myself putting it down as much for my own interest as for the information of a potential reader. And from that has grown a very different book altogether. It still deals with classic 'seventy-eights', but only those that were recorded between 1917 and 1930. It still has detailed discussion of the single titles which I have selected. But as much, and in some instances, more space is given to looking at the background of the recordings and the artists who made them, and into the jazz life of the cities in which those artists worked. It is still intended to be helpful to newcomers to jazz who want to learn more about the names of both musicians and tunes which jazz presenters such as myself drop so casually into their programmes.

But I hope, too, that the chapters contain some original thoughts and theories that will give the most seasoned collector a further lease of enjoyment in these great pieces of music.

In a way, the jigsaw fragments discussed here interlock into a rough-and-ready history of jazz in the Twenties. But the method I have adopted has its drawbacks, and I am all too aware of them. Lines have to be drawn everywhere, of which those limitations of time and space laid down by a long-suffering publisher are not the least important. The records I have chosen represent most of the musicians who had a lasting influence on jazz development—but not quite all. The omissions about which I feel most guilty involve two trombonists, Miff Mole and Jimmy Harrison, who, in that chronological order, were largely responsible for weaning the trombone away from its ponderous, military band role and towards a fluency comparable to that of the other 'blowing' instruments. Had this been a straight history, their contribution would have been duly noted and discussed. But when it came to compiling the limited list of masterpieces on which this book is based, the records which feature them fell just below the line. Another trombonist, Kid Ory, turns out to have less than his fair share of exposure.

There are other glaring omissions which I will explain by saying that it is proposed that another book will follow this one dealing with recordings between 1931 and 1944, the period commonly referred to as the Swing Era. There are some musicians—Fats Waller, Benny Goodman, Jack Teagarden among them—who made their debut on record in the Twenties but who are more generally associated with the music of the Thirties. When I decided, with some gnashing of teeth, to reject, for example, the superb Armstrong/Teagarden recording called 'Knockin' a Jug', I consoled myself with the thought that I can refer to it retrospectively at a later date. Other omissions I have had to bear stoically. It will be some time before I cease to wake up in the middle of the night muttering to myself 'How *could* you leave out Armstrong's "West End Blues"?' Or, come to that, Ellington's 'Creole Love Call', 'East St Louis Toodle-oo', 'Hot and Bothered' or 'The Mooche'? I can only say that this list is my final, difficult choice, and I am stuck with it.

A glance at the discography at the end of the book will show that, on two occasions, I have stepped out of strict chronological order in regard to recording dates. The alteration is insignificant since the recordings were only a matter of months apart. But the changes in order have enabled me to make illustrative points more easily. When it has come to describing aspects of the music, I have avoided using musical notation, which may be Greek to some readers. Instead I have relied on verbal description helped by occasional recourse to onomatopoeia (and that really *is* Greek, but it's in the dictionary!).

At the end of the book there is a bibliography which I have confined to those books I have used as reference and from which I have quoted. As far as general information and checking goes, the jazz writer is fortunate nowadays in having at his disposal the fruits of much diligent groundwork by specialists in the field. Anyone who embarks upon an assertive book of this kind without first stacking at his elbow John Chilton's *Who's Who in Jazz*, Leonard Feather's *Encyclopedia of Jazz*, and Brian Rust's extensive discography, *Jazz Records 1897 to 1942 A–Z* is comparable in intelligence to a round-the-world yachstman who leaves his navigational charts behind on the hall table. I take this opportunity of thanking them for awe-inspiring work without which we should all still be groping around in a fog of ignorance.

One more explanation is needed. Most books of this kind give details of currently available albums on which the recordings under discussion can be found. Perhaps to the authors' surprise, the books have continued to be read long after capricious recording companies have deleted the items from their catalogues. I believe that the time has come to acknowledge that jazz has its masterpieces, comparable to the great symphonies and overtures in orchestral music, which in a sane world should permanently be available somewhere for the listener to track down. There has always been something arbitrary and eccentric about the way in which recording companies handle the regular deletions from their catalogues. I can only say that, at the time of writing this book, I was able to find readily available versions, either home-produced or imported, of all the records. Most of them exist in chronological albums, which means that the reader who tracks one down will get anything up to fifteen performances by the same artist and from the same period with which to establish a fine basic collection. And if he has half the fun exploring them that I have had in rediscovering performances that I thought I knew by heart, he is in for a good time!

The Original Dixieland Jazz Band

THE ORIGINAL DIXIELAND JAZZ BAND—hereinafter referred to
frequently as the ODJB—has turned out to be something of a
scapegoat in modern jazz history. Its fall from grace was all the
bumpier because jazz historians of the Thirties, working on the
slender evidence then available from gramophone recordings,
raised the Dixielanders so far above their station. It is true that
the ODJB was the first jazz band, recognisable as such in hindsight,
to make records. I am not going to dwell here on inconclusive
speculation about the origins of the word 'jazz'. But I will include,
for its entertainment value, the information given by the band's
biographer, H. O. Brunn, that the original spelling, 'jass', was
changed by the band 'because children, as well as a few impish
adults, could not resist the temptation to obliterate the letter
"j" from their posters'.

It is also true that the ODJB was the first New Orleans Band
to cause a worldwide sensation—it overwhelmed New York in
1917, London in 1919—and start a craze that was to be the
hallmark of a decade. The similarity between what would nowadays be dubbed 'ODJB-mania' and contemporary pop crazes
emerges from H. O. Brunn's sentence, 'Night-clubbers flocked to
Reisenweber's to be frightened by this compact little group of
rebel musicians.'

Like most crazes, the Dixieland Band quite quickly found
itself out of fashion. For one thing, the Eastern musicians, as
those working in and around New York were known, prided
themselves on a certain musical sophistication and had a tendency

(which died hard in the course of the Twenties) to look down on the rough and rugged music coming from what they termed 'the West', which meant anything from the direction of New Orleans or Chicago. In 1924, Paul Whiteman, the massive leader of an increasingly massive band whose self-appointed mission it became to make an honest woman out of the wayward hussy from the New Orleans whore-houses, started an important concert at New York's Aeolian Hall with a note-for-note take-off of the ODJB's first hit record of seven years earlier, the 'Livery Stable Blues'. The stunt nearly backfired, as Whiteman himself recalled later: 'When they laughed and seemed pleased with "Livery Stable Blues", the crude jazz of the past, I had for a moment the panicky feeling that they hadn't realised the attempt at burlesque —that they were ignorantly applauding the thing on its merits.' Dignity was restored, however, when the elephantine Whiteman band went on to waddle through 'symphonic jazz' versions of 'Yes, We Have No Bananas' and the like, hitting the heights of respectability with an inaugural performance of George Gershwin's 'Rhapsody in Blue' with the composer at the piano.

History revels in irony. Whiteman's often over-dressed arrangements of popular songs have long been buried among the ephemeral bric-à-brac of the Twenties, surfacing only briefly during spasmodic epidemics of nostalgia. 'Rhapsody in Blue' survives where it belonged in the first place, in the lower reaches of the orchestral concert repertoire. The only clement in that 1924 concert that had vitality and durability in the jazz context was 'Livery Stable Blues', Dixieland versions of which still delight audiences today.

For another truth about the ODJB is that it had a profound influence on the young white musicians who bought its records avidly when they first came out. The Wolverine Orchestra, with twenty-one-year-old Bix Beiderbecke on cornet, shared none of Paul Whiteman's condescension in 1924. Making their recording debut in that year, they took many of the tunes from the ODJB's repertoire. The same tunes reappeared in 1928 when a more mature and established Bix made informal jazz with his 'Gang'. In the late Thirties, as a revival of interest in New Orleans jazz began to stir, out came the sturdy old war-horses again, in bright new harness furnished by Bob Crosby's Bobcats and Muggsy Spanier's Ragtime Band. A decade later, every capital city in the western world resounded to 'Fidgety Feet', 'At the Jazz Band Ball' and 'Tiger Rag' as jazz spread worldwide. And it is a lucky purveyor of traditional jazz whose public appearances, even now, are not dogged by stentorian cries of 'Play "Tiger Rag"!', almost fifty years after the tune made its muffled debut on record.

And here is irony again. The very movement back to the New Orleans roots of jazz which rejuvenated the ODJB's tunes in the Forties and Fifties led to the devaluation of the band's historic reputation. In magazine articles, recorded interviews and autobiographies, veteran jazzmen queued up to give their recollections of what really happened in those early days. And the notion that the ODJB gave birth to jazz single-handed in the studios of the Victor Talking Machine Company in 1917 suffered lethal damage.

What emerged from many ear-witness accounts was that the Original Dixieland Jazz Band was by no means original. It must always be borne in mind that black musicians who watched white contemporaries collect the richest rewards from the music to which they themselves had made the major contribution (and it is a recurring theme throughout jazz and pop music history) are not exactly disinterested witnesses. On the other hand, jazz musicians are usually men of staunch independence, not much given to conspiracy. And the verdicts of, for example, Sidney Bechet, Bunk Johnson and Jelly Roll Morton on the ODJB match each other so closely that they must either be true or the result of close collusion.

In his autobiography, *Treat It Gentle*, Bechet said: 'All these Dixielanders could do was play what they learned from us . . . take a number like "Livery Stable Blues", we'd played that before they could remember; it was something we knew about a long way back.'

Jelly Roll Morton told his story for the archives of the American Library of Congress in 1938, shortly before his death. In it, he calmly appropriated the ODJB's most famous composition. 'The "Tiger Rag", for an instance, I happened to transform from an old quadrille, which was originally in many different tempos. First there was an introduction, "Everybody get your partners!", and the people would be rushing around the hall getting their partners. After a five-minute lapse of time, the next strain would be the waltz strain ... then another strain that comes right beside the waltz strain in mazooka time ... we had two other strains in two-four time. Then I transformed these strains into the "Tiger Rag", which I also named, from the way I made the tiger roar with my elbow. A person said once, "That sounds like a tiger hollering." I said to myself, "That's the name." All this happened back in the early days before the Dixieland Band was ever heard of.'

We must not be elbowed into disbelief by the alacrity with which Jelly Roll laid claim to any common musical property which happened to be lying about. Bunk Johnson was not a close associate of Morton's at any time, and his account of the origins of 'Tiger Rag' puts the authorship elsewhere. Otherwise, it is remarkably close. 'This quadrille, the first eight bars of what the bands are usin' today, "Tiger Rag", that's King Bolden's first eight bars we would play to get your partner ready for the quadrille. And, in later years, t'was taken and turned into "Tiger Rag" by musicians that could read. Had Bolden knew music, probably Bolden would have made "Tiger Rag". So we had "Tiger Rag" before we had any Dixieland Jazz Band.'

Where does this leave the poor old ODJB? Well, it certainly showed up as glib all those jazz 'histories' which assumed that the ODJB was first in the field simply because it beat all comers to the recording studios. On the other hand, there was at first some over-reaction when the comments I have quoted, and others like them, came out. The New Orleans Revival—the great exploration to the source of jazz—was under way, working up a fine head of romantic steam about those black pioneers of the music whose work, and indeed existence, had up till then been ignored. It was one thing to say that the Original Dixieland Jazz Band was not particularly original. It was quite another to claim, as some commentators did, that it was simply a white 'ragtime' band whose style, greatly inferior to that of contemporary black bands, can only grudgingly be accepted as 'a form of jazz'. If the New Orleans Revival discovered anything, it was that in New Orleans in the first two decades of the century, embryonic forms of jazz were played by both black and white bands, the common denominator being a position near the bottom of the social and cultural scale.

It took all sorts to make the musical world from which jazz emanated. A good picture of this world can be found in Alan Lomax's book, *Mister Jelly Roll*, which was written around Jelly Roll Morton's Library of Congress reminiscences. From the testimony of one old-timer after another it emerges that not every black musician was a jazzman born and bred. Some were 'hot' players, some were 'sweet', some were readers, some were 'fakers' who played by ear, some produced refined music, others specialised in the rugged blues. One of them, the clarinettist Alphonse Picou, whose claim to jazz immortality lies in the traditional—and unimprovised—clarinet solo in the piece 'High Society', had some difficulty in mastering the improvised style of the rough street bands. He was himself a Creole and had received formal musical training. 'One day Bouboul Augustat, the trombone player, heard me practising in the house and ask me if I want to come to one of his rehearsals. I say, "You got any music?" "You don't need no music," say Bouboul. "That's impossible. What I'm gonna play? Just sit there and hold my instrument?" "Don't worry. You'll know." That's what Bouboul tell *me*. So I went. They were playing some good jazz that I didn't know nothing about . . .'

In this context, the Original Dixieland Jazz Band was undoubtedly a 'hot' band—the trombonist Eddie 'Daddy' Edwards was the only member who could read music, and it was he who would play over new numbers from the published sheet music until the other members of the band had learned the tune. Jelly Roll Morton alleged that the band's style came very close to that of the Original Creole Band, led by cornetist Freddy Keppard. It was this band, in fact, which preceded the ODJB on the grand tour out of New Orleans, causing quite a sensation in its own right in both Chicago and New York two years before the ODJB arrived. Indeed, had Freddie Keppard not declined a recording offer (to prevent other bands stealing his stuff, says the popular legend, but it's just as likely that he didn't take the new 'toy' seriously enough to bother), we might have been spared this lengthy explanation of the ODJB's true role!

Jelly Roll's comparison between the Original Creole Orchestra and the ODJB is corroborated to a large extent if we listen to the only comparable record which Keppard ever made. 'Stockyard Strut', by Freddie Keppard's Jazz Cardinals, was recorded in 1926, nine years after the first ODJB recordings. Keppard, like Nick LaRocca, was born in 1889, and both men lead their bands in a similar rhythmic style which derives directly from the even eight-notes-to-a-bar rhythm of ragtime. To get an idea of this basic rhythm, just repeat 'one-and-two-and-three-and-four-and' evenly and rapidly, and the result will be the machine-gun *rat-tat-tat-tat* which characterised this 'old' style. In the chapters that follow there will be frequent references to the gradual change from this 'ragtime' rhythmic feeling to the looser four-four rhythm that was introduced in the playing of Sidney Bechet and Louis Armstrong in the early Twenties and which became the basis of jazz phrasing throughout the changing fashions of the next five decades. So let us leave it now and go on to look in greater detail at the ODJB's most famous showpiece, 'Tiger Rag'.

In referring to other recordings in this collection which were recorded in more than one version within a short period of time— King Oliver's 'Dippermouth Blues', for instance, or Duke Ellington's 'Black and Tan Fantasy'—I have been careful to specify one particular version as being, by general consensus or in my own view, the best one. The ODJB's 'Tiger Rag' does not demand any such scrupulous selection, except perhaps on the grounds of audibility. For the several versions which they recorded between 1917 and 1919 are alike in practically every detail. This is one reason for the band's rejection in later years by critics who set greater store by improvisation than did many of the musicians themselves. The theory that all the great players since the birth of jazz lived by the dictum that 'we never play a tune the same way twice' doesn't stand up to even cursory examination, and would certainly disqualify more than one of the great recorded classics cited in this book.

But to work out a solo in advance or repeat a 'head' or memorised arrangement is not quite the same thing as making each per-formance a replica of the last in every detail. Even a written score is open to a wide range of interpretation. The funny thing is that 'Tiger Rag' has, over the years, been played in more ways than, perhaps, any theme in jazz history, and yet the five men who claimed authorship of it through their leader, Nick La Rocca, could only keep trotting it out with the jerky predictability of a player-piano.

However it came about, the old New Orleans quadrille, with its waltz and 'mazooka' sections, is transformed here beyond recognition. The first B flat 'get your partners' theme is, according to Jelly Roll Morton's analysis, quite close to the original, though taken here at breakneck speed. With its bugle-call theme over the two basic chords of B flat and F, it has something of a rallying cry about it. One interesting aspect of the New Orleans style is high-lighted in this opening section, and it is the tendency among trumpet-players to phrase across the beat rather than squarely on it. It was the primary function of the trumpet to 'carry the melody' in the ensemble, and with all but he improvising to their heart's content, rhythmic variation was about all that was left to him. (When I first joined a Dixieland band in 1947, I was denied even this freedom—the band had a second cornet-player who intimated the rhythmic accents with a very sharp elbow in my ribs!) A more serious explanation for this rhythmic flexibility no doubt lies in the African origins of jazz. In his book, *Early Jazz*, the musicologist and musician Gunther Schuller goes into this at great length. It will suffice me to say that one finds the same freedom in the melody line of a *genuine* Cuban rhumba or Trinidadian calypso. It has to be added that Nick LaRocca does not do it in a very subtle way—the anticipation of the last phrase in the opening four bars is so exaggerated each time that it simply sounds as if he has raced ahead of his colleagues.

We are told that the original quadrille, once the partners were settled, began with a stately waltz in the key of F major. In 'Tiger Rag', this theme is relegated to what is called a 'bridge passage', a short relief from the opening B flat theme which modulates back into it by way of an F dominant seventh. In this short section we have a foretaste of the clarinet 'breaks' by Larry Shields which were such a feature of the ODJB's version. It has become the accepted belief that 'breaks'—that is, short passages in which one instrument is left on his own to fill a gap—

were the first manifestation of the jazz solo and that, as musicians became more proficient, they were able to spread these ad lib excursions over a full chorus and beyond. It's a theory that might look all right on the blackboard of a lecture-room, but does not appeal to me. I have never understood why a musician capable of improvising his way through countless ensemble choruses should be suddenly struck dumb when left on his own. Recordings made in more recent years of primitive New Orleans bands offer at least one more down-to-earth explanation—that the jazz solo originated in human frailty, one instrumentalist being left on his own when the others got tired. It is no coincidence that most of the solo work in early New Orleans jazz was undertaken by the clarinettist, whose instrument is less punishing to lip and lungs than either trumpet or trombone.

If we look to Larry Shields for a demonstration of wit and inventiveness in his solo 'breaks', we are surely doomed to disappointment. Sidney Bechet claimed that Shields once took lessons from him. Certainly no one can deny that the clarinet in 'Tiger Rag' is accomplished—the pitching is accurate, the tone, so far as one can discern it, is rounded, and the piercing high notes that must have caused seizures in the control room reveal a sound technique. But there, alas, it ends. In the E flat section that follows a reprise of the opening theme, the clarinet 'breaks' could hardly be more dull or obvious. If we listen for what the New York jazz critic Whitney Balliett has called 'the sound of surprise', we listen in vain. These interpolations by Larry Shields are clearly worked out in advance and most of them sound uncomfortably like 'novelty' effects. We know from what other musicians have said that New Orleans music had its jokey side—'New Orleans hokum' is what they called it, and it incorporated all sorts of extracurricular noises such as horse-whinnying from the clarinet and macabre laughter from the muted cornet. In the best jazz, the jokes were offset by the music's more profound qualities. In 'Tiger Rag', they just sound like jokes, and repetitive jokes at that. Later chapters will dwell on the sobering influence of the blues on jazz through the ages. We shall try and define, as we go, the 'blues feeling' which gives passionate and melancholy undertones to the jauntiest of tempos. The blues did not feature in the musical heritage of the white musicians in New Orleans, although some of them—for example, the cornetist Wingy Manone and the clarinettist Leon Rappolo—were sensitive enough to receive the message. Despite the fact that several of their early titles incorporated the word 'Blues', the ODJB were almost totally devoid of blues feeling. In later years, exponents of 'Dixieland' jazz, delving with furrowed brow into the profundities of the blues, have often been riled by having their music labelled 'jolly jazz', 'good time music' and even 'funny hat stuff' by their antagonists. If any bands deserve such dismissal, it is those who interpret not only the music, but the spirit of the ODJB too closely.

The final section of 'Tiger Rag' moves into A flat and consists of four variations on a theme. First comes a free-for-all ensemble on what can be described as a standard harmonic sequence over thirty-two bars. Mr H. O. Brunn has it that the sequence was deliberately borrowed from the trio section of the 'National Emblem March'—which, incidentally, Louis Armstrong always used to quote in his many versions of the tune. Be that as it may, it is the part of 'Tiger Rag' which, over the years, has given the greatest scope for improvisation, consisting of long expanses of unchanging harmony over which new melody can be imposed. The ODJB start with a demonstration of the classic Dixieland ensemble style—the cornet stabbing out a leading melody in the instrument's middle register, the clarinet weaving a descant or counter-melody all around it, and the trombone playing a bass-part that conforms quite closely to the role of the trombones in a military band. (The New Orleans trombonist made freer use of the instrument's slide mechanism than was accepted in 'straight' bands, and the name 'tailgate', given to their sliding and slithering style derived from the need for the trombonist, on wagon-borne outings in the cause of advertising, to give himself elbow-room by sitting on the back end, or tailgate, of the wagon.)

After this spirited ensemble comes a chorus which, with justice, was dropped from most subsequent versions of the tune. According again to H. O. Brunn, this unsyncopated, thudding passage in straightforward 2/4 time began as a humorous imitation of the alto part in a German band. Jelly Roll Morton, on the other hand, includes it as one of the original quadrille themes. Either way, it proved to be invincibly jazz-proof material and vanished.

What remained instead as 'Tiger Rag's' primary theme was the ODJB's third variation, similar to the preceding one but this time syncopated across the beat and with the trombone making the 'tiger roar' which Jelly Roll Morton claimed to be the inspiration of his left elbow. Somewhere along the way, novelty versions of 'Tiger Rag' appended the words 'Hold that tiger!' to this theme, but this is irrelevant to the jazz history of the tune. After this straightforward variation, the band returns to a final ensemble —and offers a carbon copy of variation No. 1, though with another of Shields's standard 'breaks' substituted.

Here lies, surely, the greatest flaw in the ODJB's general performance. Sidney Bechet put his finger on it when he said, apropos the band's sudden decline in the early Twenties, 'Those Dixielanders had played all that they had learned and the thing just dropped.' We can argue ad infinitum about whether the ODJB did or did not play 'jazz', whether they should be disqualified for memorising rather than improvising their music, whether they stole all of their stuff, or only some of it, from other more talented musicians, and whether they were in any way representative of New Orleans music. What is fact, and not conjecture, is that, once they had made their initial impact on the world, 'the thing just dropped'. Of the musicians in the band who survived into the Twenties and Thirties, not one went on after their fall from grace to expand and develop his talent in other surroundings. When, in 1936, they came together again to enjoy a brief Indian summer, it was as if they had been pickled in soundproof aspic during the intervening years. 'Tiger Rag' had lost some of the explosive vigour that 'frightened' the avid customers at Reisenweber's Restaurant nineteen years earlier, and had gained nothing.

Why, you might have begun to ask yourself several pages ago, have I chosen a band so low in creativity and inspiration to launch this anthology of jazz on record? There are several reasons. For all the band's shortcomings and eventual eclipse, it did, by virtue of those first recordings, have a pervasive influence on the jazz which came afterwards. However suspect their 'compositions' may have been, they certainly collated, in neatly packaged form, many of the themes and musical ideas which were bandied about in New Orleans before gramophone recording came on the scene, and a striking number of the resulting pieces found a permanent place in the jazz repertoire. Again, by the very meticulousness with which they worked out and memorised their style they provided a sort of blue-print of how the line-up of trumpet-clarinet-trombone could be organised, and from that blueprint a lot of more creative jazz in what has come to be called the Dixieland style has stemmed. In considering their place in the early scheme of things we have revealed quite a lot about the beginnings of jazz in New Orleans, albeit negatively. And we have ensured that any reader unlucky enough to find himself at a jazz concert sitting next to one of the stentorian 'Play "Tiger Rag"!' brotherhood will at least know what the fool is on about.

James P. Johnson

THE MEMBERS OF THE ODJB were still scattered among diverse bands in New Orleans and Louis Armstrong, at twelve years old, was yet to experience his first cornet lessons in a New Orleans Waifs' Home when James Price Johnson, known to jazz historians and discographers as James P. Johnson and to friends such as Duke Ellington as 'just James', undertook his first professional engagement at Coney Island in 1912. For some time before that he had worked sporadically as a piano-player or 'tickler', a young recruit in a huge army of such entertainers who had developed ragtime along the Eastern seaboard of the United States from Washington to New York.

And yet we do not speak of James P. Johnson as a ragtime pianist but claim him as one of the founding fathers of a jazz piano style which, with benefit of hindsight, we can trace through Fats Waller, Duke Ellington, Count Basie and Thelonius Monk to the present day, when it still manifests itself in all sorts of surprising places. When is a ragtime player not a ragtime player? What was the ingredient, or recipe of ingredients, that converted music clearly descended from the rags of Scott Joplin and his contemporaries into jazz?

The answer has been given in many thousands of weighty words on the subject. Even in the somewhat cursory explanation for which I have time and space here, it is necessary to set the scene. In an interview with Tom Davin (quoted at length in a book called *Jazz Panorama*, edited by Martin Williams), James himself does this succinctly. 'In the years before World War I, there was a piano in almost every home. The piano makers had a slogan: "What Is Home Without A Piano?" It was like having a radio or TV today. Phonographs were feeble and scratchy. Most people who had pianos couldn't play them, so a piano-player was important socially. There were so many of them visiting and socialising that some people would have their pianos going day and night all week long.' In his autobiography *Music Is My Mistress*, Duke Ellington brings to life graphically a ritual which still persisted when he arrived in Harlem in the early Twenties: 'Other times, Lippy [a piano-playing colleague] and the bunch would get together, get James cornered, find a taxi, of maybe walk over to someone's house, and ring the bell. This would be 3 or 4 am. People stuck their heads out of windows, ready to throw a pot (flowerpot, maybe).

"Who's that down there?" they'd growl.

"This is Lippy," the answer would be. "I got James with me." Those doors flew open. Lights switched on. Cupboards emptied, and everybody took a little taste. Then it was me, or maybe Fats [Waller] who sat down to warm up the piano. After that, James took over. Then you got the real invention—magic, sheer magic.'

As this story implies, these piano-ticklers with an entrée into every home at whatever hour were a very special breed. Happily, their lives and times are well chronicled. Accounts such as James P. Johnson's interview or the autobiography (*Music On My Mind*) which Willie 'The Lion' Smith wrote, contain a litany of formidable and colourful names—Walter 'One Leg Shadow' Gould, 'No Legs' Cagey, Jack the Bear, Stephen 'The Beetle' Henderson, Richard 'Abba Labba' McLean, not to mention more conventionally named but no less talented players such as Luckey Roberts, Willie Gant and Eubie Blake. Rather like tennis-players in the modern international circuits, these men were, at their various times, friends *and* keen competitors, vying for the most important and lucrative jobs. Since they worked as both soloists and accompanists, the technical demands on them were high. As Willie The Lion said: 'One of the many important things you had to be able to do when playing piano in the saloons back in those days was to accompany the singer-entertainers. Some of the larger concert saloons and cabarets had as many as ten male and female singers around the joint regularly. You had to be a fast thinker to handle them. First, it was necessary to be able to play in any key, run the chords as we call it, because the entertainers worked in them all. A singer might change into any key on the piano at any time. They themselves didn't know half the time what key they worked in.' In the early days, when James P. Johnson began to earn his living at the keyboard, the required repertoire had little of the easy-going, pick-and-choose informality of later jazz. 'I played "That Barbershop Chord" . . . "Lazy Moon" . . . Berlin's "Alexander's Ragtime Band". Some rags, too, my own and others. . . . Joplin's "Maple Leaf Rag" (everybody knew that by then) . . . his "Sunflower Rag" . . . "Maori", by Will Tyers . . . "The Peculiar Rag" and "The Dream" by Jack the Bear. Then there were "instrumentals"; piano arrangements of medleys of Herbert and Friml, popular novelties and music-hall hits—many by Negro composers . . . Blues had not come into popularity then, they weren't known or sung by New York entertainers.'

It was the stress of competition from their peers, rather than any highbrow demands from employers or audiences in the often down-at-heel places where they played, that encouraged the ticklers to include several classical selections in their repertoires. James P. Johnson did rag variations on the William Tell Overture, the Peer Gynt Suite and even the relatively modern Prelude in C Sharp Minor by Rachmaninoff. The 'Polonaise Militaire' and the 'Miserere' from *Il Trovatore* (also favoured in a far distant context by Jelly Roll Morton) were two of The Lion's specialities. Anyone who can trace and hear some of the recordings made in this genre by the little-known and highly underrated pianist, Don Lambert, will know that such performances were no mere 'jazzing' of the classics in frivolous vein, but adhered conscientiously to the originals in all but their rhythmic aspect, and demanded a concert-pianist's technique and discipline.

If technical prowess was all-important to these piano 'professors', 'attitude' was not far behind. This was their word for what we would now call 'showmanship', the difference being that showmanship is dictated by the employers and enterpreneurs of the entertainment world while attitude was self-imposed. As

Willie The Lion recalled, 'It didn't take me long to notice that everybody in the entertainment business made it a point to dress sharp. It behooved us to look spectacular, not only to get and hold a gal, but to make a good impression all round.' The impression one gets from the reminiscences of The Lion and James P. is that they resembled in their way the flamboyant actor-managers of the old London theatre. 'Every move we made was studied, practiced, and developed just like it was a complicated piano piece,' said James P. Johnson. A 'real smart tickler' would wear a military or coachman's overcoat, double-breasted, full-skirted and in blue, grey or brown according to taste. This would be complemented by a distinguished hat—a Homburg with three buttons on the side or, with The Lion, a Derby worn at a jaunty angle. Having made a theatrical entrance, the great man would refrain from removing hat and coat until he reached the piano, when he would go into a highly stylized and personal routine. If he was carrying a gold- or silver-headed cane he would lay it with great deliberation on the music rack of the piano. The prized overcoat would be removed and laid along the top of the piano, folded to show off the expensive lining. Then, according to James P., 'you took off your hat before the audience. Each tickler had his own gesture for removing his hat with a little flourish; that was part of his attitude, too. You took out your silk hand-kerchief, shook it and dusted off the piano stool.' It's not hard to see where Duke Ellington's predilection for the flamboyant gesture was nurtured!

We have arrived, then, at a picture of a breed—a guild, almost —of highly-skilled and intensely professional freelance piano-players who, largely through their own pride in their calling, had mastered an enormous repertoire of works, both popular and classical. We still have to explain how the men of James P. Johnson's generation, who reached their prime in the post-war period when the recording-machine was on hand to commit their work to posterity, made the transition from a style based on rag-time to one that was recognisably jazz. The answer is embedded in black American history from the Civil War onwards. Anyone wishing to go into the question in some depth would do well to get hold of a book called *They All Played Ragtime* by Rudi Blesh and Harriet Janis, which tells the detailed story. I shall be content here to lay a trail of clues.

A comment by Willie 'The Lion' Smith starts us off on the scent. 'This story wouldn't be complete if I didn't mention one of the most fabulous piano men of them all—Walter (One Leg Shadow) Gould. He came from Philadelphia and he must have been over a hundred years old when he died in Albany, New York, in 1959. The Shadow was one of the first to start sprucing up the quadrilles and schottisches that were popular around the time of the Civil War.' The Shadow was in fact a modest eighty-four when he died, but he lived long enough to take us back even further via the researches of Blesh and Janis. 'Old Man Sam Moore was ragging the quadrilles and schottisches before I was born.' Here, then were the seeds of the tradition in which young Jimmy Johnson would interpret the popular songs of the day— the 'sprucing up' of European-style dances in a manner derived, but distinct, from the composed and formal ragtime.

But there was another, equally important influence. In *They All Played Ragtime*, James is quoted, apropos his early childhood, as saying: 'The Northern towns had a hold-over of the old Southern customs. I'd wake up as a child and hear an old-fashioned ring-shout going on downstairs. Somebody would be playing a guitar or jew's-harp or maybe a mandolin, and the dancing went to "The Spider and the Bed-Bug Had a Good Time" or "Susie, Susie". They danced around in a shuffle and then they would shove a man or woman out into the centre and clap hands. This would go on all night and I would fall asleep sitting at the top of the stairs.'

The ring-shout was a hold-over from African culture, and it has survived in the United States in both religious and secular form. In the black Baptist churches, the shout (which, having little to do with shouting, is better understood by substituting the word 'dance') has long been used to generate a state of trance-like ecstasy. Forming a circle, the congregation shuffle round with the feet barely leaving the floor and the body jerking rhythmically in a hitching motion, chanting a chorus response to the words of a spiritual uttered by the preacher or one or more lead singers. We shall come across this 'call and response' formula in subsequent

chapters, but suffice it to say now that, clearly, the rhythm
generated by the ring-shout was hypnotically insistent and compelling. Willie The Lion put it this way: 'Shouts are stride piano—
when James P. and Fats and I would get a romp-down shout
going, that was playing rocky, just like the Baptist people sing.
You don't just play a chord to that—you got to move it and the
piano-players do the same thing in the churches, and there's
ragtime in the preaching.'

One further element must now be brought in to complete the
picture. The metamorphosis of Harlem from a small Dutch
village far from the centre of New York to a city suburb and then
a densely populated black ghetto was a gradual one. Black com-
munities, which had previously clustered together in many
different districts, began at the start of the century to converge
upon the northern part of Manhattan Island. First stop was the
area of San Juan Hill, on the northern boundary of the tenderloin
district known as Hell's Kitchen. The black section of Hell's
Kitchen was known as The Jungles, and it was here that the
'ticklers', of the generation that preceded James P. Johnson,
found their most regular haunts.

In the early years of the century the population of the San Juan
Hill area was boosted by an influx of migrants from the South,
some from Alabama, some from the part of South Carolina and
Georgia that centred around Charleston. From the testimony of
both The Lion and James P., it is clear that these latter people,
known as Gullahs or Geechies, had a powerful effect on the style
of the local piano men. First Willie The Lion: 'Our soft, slow,
four-o'clock-in-the-morning music got to those folks from the
South. They danced cakewalks and cotillions; by this time we
had learned to play the natural twelve-bar blues that evolved from
the spirituals . . . the Gullahs would start out early in the evening
dancing two-steps, waltzes, schottisches; but as the night wore on
and the liquor began to work, they would start improvising their
own steps and that was when they wanted us to get-in-the-alley,
real lowdown . . . it was from the improvised steps that the
Charleston dance originated.' James P. Johnson, one of whose
Charleston-style compositions, 'The Charleston' itself, launched a
worldwide dance craze a decade later, has similar recollections.

'The dances they did at the Jungles Casino were wild and comical —the more pose and the more breaks the better. These Charleston people and the other Southerners had just come to New York. They were country people and they felt homesick. When they got tired of two-steps and schottisches . . . they'd yell: "Let's go back home!" . . . "Let's do a set!" . . . or, "Now, put us in the alley!" . . . Breakdown music was the best for such sets, the more solid and groovy the better. They'd dance, hollerin' and screaming until they were cooked.'

It was the big influx of these country people which drove the long-established black population of New York (many of whom were well acclimatised to the habits of the North and more interested in emulating the white people than in preserving their Southern culture) further north into the then quieter avenues of Harlem. We shall see, in the later chapter on Fletcher Henderson's Orchestra, how their staid and sober tastes kept the jazz influence at bay until a further massive migration from the South in World War I and afterwards broke down the defences. Their relevance here is that they provide us with a situation which is uncannily close to the manner in which jazz was procreated in New Orleans at about the same time. There a once free and proud half-caste or Creole population with a strong European cultural tradition lost status and privileges through the general emancipation of Negroes after the Civil War, and, in their decline, met the descendants of freed slaves on the way up. The fusion of the European traditions of the Creoles and the African traditions of country people who came in from the plantations resulted in jazz.

If we substitute for the Southern creoles the long-established Negro families around New York, some of whose forebears had come there as Negro freemen before the Civil War, we find a parallel situation. Consider the influences which came to bear upon young Jimmy Johnson once he started as a professional piano-player. The ethos of the black New York establishment in which he was brought up was modelled on that of 'respectable' white society, from whom a knowledge of, and respect for, the European popular classics derived. The musicians of his immediate experience were not concert pianists but friends of his older brothers: 'They were the real ticklers—cabaret and sporting

house players. They were my heroes and led what I felt was a
glamorous life—welcome everywhere because of their talent.'
From these men he learnt the Eastern style of ragtime, less formal
and rhythmically more 'spruced up' than the parent style that
had emanated from Missouri in the Mid-West. As with jazz
itself, much of the rhythmic impetus of this Eastern ragtime
derived from the African dance, probably more varied than the
single term 'ring-shout' implies, which survived in the black
Baptist church ritual and spilled over from there into Negro
social life. As Willie The Lion said, when playing for 'shouts',
you had to move it. The Gullahs or Geechies who had come up
from the South put further demands on the piano-tickler. When
they shouted 'Let's go back home' they wanted lowdown music,
tinged with the blues, to match their improvised steps until such
time as they or the piano-player dropped.

It would be surprising if a musician whose formative years were
assailed by such diverse influences emerged at the other end as a
mere backroom piano-tickler. In the course of a long career, which
ended in his death in 1955, James P. Johnson wrote several
symphonic works, a one-act opera, some Broadway shows and
popular songs (of which the best-known today are 'The Charleston', 'If I Could Be With You' and 'Old Fashioned Love'), at
least one classic piano blues ('Snowy Morning Blues') and a large
number of rags and 'shouts'. As an executant he also appears in
the discographies as a prolific blues accompanist—of Bessie
Smith among others—and as the pianist in all kinds of jazz bands.
But out of all this widely-spread endeavour, it is as the Father of
Harlem Stride Piano that James P. Johnson will always be best
known.

I have no idea when, and by whom, the term Harlem Stride
Piano was coined, nor do any of us know, other than by hearsay
and deduction, whether Johnson was indeed the father of the
style or simply one of several equally impressive uncles. Willie
The Lion was vague on the subject. 'The writers who make up
titles for the ways of playing music have called our piano style
here on the eastern seaboard Harlem Stride Piano. I'm not very
sure I know what they are talking about.' It has to be said that,
having coined the term, the writers themselves have not been

very sure what they were talking about. For example, in one of
George Hoefer's 'interludes' in Willie The Lion's book, John S.
Wilson of the *New York Times* is quoted as giving the popular
definition of the term 'stride': 'The stride effect is produced by
the left hand hitting a single note on the first and third beats and
a chord of three or four notes on the second and fourth beats.' On
the other hand, Whitney Balliett of the *New Yorker* brings the
right hand into account, too. 'Stride piano is characterised chiefly
by an oompah left hand (a two-beat seesaw, whose ends are a
powerful mid-keyboard chord and a weaker single note played an
octave or a tenth below) and by an arabesque of right-hand
chords and arpeggios, fashioned in counter-rhythms.' Apart from
seemingly reversing the bass figure to provide a pah-oom bass,
Balliett's is an accurate picture of the sound of stride piano. But
James P. Johnson himself adds to the confusion by saying that
'the characteristic strides were performed by the *right hand*' (my
italics). It seems as if, like the word 'shout' in the same context,
'stride' simply exists to confuse the layman. Happily, the phono-
graph developed in time to give us audible examples of a style
that came to be most widely known through the work of Johnson's
protégé, Thomas 'Fats' Waller. Furthermore, the style has shown
remarkable powers of survival. While ragtime long since died, to
be resurrected only during bouts of nostalgia, stride piano goes
on and on. It lay at the heart of the piano styles of Duke Ellington,
Count Basie and Art Tatum, who carried it into the Swing music
of the Thirties. In the Forties, as an off-shoot of the retrospective
New Orleans Revival, it was itself revived in its basic form by a
generation of young musicians which included Ralph Sutton,
Don Ewell and Dick Wellstood in the States, Dill Jones, Dick
Katz and Lennie Felix in Britain, Eddie Bernard and, for a while,
Bernard Peiffer in France and Henri Chaix in Switzerland. Even
when modern jazz seemed intent upon erasing all evidence of
earlier jazz conventions, there was Thelonius Monk building his
sparse and harmonically austere music on at least a scaffolding of
earlier stride. Since then, any number of modern jazz performers
—one thinks of Roger Kellaway, Jaki Byard, Nat Pierce,
Britain's Mick Pyne and, of course, Oscar Peterson—have taken
trouble to assimilate stride piano into their technical armoury.

I would guess that all of them have, in private, had a tilt at James P. Johnson's 'Carolina Shout'.

'My first encounter with James,' wrote Duke Ellington, 'was through the piano rolls, the QRS rolls. Percy Johnson, a drummer in Washington who told me about them, took me home with him, and played me "Carolina Shout". He said I ought to learn it. So how was I going to do it, I wanted to know. He showed me the way. We slowed the machine and then I could follow the keys going down. I learned it!' It was when James P. went to Washington in person a short time afterwards that Duke, by playing 'Carolina Shout' back at him at his own supporters' insistence, earned his respect and friendship. It was not the first, or the last time that 'Carolina Shout' was used as a piano test-piece. Indeed, so obligatory did it become for aspiring stride-men to master it that I was once able, for my own amusement, to compile from recordings a 'cutting contest' consisting of versions by Johnson himself, Willie The Lion, Don Lambert, Fats Waller, Dick Wellstood, Cliff Jackson and Henri Chaix. With unscrupulous use of a portable tape-recorder I could have captured a Duke Ellington version at one of his latter-day concerts when he was apt to trot it out, albeit a trifle creakily, as an encore.

James P. Johnson, playing the piano for dancing in a 'dancing school' called the Jungles Casino (it was easier for Negroes to get a licence for a dancing school than a dance-hall), liked to inject a little ring-shout fervour into the music. The 'pupils' danced two-steps, waltzes, schottisches and a new step called the 'Metropolitan Glide'. 'I played for these regulation dances, but instead of playing straight, I'd break into a rag in certain places. The older ones didn't care too much for this, but the younger ones would scream when I got good to them with a bit of rag in the dance music now and then ... The Charleston, which became a popular dance step on its own, was just a regulation cotillion step without a name ... My "Carolina Shout" was another type of ragtime arrangement of a set dance of this period.'

Even in its earliest version, recorded by James P. in 1921, 'Carolina· Shout' reveals those qualities of swing and fervour which made the younger dancers at the Jungles Casino scream in ecstasy. We have all been well-enough acquainted, through Scott

Joplin's rag 'The Entertainer', with the stately rhythms of formal Mid-Western ragtime to know at once that this is something quite different. From the introduction onwards, the music rolls forwards in an even four-beats to the bar. The bass rhythm is anything but the limited oom-chah that some of the definitions suggest. In the first chorus the single notes on the first and third beats, played in broken octaves, often take over all four beats in the bar to define a counter-melody to the romping right hand. In the second chorus, a left-hand device that was a favourite of James P., if not his actual creation, makes its appearance. It is just the kind of invention, technically tricky and at the same time musically dazzling, with which the combatant ticklers would challenge their opponents. It involves a sporadic reversing of the oom-chah bass figure—in parade-ground terms, a 'change step'—by playing, for example, a passage that goes *oom-chah-oom-chah-chah-oom-chah-chah*, weaving an intriguing rhythmic pattern out of the strong and weak beats. The variation of the cascading opening theme that the right hand plays over this shifting rhythm is the very epitome of stride piano. Keeping to the broad shape of the original, it skips and dodges and pirouettes on its way, managing to impart a sense of exhilaration even through the dulling mists of antiquated recording.

Had 'Carolina Shout' been a conventional rag in the Mid-Western style, the tuneful opening strain would have given way to another equally melodic, perhaps reverting to the first theme before moving on to a trio section in a contrasting key. But it was not for nothing that James P. Johnson called his piece a shout. The prime function of the pianist in this circumstance is not to weave elegant melodic variations but to 'move it' according to Willie The Lion's prescription. So we shall see that, in each successive variation from now on, Johnson feeds the dancers' feet with a fresh rhythmic idea. Having moved on to a simpler theme in the third chorus, he first of all establishes a rolling, hand-to-hand rhythm which, appropriately enough, came to be known in later jazz as a 'shuffle rhythm'. Then, on the same harmonic theme, he moves into a 'call and response' pattern in which we see the origins of the repeated figures or 'riffs' of which later jazz, especially in the big band field, made effective and sometimes excessive use. For two choruses running he matches riffs in the right hand with answering figures in the left, pushing ahead of the beat to build a powerful momentum. This leads to a change of theme with an equally simple harmonic pattern over which, with the pumping left hand working up a fierce head of steam in the stride manner, his repeated phrases in the right hand are strikingly similar to those used by Morton in the final section of his 'King Porter Stomp'. This is neither coincidence nor plagiarism. Johnson records in the Davin interview that Morton once told him that 'King Porter Stomp' was, like 'Carolina Shout', taken from cotillion music.

At this point the reader can be left to marvel at the way in which, reverting to the call and response pattern, James P. Johnson varies and breaks up the left hand figures while maintaining the momentum with his right hand. We get three variations here, and, in each successive one, more is made of the halting, almost hiccuping bass response, until in the final chorus it rumbles prodigiously. In the second variation, the right hand reminds us of much of Duke Ellington's piano-playing in this idiom. It has another of the stride men's favourite effects, an octave struck at the beginning of the phrase and given an added fillip by the addition of a grace note half a tone below the upper note. Try it on the piano by striking a G octave with thumb and little finger of the right hand and just flipping the F sharp with the fourth finger (counting the thumb as 1) a fraction of a second before the octave is sounded. It gives a very spritely attack.

One can see how 'Carolina Shout' came to be the test-piece for all aspiring pianists in Harlem in the early Twenties. It incorporates all the elements of a style which has to be assiduously learnt—even today there are technically advanced pianists who would hesitate to tackle it for the first time without some diligent practice. Every one of James P. Johnson's variations presents a challenge which cannot be shirked. And yet it is in the nature of the shout idiom that it should be capable of almost limitless extension to keep up with the dancers' enthusiasm. And so we find in some subsequent versions—Fats Waller's is a good example—that having got their fingers around James P. Johnson's variations, the players went on to add some of their own. There was nothing to hinder them. The smooth, four-beat foundation was in keeping with, not to say ahead of, the modern rhythms of the emerging jazz music (in this respect James P. offered a better example than Jelly Roll Morton, whose own extension of ragtime into jazz, influenced by the contrapuntal style of New Orleans band music, retained more of the somewhat sedate rhythms of ragtime). And Johnson's themes, being more rhythmic than melodic, gave the same scope for improvisation as the chord sequences of popular tunes to which jazz musicians have long been indebted.

In short, from its jaunty introduction to its witty and ingenious coda, 'Carolina Shout' is jazz. What's more, the style which it epitomises—Harlem Stride Piano—has proved to be one of the most durably satisfying of jazz forms. To hear Dick Wellstood, one of the younger ticklers, applying its principles to the harmonically-complex John Coltrane composition, 'Giant Steps', is to marvel at its infinite adaptability. At the Montreux Festival in 1977, Count Basie was playing a stalking, middle tempo blues with a trio when he suddenly doubled the tempo and went into some time-honoured stride piano in the manner of James P. Johnson. Both the huge audience and the all-star band onstage broke into spontaneous cries of delight, as if an old and valued friend had unexpectedly walked through the door.

King Oliver

BY 1923, JOE OLIVER was past his prime, according to ear-witnesses. Born in 1885 not far from New Orleans, he had been proclaimed 'King' in his early twenties when the connoisseurs who crowded round the stand at the Abadie Cabaret at the corner of Marais and Bienville Streets concluded that he had outplayed the reigning monarch, Freddie Keppard. (Joe must have been a slow starter, for Keppard was four years his junior.)

Joe Oliver was playing at the time in a quartet led by the pianist Richard M. Jones, and one of the more fanciful legends in jazz mythology tells of one night when, provoked by hearing other musicians speaking well of his rivals, he growled 'Beat it out in B flat, Jones!' and walked out on to the sidewalk to unleash a few challenging blues choruses in the direction of Pete Lala's Cabaret a block away, where Freddie Keppard held sway. The legend goes on predictably to record that the customers streamed out of Pete Lala's and followed Oliver like the children of Hamelin back into the Abadie. It doesn't tell us if Jones was still patiently beating it out in B flat.

Shortly after this incident, Keppard left New Orleans at the head of the Original Creole Orchestra, the band which preceded the Original Dixieland Jazz Band in blazing the trail for the new ragtime style from New Orleans northwards to Chicago and New York. The story of how the fruits of their pioneering tours were reaped by the ODJB has been told in a previous chapter. But Keppard and his men did have their own successes, and, in the years between 1911 and 1917, they opened up the market in

Chicago for New Orleans musicians.

Again, legend has put the gloss of romanticism on the move of jazz musicians away from New Orleans up to Chicago, suggesting a mass exodus following the closing down by City ordnance of the Storyville brothel and entertainment district of New Orleans which had been the nursery of jazz. (In the ludicrous but enjoyable film *New Orleans*, made in 1947, this exodus was actually depicted, with Louis Armstrong and his 'girl-friend', Billie Holiday, leading the throng!) No doubt the Storyville episode did act as a spur, but the migratory movement had been under way for some time. As Alan Lomax wrote in his study of Jelly Roll Morton, *Mister Jelly Roll*: 'The shift of New Orleans musicians to Chicago was only a grace-note in a big movement. The factories and mills of wartime America needed fresh supplies of labour and for the first time they were hiring great numbers of Negroes . . . in five years a half-a-million Negroes moved North, one tenth of them settling in Chicago's South Side.'

This was the new audience of which Keppard and his musicians spoke with enthusiasm whenever they communicated with friends and colleagues in New Orleans. And it was inevitable that the ambitious and skilled musicians would flock to where the action was. Joe Oliver travelled to Chicago in 1918 and soon formed a band of his own. In June 1922, King Oliver's Creole Jazz Band, returning from a stint on the West Coast, was offered a residency at a big dance-hall on Chicago's South Side called the Lincoln Gardens (formerly the Royal Gardens immortalised in the 'Royal Garden Blues', a favourite old jazz standard by the unrelated Spencer and Clarence Williams). The line-up of the band which opened at the Lincoln Gardens is as listed, with the exception of Louis Armstrong, who came North to join Oliver a few weeks after the opening.

Various guesses, informed and otherwise, have been made as to why Joe Oliver, established in Chicago with a band of conventional line-up and apparently set fair for a great popular success, sent off a telegram in the summer of 1922 to Louis in New Orleans inviting him, in the tones of a Royal Command, to join his band. In New Orleans, when Joe was unchallenged king, the teenaged Louis had become his protégé, to the extent that Louis, whose childhood had involved a dimly-remembered father and a procession of 'stepfathers', accepted Oliver in loco parentis and called him 'Papa Joe'.

Paternal feelings, then, may have come into Joe Oliver's reckoning, although the fierce and ruthless competitiveness that went into the making and breaking of trumpet 'Kings' in New Orleans can have left little room for sentiment. Louis had already shown prodigious talent back home and, after Oliver headed North, stepped effortlessly into his jobs, establishing a reputation which must have reached the older man's ears on his travels. There may, then, have been truth in Lil Hardin Armstrong's assertion years later that King Oliver said to her one night that Louis could play better than he could. 'He says, "But as long as I keep him with me he won't be able to get ahead of me. I'll still be the King!" '

Whatever the reason for Oliver's decision, it transformed his Creole Jazz Band into the most creative and influential jazz unit of its time, whose thirty-seven recordings, made between April and December 1923, provide us with the audible source of the jazz 'mainstream'.

'Dippermouth Blues' (the title was a stock nickname for anyone with a capacious mouth in general, and for Louis Armstrong in particular) was King Oliver's speciality, the piece for which his audiences on the Chicago South Side clamoured nightly. It is a loosely-constructed blues which the Creole Band recorded twice. In contrast to the ODJB's rigid treatment of 'Tiger Rag', Oliver's two versions of 'Dippermouth Blues', made for the Gennett and Okeh labels respectively, vary considerably in detail while conforming to the same overall pattern.

I have chosen for special consideration the earlier Gennett version, recorded at the band's first session. Even by pre-electric standards, Gennett seem to have been less well-equipped for sound than the Chicago studios of Okeh. Listeners brought up, not to say spoon-fed, on hi-fi might wonder why I do not go at once for the version that is considerably easier on the ear. I had to ask myself whether it was not pure sentiment and nostalgia that made me choose the recording which I first bought some time in the late Thirties on a Brunswick '78' and to which jazz-loving friends and I listened in a posture not unfamiliar to junior jazz buffs of any era—namely, kneeling round a gramophone on the floor with our ears pressed to the speaker, looking like ostriches in search of concealment.

Having given both versions the same sort of concentrated attention over and over again, I am convinced that, sound quality apart, the Gennett version is in most other respects the better performance. The tempo is gloriously relaxed, a consistently-neglected object lesson to the traditional jazz bands (not excluding the otherwise exemplary Muggsy Spanier Ragtime Band of 1939) who have since spurred the tune into a brisk canter. Through the mists of time, it is just possible to hear the interplay between the two cornetists in the opening choruses. In the 1940s, several 'revivalists' bands—Lu Watters and his Yerba Buena Band in America, George Webb's Dixielanders in Britain, Claude Luter's early band in France—adopted the two-cornet line-up, allegedly under the influence of recordings by King Oliver's Band. But they all used the two instruments in a different and more obvious way, coupling them together closely in parallel harmony like musical Siamese twins. In effect, theirs were conventional three-part front-lines of cornet, clarinet and trombone with the cornet line 'thickened' by an additional harmony.

The Oliver band's two cornets were separated in the recording studio in more senses than one. Lil Hardin, the pianist with the band who, a year later, became the second Mrs Louis Armstrong, recalled their first recording session in 1923. 'At the first session . . . the band was around the horn, and Louis was there, as he always was, right next to Joe . . . it didn't work out. Couldn't hear a note Joe was playing. So they moved Louis way over in the corner away from the band. Louis was standin' there looking so lonesome—he thought it was bad for him to have to be away from the band . . . and that's the only way we could get the balance—Louis was at least fifteen feet from us, on the whole session.'

Apart from this physical separation, the two cornets in Oliver's front-line operated, except in their co-ordinated breaks, as separate voices in the ensemble. Other more clearly-recorded performances reveal young Louis playing a free harmonic role in mid-ensemble, aided by the unconventional role which the trombonist Honoré Dutrey adopted. One hardy jazz legend attributes Dutrey's curious, wandering ensemble style to the fact, reported by his contemporary and fellow-trombonist Preston Jackson, that he learned new tunes from the cello parts. 'I used to sit behind Dutrey every night and watch him play cello parts because cello parts were easier to get than trombone parts.' Apart from the formally-trained Lil Hardin, Dutrey was probably the only member of Oliver's band who could read music at all in those days. It is hardly conceivable that any cello part ever found its way into the preparation of 'Dippermouth Blues', but it is true that Dutrey's carefully worked-out trombone part, almost identical in each version of the tune and sounding rather more like a euphonium than a cello, has little to do with the conventional 'tailgate' role of the New Orleans trombone. That role, as exemplified by 'Daddy' Edwards in the Original Dixieland Jazz Band and, in later recordings, by Kid Ory, derived from the military band trombone part with its insistence on the root harmonies in the ensemble. Dutrey's mournful moo-ing in the Oliver band was altogether less rigid and dictatorial, and it allowed Louis quite a lot of scope among the harmonies left unattended. Glimpses of the way in which he moved among those harmonies with great sensitivity show through the murk of 'Dippermouth's' opening chorus, although it is better heard on later recordings such as the Okeh versions of 'High Society', 'Riverside Blues' and the superb 'Mabel's Dream'.

Another reason for my preference for the earlier version of 'Dippermouth Blues' lies in the clarinet solo by Johnny Dodds, played against interrupted 'stop-chords' from the rest of the band. This solo, like that taken by Oliver himself later on, exemplifies the 'set pieces' which were an accepted feature of New Orleans jazz—the pinch of salt, if you like, with which the theory of constant improvisation must be taken. In this first recording, Dodds plays two twelve-bar choruses. The first descends from an upper keynote in a mournful phrase that is redolent of the blues, as was Dodds's playing at all times. The second starts an octave lower and wanders upwards to provide a nicely balanced contrast. This solo, which successive clarinettists have always reproduced in essence as being an indispensable part of 'Dipper-mouth Blues', was clearly worked out in advance. It is there again in the later recording, but this time Dodds omits the second, contrasting twelve-bar variation and simply repeats the first—a victory, perhaps, of improvisation over concentration!

After the Dodds solo it is Louis Armstrong who takes over the cornet lead in a reprise of the opening theme. Although differences in the cornet styles of Oliver and Armstrong are blurred by the recording requirement that the horns should be muted (and for the same reason the ebullient drumming of Baby Dodds was restricted to deathwatch beetle caperings on the woodblock and some indistinct thumping on a muffled tom-tom), it is still possible to hear two strongly contrasted styles. Oliver's sound on the 1923 recordings—and I am talking now of the straight-forward muted sound and not the 'wa-wa' effects—is vigorous, attacking and almost sternly commanding. His cornet lead bears down on the melody in an inexorable way which is often emotion-ally moving through its very lack of overt sentiment. Some of the notes end with a rapid 'shake' but otherwise the tone has very little vibrato to soften it.·

Louis Armstrong's style is draped all over with ostensible Oliver influences. The downward leap of an octave on the dominant note (from G to lower G in the key of C) at the end of a chorus was one trade mark which he took over from Oliver for a while, and there were several other turns of phrase which he inherited. But his musical approach was fundamentally different. If, as a reflection of the human personality, music can be said to have masculine and feminine elements, then Louis' style, though palpably virile, showed from the start a generous endowment of the latter. There was a softness, an absence of aggression, manifested in the way the tone was ameliorated by a pulsating vibrato, the angular corners of the phrases were rounded off and the most functional cadences were imbued with a caressing warmth far beyond their purely structural requirements. In interviews throughout his life Louis always laid great stress on his over-riding belief that music should be 'pretty'. When in later years angry and aggressive modern sounds erupted all around him, he growled his disapproval of musicians who paid little heed to the melody and trumpet-players who sacrificed tone and accuracy for speed and a stratospheric range. 'We always used to make sure that our notes were *covered*!' he used to say, by which I take it to mean that they were hit bang in the middle and surrounded by a comfortable cushion of tone. Fortunately, Louis Armstrong's remarkably consistent and reliable musical taste almost invariably offset the 'prettiness' by a strong instinct for construction and a feeling for the noble phrase. As a result, what he intended as 'pretty' reached the listener as sheer beauty. In later examples of Louis Armstrong's work we shall appreciate this more clearly. The rather busy and angular theme of 'Dippermouth Blues' offers him little scope to do other than demonstrate the leaping energy which set all who heard him at that time back on their heels.

But this is, after all, Joe Oliver's record. There is a practical reason for his absence from the ensemble that follows Dodds. He is preparing himself for a dramatic entry into his own set piece. The inaccurate balance of this early recording has led us into the habit of referring to Joe Oliver's three declamatory muted choruses as a 'solo', but Armstrong, Dodds and Dutrey can be heard maintaining the ensemble behind, simply standing back a little to give him air. Another common assumption about these three choruses is that they were played with a 'plunger' mute. I do not agree. The plunger mute is in fact usually a combination of two mutes—a small metal or fibre mute that fits flush into the cornet or trumpet bell, and an ordinary rubber sink-cup or plunger that is waggled in front of the bell to make a 'wa-wa' sound.

It is difficult to find any eye-witness evidence that King Oliver used this sort of mute at the time of the Creole Band recordings. Fellow-trumpeter Mutt Carey, who emulated Oliver's muted style, recalled many years later: 'He was the greatest freak trumpet-player I ever knew. He did most of his playing with cups, glasses, buckets and mutes.' Trombonist Preston Jackson, who followed the Oliver band closely during the Chicago period, was more specific: 'He used a half-cocked mute, and how he could make it talk.' Buster Bailey, who joined Oliver's band for a short while at the end of 1923, adds a further clue: 'King Oliver was a great musician with a mute. With an ordinary tin mute, he could make the horn talk.' Most conclusive of all is Garvin Bushell's recollection, quoted more fully in the chapter on 'Black and Tan Fantasy', of Bubber Miley copying Oliver by 'using his hand over the tin mute that used to come with all cornets'.

One would have thought that, if Oliver used a plunger in the period under discussion, someone would have mentioned it. Danny Barker, the veteran New Orleans-born guitarist and jazz archivist, goes so far as to say, apropos a primitive New Orleans trumpeter called Chris Kelly, 'He was the first one I saw play with a plunger. Although New Orleans never featured it, he could play with it.' One last bit of circumstantial evidence—examination of all the available photographs of King Oliver's Creole Jazz Band shows no sign of a rubber plunger although in most of them the band's instruments and accoutrements are laid out like exhibits at the musicians' feet. On the other hand, several of the pictures show Oliver using the small tin mute (of the pear-shaped variety that is little used today) at half-cock—in other words, half out of the bell and cupped in the hand. I hesitate to be didactic about a sound which reaches us through such a fog of low-fidelity sound, but having experimented with a similar mute, I think it probable that this was the method that Joe Oliver used to make the peculiarly plaintive, softly articulated 'wa-wa' sound that distinguished his 'Dippermouth Blues' choruses.

Several highly distinguished trumpet-players—among them Louis Armstrong (several times), Rex Stewart, Harry James, Yank Lawson and Muggsy Spanier—have reproduced Oliver's variations, using a selection of mutes or, as in some of Armstrong's versions, no mute at all. They have made them jaunty, fervent, imperious, savage, blue. None has even tried to match the peculiar eerie, nocturnal sound that Oliver imparts to them in this first recording. But it is not only the sound which they have found elusive. Joe Oliver's phrasing, too, has a subtlety which which later versions miss. For a chorus which is alleged to have stirred the audiences at the Lincoln Gardens to a frenzy, it is remarkably restrained in its construction. The first chorus hangs on the blue-est of blue notes, not a straightforward minor third as most subsequent interpreters have assumed, but a marginally flattened third which establishes the eerily plaintive sound straight away. This is about the earliest manifestation we have on record of 'preaching' trumpet, a jazz device which derived immediately from black American sources—the call and response of preacher and congregation, of work-leader and railroad gang, of blues singer and accompanist—and beyond that, from African song forms. It is no mere flight of fancy to think of Joe Oliver here in the role of orator haranguing a responsive audience.

The three choruses build in declamatory fervour by the most economical means. The second chorus raises its point of focus from the 'blue' third to the fifth note, then the third chorus hammers away at the sixth note in rousing exhortation. All this fervour and exultation take place virtually within a range of six notes, building to a climax which leads quite naturally, if faintly absurdly, to the cry of 'Oh, play that thing!' that is as much a traditional ingredient of 'Dippermouth Blues' as the clarinet and trumpet sections. (Since the spread of the New Orleans Revival and the subsequent 'Trad boom' in the late Fifties, there is hardly an accent, from true-blue British to rugged Glaswegian, from guttural Teutonic to sing-song Oriental, which has not been heard mangling the ritualistic incantation 'Oh, play that thing!')

The final chorus of 'Dippermouth Blues' canters proudly up the home straight, the epitome of Joe Oliver's forthright and positive ensemble style. The form of it is exactly right, neither straining to improve on the climax already reached nor reverting tamely to the opening theme. Careful listening to some of the later 1923 recordings made for the Okeh company in which the two cornets are well-favoured will show Oliver's same unfailing sense of structure in what we know, from comparing alternative versions where they exist, to be largely improvisation. Two examples which I warmly recommend are the Okeh recording of 'Snake Rag' and the overwhelming, all-ensemble performance of 'I Ain't Gonna Tell Nobody' which under Oliver's inspired direction achieves the momentum of an express train. For years I was rather puzzled by Louis Armstrong's often reiterated statement that 'When you hear them four or five trumpets cut loose in the swing bands, what you're hearing is Joe Oliver.' Louis seldom if ever talked idle nonsense on the subject of music, but this did seem to carry homage to his former mentor too far. But having listened again extensively to the Creole Band recordings, I see the point. In the full fervour of the Swing Era, few arrangers, bent on building a stirring climax with full benefit of eight brass and five reeds, improved on King Oliver and his imperious cornet. To-day, it is usual to take for granted this instinct for structure—'chorus-building', it is sometimes called—in good jazz ensembles or solos. It is nevertheless impressive to hear it so fully-fledged in Joe Oliver's playing in 1923, especially when fellow-musicians have testified that he was past his prime.

This alone would have justified me in referring earlier to King Oliver's Creole Jazz Band as the primary source of the jazz mainstream. But so many other things were going on within this musical power-house. In Joe Oliver and Johnny Dodds it had two men thoroughly steeped in the blues. We shall be dealing later in more detail with the relationship of the vocal tradition of the blues with instrumental jazz. It is enough to say here that what jazz writers have rather vaguely called 'blues feeling' is a quality, only partially explicable in purely musical terms, which throughout jazz history has given to the most superficially light-hearted performance a backbone of what I can only call *seriousness*. In analysing the jazz tone, Leonard Bernstein once used the admirable phrase 'the hint of pain', and I would extend that to the jazz performance as a whole. Certainly there was in the Oliver band's most jaunty pieces a power to stir the listener's emotions which the Original Dixieland Jazz Band lacked entirely.

Just as importantly, the King Oliver Creole Band in its rhythmic 'feel' stood on the threshold of a new era. In discussing the ODJB, I noted that it played in the two-beat rhythmic style of piano ragtime, an even 'One-and-two-and-three-and-four-and' rhythm which, in the conventional 4/4 notation in which jazz is usually set down, would appear as eight even quavers or eighth notes to the bar. This was the rhythm which, in recordings as late as 1926, Freddie Keppard's Band still used. It is the basic rhythm also of another black band from New Orleans, Kid Ory's Sunshine Orchestra, which recorded a few sides in 1922. Like me, the New Orleans bassist George 'Pops' Foster favoured an

onomatopoeic description when he spoke of Keppard playing
'what I called walkin' trumpet—it was Ta-ta-ta-ta-ta. They
were straight, clear notes.' This was not the only rhythm prevalent in the dance music of the early Twenties. Listen to early
recordings by bands as diverse as the Wolverine Orchestra and
Fletcher Henderson's Orchestra and you will hear what is in
effect a variation on the even-quaver two-beat rhythm. In his
contentious book *Shining Trumpets*—the most thorough exposition
of the 'purist' philosophy underlying the New Orleans revival—
the American writer Rudi Blesh brings in onomatopoeia to help
him give an accurate picture of this rhythm. Discussing the
Wolverine Orchestra, he says, 'Their rhythm is deformed by the
peculiar, jumpy pattern often called *vo-de-o-do*. Say *do-do-vo-de-o-
do* aloud and you have the pattern as it was derived . . .' Blesh's
book was a fine piece of special pleading for the supremacy of
Negro musical concepts, hence his use of the pejorative word
'deformed'. I don't know any evidence that suggests that this
rhythm (which would be set out in 4/4 time with the eight even
quavers of our 'ragtime' example altered to combinations of
dotted quavers and semi-quavers to give a jerky 'one a-two a-three
a-four' effect) derived 'probably from attempts of white singers of
popular tunes to imitate the rhythmic Negro scat song and the
stomp rhythms of the band'. It seems to have been the fashionable
rhythm of much American dance music, black or white, from the
war years onwards.

We shall see that both the 'ragtime' and the 'vo-de-o-do'
rhythms with their underlying two-beat feeling died hard during
the Twenties and were still perceptible in recordings made near
the end of the decade. Inside the Oliver band, a new rhythmic
concept was stirring. For one thing, the rhythm section, in which
the most consistent components were piano, banjo and drums,
did not lean heavily on the first and third beats of the bar but
gave all four beats an equal value. The banjoists in particular
eschewed the plinky-plonky upstrokes that the dance bands of the
period favoured, and instead kept a steady and uncluttered four-
in-a-bar going which was complemented by the 'walking' left-
hand arpeggios of pianist Lil Hardin.

Over this even, and utterly relaxed, rhythm a different and

more subtle rhythmic concept was beginning to emerge. And the man who felt it most clearly and decisively was the young Louis Armstrong. In this respect he was ahead of his colleagues—and indeed, of practically every other musician currently appearing on record. The performance which best summarises the difference between the new and the old concepts of rhythm is the Okeh version of 'Riverside Blues' by King Oliver's Band, recorded not long after 'Dippermouth Blues'. This number incorporates solo 'breaks' by, in turn, Johnny Dodds, Honoré Dutrey and Louis. Both Dodds and Dutrey phrase, as does Joe Oliver in the opening chorus, in the 'one-and-two-and-three-and-four' ragtime manner, albeit in a much less rigid way then either the ODJB or Keppard. When they come to their short unaccompanied passages, this phrasing lands them in what, to modern ears, sounds like rhythmic trouble. The best way I can describe it without elaborate notation is to say that they are like explorers trying to cross a yawning chasm by means of a rope-ladder with its rungs too widely spaced. They get to the other side of the 'break' somehow, but it is not an elegant crossing. Now, throughout this whole recording we hear Louis Armstrong's second cornet part predominating, and, lo and behold, he is up to something quite different. There is no 'one-and-two-and' feeling here, but a loping stride which formal notation would describe as in 12/8 time and which can be demonstrated phonetically as 'one-and-a-two-and-a-three-and-a-four'. (In conventional 4/4 notation, this would be written as four sets of quaver triplets to the bar.)

When Louis stalks out of the ensemble with measured tread to play his own solo chorus at the end of the piece (I once described this ascending phrase in a broadcast as 'the sound of genius emerging' and was inordinately pleased with the notion), it is clear that he has the answer to the rhythmic problem posed by that high-wire break at the end, and, sure enough, he plays it with enormous poise. To revert to the rope-ladder analogy, his 12/8 rhythmic conception gives him rungs which are more frequent and more closely-spaced, and he can plant his feet more accurately.

The notion of subdividing the four beats in a bar, not into eight quavers as in 'ragtime' and 'vo-de-o-do', but into twelve quavers arranged in triplets, was no doubt instinctive to Louis, who was no musical theoretician. It would be rash to say that Louis was the only musician around to feel his music in this way—when Sidney Bechet first appeared on record a few months later, he seemed to have a pretty good grasp of it, as did Bessie Smith in her earlier work. We *can* say that no musician whose work is available to us on early jazz recordings showed such assurance in what was clearly a new concept. It would, I think, have been this quality in his playing which led Tommy Brookins, a youthful eye-witness to the King Oliver Band in Chicago, to say: 'Opposite the young Louis, who was already prodigious, Oliver's style rapidly appeared to date a little and it was frequent to hear musicians talk among themselves of the "old style".'

I am no believer in the theory of immaculate conception with regard to musical innovations. All sorts of influences, some quite unknown to us, must have gone into the formation of Louis Armstrong's style. We should not discount Joe Oliver among them. He may have played in an old style, but within that style his rhythmic subtlety and sure-footedness were masterly, and there is nowhere any sign of the stiff-necked rigidity that later came to be called 'corny'. I have no doubt that the rhythmic assurance of Oliver within what, for convenience, I have called the 'ragtime' framework, was father to his protégé's discovery of a freer rhythmic form.

It was, as I have said, to be another decade or so before jazz improvisation became completely at home with the 'new' 12/8 feeling that stirred within the 1923 King Oliver Band. For this reason alone, it is permissible to think of the Oliver Band as the first jazz band in the modern sense. If you doubt this, go back to 'Dippermouth Blues' and consider, when comparing it with later Dixieland and Swing versions of the same tune, how little had to be altered to keep up with the times. Most of it was there in the first place.

Sidney Bechet

'WILD CAT BLUES', once an extreme rarity, serves here as an introduction to Sidney Bechet. Today's newcomer to jazz has the advantage over those patient and painstaking enthusiasts of the Thirties whose quota of jazz '78's, mostly geared to popular taste, emerged in monthly rations of two or three. We used to read occasionally about Bechet in *Melody Maker* or *Rhythm*, but the fact that he was usually called 'the legendary Sidney Bechet' speaks for itself. The first time the legend became a fact of any real substance was towards the end of the Thirties when recordings by his own New Orleans Feetwarmers began to join Benny Goodman, Tommy Dorsey and Fats Waller in the catalogues.

By this time, Bechet was approaching his fifties and already showed a fair crop of those prematurely white hairs which made him in journalistic eyes a Grand Old Man before his time. In the reference books, Bechet's date of birth is tentatively put forward as 1897, although some musicians who remember him in New Orleans suggest that it was earlier. In his autobiography (*Satchmo: My Life in New Orleans*), Louis Armstrong spoke of Bechet as a 'youngster from the Creole quarter', but went on to describe him in such reverential terms that it is not improbable that Bechet was a little more than three years older: 'The first time I heard Bechet play that clarinet he stood me on my ear ... My [next] great thrill was when I played with Bechet to advertise a prize fight. I have forgotten who was fighting, but I will never forget that I played with the great Bechet.' Sidney Bechet recollected what must have been the same incident in his own memoirs, though the details are slightly different. 'I had a little job for an advertisement that I was doing twice a week for a picture theatre . . . so I hired Louis to come with me on this advertising and, you know, it was wonderful . . . That was the first time I ever heard Louis play cornet.' But elsewhere, Bechet recalls that, when he was working with Bunk Johnson in the Eagle Orchestra, he was urged by Bunk to 'go hear a little quartet, how they sing and harmonize'. This was the juvenile quartet with which Louis earned a few nickels on the streets before he ever took up cornet. He cannot have been more than twelve years old then. 'I went many a time to hear this quartet sing,' Bechet goes on, 'and I got to like Louis a whole lot, he was damn' nice. I was a little older than him. At that time he sort of looked up to me, me playing in bands and being with the big men.' If we believe Bechet when he says 'I was about seventeen when I first started playing with the Eagle Orchestra', then he was five years older than Louis.

What is more interesting than speculation about dates is the insight which these recollections provide into the hierarchical nature of the New Orleans jazz fraternity. Both men were well advanced into middle age when they produced their memoirs, and yet, as if through total recall, Bechet assumes a note of condescension, Louis one of boyish hero-worship, in their memories of each other. This is all the more strange in the light of what happened later. In 1925, Louis and Bechet met in the recording studios in New York. Louis was then with Fletcher Henderson's Orchestra, Bechet was moving through a succession of jobs which included a short stint with Duke Ellington's new band. The records which the two young men from New Orleans made together under the direction of Clarence Williams survived into the Thirties as much sought-after collector's items. It was inevitable that, when each of them had attained a certain eminence, a move would be made to reunite them. It happened in 1940, the occasion being an album devoted to New Orleans music. Louis Armstrong was at this time rather more famous than Bechet and this, coupled with the feeling of seniority which Bechet appears to have retained from those youthful New Orleans encounters, may account for the stern and rather sour strictures which he passed on Louis' contribution to the recordings. In short, he accused him of ignoring the prearranged routines and hogging the limelight to the detriment of the ensemble.

The idea of Sidney Bechet being challenged, let alone over-whelmed, by any trumpet-player from the Archangel Gabriel downwards will no doubt seem richly entertaining to anyone well-enough acquainted with his imperious style. Certainly there is no evidence on the recordings themselves that Louis was intemperate or Bechet subdued. So far as I know, Louis didn't enter into this particular controversy, but, apart from the strictly retrospective admiration to which I have referred, he was markedly cool about his boyhood hero in later life. To understand this, we have to dispel a popular myth which New Orleans musicians themselves have propagated through their gushing reminiscences of the good old New Orleans days. From references in potted jazz histories to the music 'moving up-river to Chicago' in 1917, we gather the impression of a concerted exodus, a sort of school-leaving ceremony with all the young musicians setting out arm-in-arm and glowing with camaraderie to face a new life in the big outside world. As the short biographies in this book reveal, things happened very differently. Several of the New Orleans men, Bechet included, were born 'loners' who were up and away while the New Orleans era was still in full swing. Others stayed together for a while in the intensely competitive atmosphere of Chicago in the Twenties, but sooner or later adopted the philosophy of 'each man for himself'. Indeed, many musicians born and bred elsewhere than New Orleans have remarked at one time or another upon the jealousy bordering on violent detestation with which New Orleans musicians appeared to view each other while at the same time generalising ecstatically about the great times they all had years ago.

Several explanations present themselves. Lone wolves in pursuit of the same elusive prey cannot be expected to assume the team spirit just because they were reared in the same lair. Furthermore, the sense of an unchanging hierarchy, based on age and length of experience, has always been very real among New Orleans men and, as jazz historians fumbled to unravel the tangled threads of early jazz history, it was more and more frequently offended. 'The critics and guys who write about jazz think they know more about what went on in New Orleans than the guys that were there,' roared Pops Foster, the doyen of New Orleans bass-players, in a taped autobiography. 'They don't know nothing . . . We had a whole lot of trumpet-players around New Orleans besides Oliver and Armstrong.' Pops Foster played with all of the lone wolves at one time or another, and from his vantage point at the rear of the bandstand he took a poor view of them as colleagues. Bechet—'the most selfish, hard to get along with guy I ever worked with—a tough baby and all for himself.' Louis— 'real jealous of other players who put out . . . he works too hard because he don't want nobody to do nothing but him.' Albert Nicholas, the New Orleans clarinettist with whom Foster played for some years in the Luis Russell Band—'very hard to get along with, he had his own ways and he didn't want nobody to tell him nothing.'

This assessment will come as little surprise to jazz fans who visited the Parisian jazz scene in the Fifties when both Bechet and Nicholas were resident in different parts of the city. Albert Nicholas was the same age as Louis Armstrong and, as Bechet himself recalled, 'Albert was younger than me, and afternoons we'd sit together on the back steps and we'd play along together and I'd kind of advise him.' Thirty-odd years later, this cosy comradeship had evaporated. Ingenuous jazz buffs meeting either of the men in Paris would invariably ask after the other. The best they would receive was a monosyllabic reply and a blank, un-compromising look. I should perhaps inject the comment here that I worked alongside the admittedly formidable trio of Louis Armstrong, Sidney Bechet and Albert Nicholas at different times, and I do not believe that the sensitive, courteous and indeed, kindly side of each man that I saw was entirely due to the 3,000-mile gap between New Orleans and Windsor, England where I was born! But on one occasion when I was touring in his com-pany and talking long into the night, Albert Nicholas unburdened himself of his own unashamedly jealous grievance against Sidney Bechet. 'Everybody talks about Bechet did this and Bechet did that. Listen, when we were making all that jazz history, Bechet wasn't even there.'

I know what he meant, and it explains why any recording of

Bechet's from the few that he made in the Twenties will serve more as an introduction of his name into this survey than an account of his impact upon jazz in that decade.

It was in 1914, not long after his encounters with young Louis, that Sidney Bechet left New Orleans on his travels. Thenceforward, he was to return to the city only for intermittent visits which covered a few months in all between 1914 and 1917, when the break became permanent. There was a brief spell in Chicago, but Bechet was not a man to settle down even in the conducive ambience that Chicago offered to musicians at the end of World War I. With Will Marion Cook's Southern Syncopated Orchestra he came to Europe in 1919, playing in London (on one occasion before King George V) and moving on later to Paris. This phase of his travels ended when, back in Britain, he fell foul of the law (in a fight with a prostitute) and, though acquitted, was ordered to be deported back to America. It was in the short period between 1923 and 1925 that he made the New York recordings which are his sole legacy from the Twenties. In September 1925 he was off again to Europe, popping up in Paris, Russia and all stations between in groups that ranged from big stage orchestras to small jazz bands. And by the time he returned to America the Roaring Twenties had roared their last.

During Sidney Bechet's first trip to Europe, in 1919, the Swiss orchestral conductor, Ernest Ansermet, made some remarkably perceptive and prophetic comments on the music of the Southern Syncopated Orchestra. He reported: 'There is in the Southern Syncopated Orchestra an extraordinary clarinet virtuoso who is, so it seems, the first of his race to have composed perfectly formed blues on the clarinet . . . I wish to set down the name of this artist of genius, as for myself, I shall never forget it—it is Sidney Bechet.' Later, he went on, 'What a moving thing it is to meet this very black, fat boy with white teeth and that narrow forehead, who is very glad one likes what he does, but who can say nothing of his art, save that he follows his "own way", and when one thinks that his "own way" is perhaps the highway the whole world will swing along tomorrow.'

In the light of what was known about jazz in Europe, or indeed America, in 1919, Ansermet's remarks were almost clairvoyant.

The word 'blues', for example, was then known to the world at large only through published songs from Tin Pan Alley which carried the word, or from recordings by the Original Dixieland Band and others in which tunes labelled as 'Blues' were very often nothing of the kind. It is probable that Ansermet likewise used the term as a generalisation for jazzy, syncopated music. And yet, in the recordings that he made twenty or more years later, Bechet was to show that he was, indeed, a master of the perfectly composed blues. What else are masterpieces such as 'Really the Blues', 'Out of the Gallion' or, the greatest of all, 'Blue Horizon'? It is uncanny, too, that Ernest Ansermet should have hit intuitively upon the word 'swing' which was, in 1919, more than a decade away from acquiring a special significance in the jazz vocabulary.

In order to lead the reader back to a point as near as possible to that from which Ernest Ansermet made his observations, I have chosen the earliest Bechet recording hitherto issued. In July, 1923—a magical year, as it will transpire—Bechet was booked for a recording session by a New Orleans compatriot, Clarence Williams. Williams, a rather indifferent pianist, had emerged ten years earlier as New Orleans music's first entrepreneur. It would not be unfair to say that his music publishing business was founded on the rubble of unclaimed, unattributable material that the city's prolific but feckless music-makers scattered around. In those days, and for some years to come, jazz musicians were more interested in cash-in-hand than pie-in-the-sky, so original melodies would often change hands across the table in exchange for the price of a week's rent. If the publisher—and, as a result of the transaction, 'composer'—happened also to be a musician and a man in good standing with a recording company, a recording of the tune would result and royalties beyond the original composer's wildest dream would accrue. Bitter would be the cries of 'Horse-thief!!' when this was discovered! Even when the real composers themselves began to get their due acknowledgement, it was a long-standing custom for publishers and/or bandleaders who recorded a tune to add their names to the composer credits. In most cases there was a certain rough justice in this, since much of the material would never have earned a penny without entrepreneural assistance. 'You write it, I'll sell it' was undoubtedly the principle of many of the collaborations in which Clarence Williams's name appeared.

'Wild Cat Blues' was brought to Williams by a twenty-year-old pianist called Thomas Waller (nicknamed 'Fats' for visibly obvious reasons) who frequented the Harlem saloons and dives where good piano-players were at a premium, and whose habit of throwing off brilliant keyboard compositions without a thought for their future had been the despair of the businesslike Mr Williams. Having acquired the composition—Fats's first to be published—Clarence Williams quickly assembled one of his studio bands to record it.

The tune—or, more accurately, series of themes—suited Bechet perfectly. While he had been in Europe with Will Marion Cook, he had been attracted to the sound of the soprano saxophone, experimenting first with a standard curved model and eventually purchasing in London the straight model with which he became permanently associated. This instrument, which handled like the clarinet on which he was already a virtuoso and which jutted and flared aggressively like a trumpet, was custom-built for Bechet's personality. Louis Armstrong recalls having heard him in New Orleans playing cornet at the head of a parade, and it is true that his style, as revealed on this earliest record, combined the fluency of the New Orleans clarinet style with the strutting, rallying, domineering voice of the parade trumpet. It has become a cliché in jazz commentary to speak of Bechet overwhelming all but the most assertive trumpet players in the ensemble. The fact is that Sidney Bechet was not particularly interested in just transferring the decorative role of the New Orleans clarinet to the stronger instrument. Had that been his intention, it's difficult to see why he was drawn so compulsively to the soprano saxophone. He intended to dominate the ensemble, and expected trumpet players to find a satisfactory role in support. As one who played and recorded with Bechet, I can testify that this was not easy. 'Don't be afraid to play that lead,' he told me after our concert together in 1949. By 'lead' he meant the clear statement of the melody which is the function of trumpet or cornet in a New Orleans or Dixieland ensemble. Flanked by gruff trombone or shrill clarinet, the trumpet usually assumes, through its central role and tonal strength, absolute leadership of the ensemble. I doubt if I was the first or last trumpet-player to find, with Bechet at his elbow, that the ability to command was sapped!

In the long-defunct magazine *Jazz Music*, the French critic Hugues Panassié drew attention in 1948 to 'Wild Cat Blues' and its coupling, which were then extreme rarities in Britain: 'A remarkable thing about these two sides is that Bechet assumes the lead from the first bar to the last; the rest of the band is there merely to support him. These are really two great soprano saxophone solos. In them Bechet shows himself in his grandest manner and I doubt if he has ever played better than on this record.'

It is unlikely that the cornetist Thomas Morris minded taking a supporting role in 'Wild Cat Blues'. Fats Waller's piece is essentially a piano composition, clearly derivative of ragtime in its series of well-balance themes but with the overriding four-in-a-bar momentum which characterised the Harlem 'stride' piano of Waller's teacher and mentor, James P. Johnson. Indeed, there is a strong family likeness between this first published composition of Fats Waller's and the classic 'Carolina Shout' by Johnson. With the added mobility afforded by the soprano sax, Bechet found he could get around these fluent melodies more easily than a trumpet-player, and he loved them. All through his recording career, similar pieces crop up—'Polka Dot Rag', 'Temptation Rag', 'Coffee-grinder' and so on. In the same issue of *Jazz Music* from which Hugues Panassié's quotation comes, there is an article on Bechet by Bob Wilber, now a firmly established musician in his own right but, in 1948, still strongly under the influence of Bechet, with whom he studied for several years. 'As a listener, Sidney has the intuitive ability to sense the value of any music he hears. I've never heard him say "That's an awful tune." He loves all music because he sees the way to play it . . . He plays the melody, and when he improvises, improvising on the melody. That, in brief, is his theory of jazz.'

Presented with the melody of 'Wild Cat Blues' by Clarence Williams, Bechet knew exactly how to play it. In the chapter on 'Dippermouth Blues' by King Oliver, I suggested that Louis Armstrong was the first musician to have an instinctive feeling for the rhythmic freedom of 12/8 time, though I added that 'Sidney Bechet seemed to have a pretty good grasp of it.' My caution in this instance derived from several other Bechet performances from the same period (hear a rather dreadful piece called 'Oh Daddy Blues' for a perfect example) in which he conforms with the ricky-ticky rhythmic conventions of the time in a way that Armstrong could not have done had he so wanted. This is slender evidence, I readily agree, upon which to withhold the conclusion that, in terms of complete rhythmic freedom and elasticity, Bechet and Armstrong were 'modernists' almost a decade ahead of their time.

Without doubt, Bechet's playing in 'Wild Cat Blues' shows that his familiar style of the Forties onwards was fully mature in 1923. In achieving this 'modern' sound, he was not entirely unaided. The even four-beats-to-a-bar upon which relaxed phrasing in 12/8 time depends is provided—happily without any audible assistance or hindrance—by the superb banjoist, Buddy Christian, a New Orleans man of Bechet's generation who does for Bechet what Johnny St Cyr did for Louis Armstrong, and with as much suppleness and accuracy. Nowhere is the maturity of Bechet's rhythmic approach more striking than in the series of breaks which the composition provides from the halfway key-change onwards. Once again, one is drawn into comparisons with Louis Armstrong, who was himself engaged at this time in making his first recordings with King Oliver's band. The way in which both men pounced with predatory zeal upon the opportunities for solo expression that such breaks offered (hear Louis in the Oliver recording called 'Tears') links them together again as the first 'modernists' to sense the full potential of solo improvisation.

One cannot leave Bechet at this point without touching upon the prickly subject of vibrato. When Bechet made his belated and much-acclaimed return to the centre of the jazz stage in the late Thirties, some otherwise well-disposed critics and fans complained of his broad vibrato, which was variously described as 'whinnying' and 'nannygoat'. Vibrato is the word for the artificial introduction of a throb or pulse in a note to give it added expressiveness. In 'classical music', violinists and cellists have always used quite broad vibrato, achieved by a controlled shaking of the left hand on the fingerboard when the strings are depressed. In orchestral playing, the wind instruments make much less use of applied vibrato, relying for the most part on the natural pulsation of the sound. At the unschooled or self-taught folk-music end of the musical spectrum, where hearts are worn more ostentatiously on sleeves, vibrato is used without restraint on all instruments, achieved by shaking the instrument against the mouth or, in reed instruments, rapidly moving the lips or jaw around the mouth-piece. It follows naturally from the above that, in New Orleans, the music which stemmed from the schooled background of the Creoles, as exemplified in the clarinet playing of Lorenzo Tio, Jr., George Bacquet, Jimmy Noone and Albert Nicholas, made modest and restrained used of vibrato. Sidney Bechet was a Creole, but he was also a self-taught rebel who naturally gravitated towards the more violently self-expressive music of black New Orleans that owed nothing to conservatory training. As a trumpet-player *manqué*, too, he was probably attracted to the rapidly-shaking, 'shimmering' sound which many of the New Orleans trumpet-players have adopted through the years.

Much of the hostility to Bechet's vibrato arises from the fact that his playing became well-known late in the day, by which time the advance of more formal teaching into jazz had modified the use of vibrato. (This has been a progressive tendency, reaching a point, in modern jazz, at which Miles Davis, decrying the use of any applied vibrato at all, recalled his first teacher telling him 'Play without any vibrato. You're gonna get old anyway and start shaking.') What's more, the sort of broad, rapid vibrato that had become an accepted part of the style of Louis Armstrong and Johnny Dodds and their respective followers had never been applied to the saxophone—or if it had, it had been discarded (in most instances, wisely) as a bad idea. In the article quoted earlier, Bob Wilber accurately describes Bechet's vibrato as 'steady and controlled and somewhat akin to a violin'. Significantly, few ever complained about the vibrato in Bechet's clarinet playing—and had he played trumpet or violin, the objections would probably have been equally muted. As it is, the Bechet sound, vibrato and all, must always be a matter of taste. My own view is that a musician's creative personality is indivisible. One has only to hear the weak and whining noises which less committed players got from the soprano in the Twenties—Buster Bailey, for instance, or Omer Simeon, both of them fine clarinettists—to recognise the intense passion which endowed Bechet's handling of the instrument with such command. The vibrato was not just a mannerism but a deeply-rooted expression of that passion.

In the light of what still appears to us, through the fog of primitive recording, to be splendid and formidable playing on a grand scale, it is astonishing that this chapter does not end with brief account of the influence which Bechet exerted on his contemporaries. Duke Ellington recalled, 'Sidney Bechet was one of the truly great originals. I shall never forget the first time I heard him play, at the Howard Theatre in Washington around 1921. I never heard anything like it. It was 'a completely new sound and conception to me.' The Duke translated his admiration into action when, for a brief time, he employed Bechet in his band in New York. Some time after the migratory Bechet had flown again, Ellington perpetuated some of his influence in the band by employing Johnny Hodges, a young Boston musician whom Bechet had taken under his wing and who, in both his alto and soprano playing, inherited some of the older player's lyricism and feeling for the blues. Apart from this, and the mild and unsuccessful flirtations with the soprano sax to which I have alluded, there is no aural evidence that Bechet made any lasting impact on the jazz of the Twenties. Much of the blame for this must go to his apparently unerring instinct for the wrong thing, the wrong place and the wrong time.

In the period between 1917 and 1921, when most of his New Orleans compatriots were establishing themselves in Chicago, Bechet was jaunting around Europe. He returned not to Chicago but to New York, where, as Louis Armstrong was to discover when he joined Fletcher Henderson in 1924, musicians had their own thing going and were resistant to ideas coming in from 'the West'. He never settled in a band long enough to allow his talent to infect other musicians, in the way that Louis passed on the ability to 'swing' to the stuck-up and cliquey Henderson men. By choosing to overcome the outcast in the saxophone family, he established himself as a 'loner'. It is no accident that jazz historians of today still cite Coleman Hawkins and Johnny Hodges as the first men to elevate the saxophone to a convincing jazz role, relegating Sidney Bechet and his soprano to the limbo of what the jazz popularity polls categorise as 'miscellaneous instruments'. Yet what 'Wild Cat Blues' reveals above all else is that Sidney Bechet was, by an impressive margin of several years, the first great jazz saxophonist.

ORIGINAL DIXIELAND JAZZ BAND

Best Wishes To Our Pal Billie Jones
The Original Dixieland Jazz Ba...

CREATORS OF JAZZ

...die Edwards, Larry Shields, Tony Sbarbaro, J. Russell Robinson, Nick LaRo...

James P. Johnson.

KING OLIVER'S CREOLE
JAZZ BAND. *Left to right,
Baby Dodds, Honoré
Dutrey, King Oliver,
Louis Armstrong, Bill
Johnson, Johnny Dodds,
Lil Hardin.*

*The veteran Sidney
Bechet.*

Bessie Smith

THERE ARE MOMENTS when anyone setting out to discuss the blues must wish devoutly that the term had never been coined. To start with, there is the purely grammatical ambiguity which makes one vacillate feebly between the singular and the plural. In this context I had better make it clear that I work by no firm rule but use whichever form looks and sounds right at the time.

Then there is the problem of accurate definition. During the Jazz Age of the Twenties, the term 'blues' became fashionable and was used indiscriminately to denote a whole range of moods from hangover and ennui at one end of the scale to deep depression at the other. It is quite clear that what Noël Coward meant by his 'Twentieth Century Blues' was a million light-years removed from the subject matter of Bessie Smith's 'Empty Bed Blues'—but it is no easy matter to explain why.

As if this were not enough, confusion surrounds the actual musical definition of the blues. It is simple enough to establish that the basic format of the blues is a stanza or chorus of twelve bars in length with the three basic chords of tonic, subdominant and dominant—or, in the key of C, of C major, F major and G seventh. But one will very soon have the awkward task of explaining away a primitive blues by Big Bill Broonzy or Leadbelly that over-runs into anything from thirteen-and-a-half to fifteen bars or, worse still, of laughing off familiar 'standards' such as 'Limehouse Blues' or 'Jazz Me Blues' which are not in any sense of the term blues at all.

Let us content ourselves here with the tersest of definitions.

When an instrumentalist announces that he is going to improvise
or 'jam' on the theme of a twelve-bar blues, he means that he is
about to harness his improvisation to a harmonic sequence that
lasts, each time round, for twelve bars and in which, in the key of
C, the chords will be as follows:

bars	1	2	3	4	5	6	7	8	9	10	11	12
chords	C	C	C	C7	F	F	C	C	G7	G7	C	C

Of course, jazz has acquired harmonic sophistication over the
years and these basic chords have been enriched with extensions
and substitutions. But strum them out on the piano or guitar and
you will recognise them as being the basis of well-known instrumental 'standards' such as 'In the Mood' and 'At the Wood-
choppers' Ball' as well as literally countless jazz compositions
and spur-of-the-moment inventions.

When a blues singer of great antiquity from a remote area of the
Deep South advances on a microphone, guitar at the ready, to
sing the blues, he will have something rather different in mind.
Using the same basic harmonic structure, he will sing a line—
say, 'I lay down las' night, turnin' from side to side'—which will
occupy, and slightly overrun, bars 1 and 2. Over bars 3 and 4 he
will fill in with an answering phrase on guitar, taking care of the
progression to the new chord in bar 5. The same words will be
repeated over bars 5 and 6, and bars 7 and 8 will again have some
instrumental response. Then, over bars 9 and 10, he will sing a
new line—'I was not sick, I was jus' dissatisfied'—that serves to
resolve the thought or sentiment expressed in the first two repeated
lines. And again, instrumental backing fills out bars 11 and 12
and leads to a new stanza. It is in this area of instrumental response
between vocal lines that the very early blues often strayed from
the rigid twelve-bar formula, as the singer virtually strummed
away until he was ready to deliver the next line.

On the musical side, one further thing needs to be said. Far
back in time, the blues evolved from the meeting of African and
European musical cultures. On the European side there is the
harmony which, as we have seen, can quite easily be set out in
conventional musical symbols. When it comes to melody we find

the two cultures in head-on collision. It is quite possible to set out the melody of a blues using the key signature, the diatonic scale and the notation of European music. Doing this, we would notice that, invariably, much use would be made of the flattened third, seventh and, sometimes, fifth degrees of the scale. These are the notes which are often referred to as 'blue notes' because their use gives the melody line of the blues its dark and melancholy quality. But if we compare the notes which we have written down with what a blues singer actually sings, we find that our blunt-fisted European notation is inaccurate. The 'blue notes' are rarely flattened by a true semitone, but are bent and twisted in a subtle way which defies notation.

As for the actual character of the blues, it is as complex and perverse as human nature itself. In its primitive early form, the blues was the medium through which the oppressed and subjugated black American on Southern plantation or levee ventilated his feelings about life. In view of the condition of that life, it is surprising to discover that the theme of the blues is not always one of hopelessness and despair. There is a fine blues by the pianist Richard M. Jones whose words, no doubt borrowed from some common store, speak for all the blues: 'Trouble in mind, I'm blue, but I won't be blue always—the sun's gonna shine in my back door some day.' Trouble there is in the blues, and plenty of it, ranging from the personal disasters of poverty, starvation, prison, booze, sickness and ill-fated love to the shared calamities of flood, drought or pestilence. But the blues were sung to alleviate pain, not to intensify it, and everywhere the unhappiness is tempered by hope, defiance or a wry philosophy. If good luck befell or a love affair succeeded, then the celebration of it in the blues song was, in its turn, modified by a deeply-instilled realism. In the stanzas of the blues, love may be passionate, tender, bawdy, violent or tragic, but never romantic.

From the blurred and indistinct picture that has so far emerged the reader will gather that the blues is as hard to ensnare and pin on to a specimen board as jazz itself. Like jazz, it has undergone growth and development and transplantation, surviving misconceptions, corruption and indignities along the way. Purists have pursued, as if it were the Holy Grail itself, the notion of ultimate 'authenticity', studiously separating the wheat of 'genuine blues singers' from the chaff of 'singers of the blues' who were not born to the style but acquired it. Nobody will ever know for sure when and where the first recognisable blues was sung. Since many of the earliest exponents were itinerant musicians who wandered far and wide across the Southern States, the trail rapidly became criss-crossed and confused.

Having once been something of a purist myself, I can recount a cautionary tale which illustrates the dangers of pontificating about authenticity. One night in the mid-Fifties, a gladiatorial contest took place in my club in Oxford Street between Big Bill Broonzy from Scott, Mississippi and Josh White from Greenville, South Carolina, both of whom were in London on separate engagements. Big Bill was at the time enjoying a professional Indian summer as 'the last of the Mississippi blues singers' (the first, as it turned out, of a long procession of surviving Mississippi bluesmen to visit Britain as the blues revival gathered momentum in the Fifties and Sixties). Josh White had moved to New York in his early twenties to embark on a successful cabaret career as a purveyor of folk-song that included black blues, work-songs, spirituals and penitentiary songs as well as folk-songs of England, Scotland and Ireland.

At the club on this occasion, Josh had to endure persistent ribbing from Bill Broonzy, who was in ribald mood and kept haranguing the audience with 'He cain't sing the blues! He's from the North—ain't never heard no one from the North sing the blues!' Singers from the Mississippi States always tended to regard the blues as their special preserve, much as the old New Orleans men talked of jazz. And doubtless Bill spotted the effect that a long sojourn in the alien field of sophisticated cabaret had had on Josh's style. But critics in the audience, myself included, nodded sagely at Bill's comments. This is what we had always said—Josh White was not an 'authentic' blues singer and here it was being confirmed, as it were from the horse's mouth! A few weeks later, from the same horse's mouth, came the admission that Big Bill Broonzy, whose career as a blues singer flourished in the Thirties in the urban environment of Chicago, had had to brush up and, in some instances, learn from scratch the country blues and folk-songs which his European promoter wanted him to sing.

I cannot answer for the other witnesses to that epic contest (it ended with both men singing a string of amicable and entertaining duets), but I thought then, and think now, that Josh White was not in the same class as Broonzy and that he didn't sing the blues very convincingly. But authenticity had nothing to do with it. Having acted in his youth as guide to several blind bluesmen of the calibre of Blind Lemon Jefferson and Blind Blake, he must have had a headful of the real stuff and could have learnt it as well as anyone had he the ear and voice to do it.

It is important to have got any preoccupation with authenticity out of the way, because by the time we join the story of the blues, it had undergone a metamorphosis. The British blues historian, Paul Oliver, has written a pictorial survey actually called *The Story of the Blues*, which I highly recommend and in which we can see, through the selected photographs, the change taking place. The early chapters, discussing the evolution of the blues, show pictures with a predominantly rural background. Guitar players and bandsmen clutching home-made instruments pose on ramshackle porches or in dusty-looking fields, wearing flimsy vests or awkwardly-fitting country suits. And then, after fifty-odd pages, the scene suddenly changes and we are confronted with an imposing regiment of women, theatrically-dressed against formal backdrops and looking more like prima donnas than purveyors of a simple folk-music. And that is exactly what they were, for by the start of the century the blues had become a formal song-form which was susceptible to theatrical presentation. In other words, it had made the quite considerable step from a folk-music to a popular music. And because its roots were so firmly embedded in the life of Negroes in the South, it became, in every area to which black entertainment spread, very popular indeed.

With some justice, the photograph which looms largest in the early part of this phase in Paul Oliver's story is that of a homely lady dripping with ornate jewellery and revealing in a broad grin a veritable Fort Knox of gold fillings. This is Gertrude 'Ma' Rainey, the first great exponent of what have come to be called the 'classic' blues. Ma Rainey (she never liked the title, preferring to be addressed as Madame Rainey) was born Gertrude Pridgett in 1886, and by the age of eighteen was married to one Will Rainey and was working with him in a travelling show under the name of Rainey and Rainey, 'The Assassinators of the Blues'. Contrary to widespread belief, 'Nigger Minstrel' shows were not the sole invention of paternalistic and condescending white entrepreneurs for the amusement of white audiences. In the last two decades of the last century, all-black minstrel shows were established in which, for some years to come, black entertainers would have the opportunity to work their apprenticeship. A good idea of the nature of these shows comes from Paul Oliver's description of one of the best known of them all, F. S. Wolcott's Rabbit Foot Minstrels. Writing of this team and its chief rival, Silas Green's from New Orleans, he says: 'It was the central location of both shows on the Mississippi that enabled them to draw so freely on blues singers, but they also featured a variety of acts. Wolcott's show had jungle scenes and olios, wrestlers, comics, jugglers and vaudeville teams as part of the show. The "Foots" travelled in two cars and had an 80′ × 110′ tent which was raised by the roustabouts and canvasmen while a brass band would parade in the town to advertise the coming of the show . . . the stage would be of boards on a folding frame and Coleman lanterns—gasoline mantle lamps—acted as footlights. There were no microphones; the weaker-voiced singers used a megaphone, but most of the featured women blues singers scorned such aids to volume. Few "classic" blues singers of note became famous without serving a tough apprenticeship in the tent shows, barnstorming from settlement to township to plantation, from Florida to Fort Worth, from North Carolina to New Orleans and from Missouri to Mexico.'

There is a famous story, almost certainly apocryphal, which serves to describe the special, theatrical quality which these women brought to the performance of the blues. It is alleged that Ma Rainey was onstage in a tent show, bringing all the majesty of her fine contralto voice to bear on her speciality, 'C. C. Rider', when the frail stage on its folding frame began to collapse. Without a tremor in the voice or a falter in the tempo she kept on singing with such authority that there was neither mirth nor alarm among the audience as she slowly sank from view in a welter of disintegrating timber. True or not, the heart of the story is to a large degree confirmed when we listen today to the many available recordings of Ma Rainey. Through the suspirating mists of ancient recording we hear the authentic sound of the 'classic' blues—a strong, clear, unequivocal melody line, rich in blue notes and delivered in tones which are not only poignant, melancholy and intensely moving but have, even at this distance, a regal command.

Authentic—that dangerous word reappears. I will justify it by claiming that, whether or not she was first in the field, Ma Rainey was the one who defined the 'classic' style by which we judge the work of her eminent rivals such as Ida Cox, Bertha 'Chippie' Hill, Clara Smith, Sippie Wallace and Bessie Smith herself. As for historical authenticity, a clear denial emerges from one sentence in Paul Oliver's book: 'She first heard the blues, she told John Work, when she heard a young girl singing a "strange and poignant" lament in a small Missouri town in 1902.' She was sixteen at the time and already embarked on a career as an entertainer. From that point onwards she used a blues of her own composition as an encore. But as time went on and the blues attained the status of popular music in Negro entertainment, she turned to them almost exclusively.

For some years the legend persisted that Ma Rainey and her husband heard Bessie Smith in her hometown of Chattanooga, persuaded—some versions say 'kidnapped'—her into joining their show, and that Ma Rainey then taught her how to sing the blues. Clearly the legend arose not only from the stylistic similarity between the two formidable contraltos but also from a need to find a link between the blues that Bessie sang and their rural and primitive origins. The truth, as it emerges in the fine biography of Bessie Smith by Chris Albertson (*Bessie*), seems to be that it was not the Raineys who 'discovered' Bessie, but a couple called Lonnie and Cora Fisher for whose show she auditioned in Chattanooga in 1912, when she would have been about fourteen years old. According to Paul Oliver, she always spoke of Cora Fisher as her inspiration. However, this is not to discount entirely the Rainey influence—Ma Rainey and Bessie did meet during Bessie's adolescence, worked together for a short while and established an allegedly strong mother-to-daughter relationship. Furthermore it seems probable that, through Ma Rainey's pre-eminence in the field of what one could call the 'theatrical' blues, the precepts which Cora Fisher handed down were essentially those of Rainey.

There is no need here to trace Bessie Smith's early career in minute detail. The Oliver and Albertson books, not to mention the eye-witness accounts that appear in Hentoff and Shapiro's *Hear Me Talkin' To Ya*, give a full account. One fact emerges— that Bessie Smith was a natural, unaffected artist with a 'presence', even in her teens, that overcame a rough manner, a non-existent dress sense and a tendency to overlay her statuesque beauty with ungainly fat. The most revealing picture comes from the New Orleans guitarist Danny Barker in *Hear Me Talkin' To Ya*: 'Bessie Smith was a fabulous deal to watch. She was a pretty large woman and she could sing the blues. She had a church deal mixed up with it. She dominated the stage. You didn't turn your head when she went on. You just watched Bessie . . . if you had any church background, like people who came from the South as I did, you would recognise a similarity between what she was doing and what those preachers and evangelists from there did, and how they moved people.' Years later, in the 1950s, a fine gospel singer came to fame who demonstrated this theory in reverse. Though Mahalia Jackson renounced the blues and jazz as 'sinful music', she did admit to having heard Bessie Smith as a child, and in her spellbinding style the influence was undeniable.

Sidney Bechet, whose recollection of a turbulent love affair with Bessie Smith was probably true in essence if not in detail, threw a light on the darker, offstage side of her nature which went deeper than the view of other contemporaries that she was 'rough'. 'She had this trouble in her, this thing that wouldn't let her rest sometimes, a meanness that came and took her over.' Speaking of her death in a car accident in 1937, he showed an insight into her real tragedy that is all the more forcible coming from a man who was no stranger to 'meanness' himself: 'Someways, you could almost have said beforehand that there was some kind of accident, some bad hurt coming to her. It was like she had that hurt inside her all the time, and she was just bound to find it' (*Treat It Gentle*).

It would take a psycho-analytical treatise for which I am in no way equipped to plumb the source of Bessie Smith's trouble. She was born into abject poverty—but so was Louis Armstrong who, through similar early vicissitudes, established a mood of sunny optimism which seldom deserted him through the rest of his life. In escaping the fate of a lifetime of ill-paid servility by the only route available—that of an entertainer in a black travelling show—she had a remarkable early success. In terms of comfort or glamour, the theatre circuits which she toured hardly deserved star rating, but before the demanding and highly critical audiences of her own people, she herself rapidly became a star. That she was called upon to do more than sing is evident from the recollection of James P. Johnson's wife, May Wright, who in *Hear Me Talkin' To Ya* described seeing Bessie's own show in Atlanta in 1921: 'You won't believe this, but Bessie was the smallest woman in that show. And you know how big *she* was. Well, that opening number was the funniest thing I ever saw. The curtain went up, and the floodlights came on, and there was the entire chorus dressed in close-fitting bloomers, bent over with their backs to the audience. The orchestra struck up "Liberty Bell", and there was that whole chorus shakin' every muscle in their bodies.' Singing, acting, dancing, hip-shaking were all part of the travelling entertainer's stock-in-trade, but it is improbable that Bessie, with her unbridled sexuality, her bawdy manner and her insatiable appetite for 'good times', harboured any resentment or frustrations over these intrusions into the sanctity of her 'art'. She seems to have been a heavy drinker almost from childhood and this no doubt contributed over the years to the mounting violence of her temperamental storms. But the stories of her portentous rages, tempestuous love-affairs, wild bouts of generosity, epic binges and not infrequent recourse to devastating fisticuffs—all of which stretch back as far as her public career itself—leave us with the impression of a totally untamed creature who remained, to the end of her days, immune from the restraints of manners or convention. Something of this uninhibited, almost menacing vitality emerges from the grainy images of a seventeen-minute film called *St Louis Blues* which Bessie made in 1929. The flimsy story line, for all it triteness, was at the same time centred firmly within Bessie's own personal experience. The woman she portrays, who is given the name Bessie, finds her boyfriend in what is known, in very un-Bessie-like language, as a compromising situation with a rival. She hurls the girl out of the room but is herself struck to the floor by the boyfriend who leaves her to drown her sorrows in, among other things, a dramatic version of 'St Louis Blues'. There is a brief but hollow reconciliation and the film ends with Bessie once again singing the blues. Everything that is good about the film emanates from Bessie Smith who overcomes the crackly sound track and a dreadfully unbecoming costume with voice and movements that are truly majestic.

To agree with Sidney Bechet that Bessie Smith's 'hurt' was probably deep within herself is not to discount the frustrations which confronted a black entertainer in America as the Twenties approached. An impresario called Irving C. Miller, who had touring shows in the South around 1912, remembers the young Bessie in the chorus of one of them: 'She was a natural singer, even then—but we stressed beauty in the chorus line and Bessie did not meet my standards as far as looks were concerned. I told the manager to get rid of her, which he did.' The slogan of Mr Miller's shows, 'Glorifying the Brownskin Girl', explains what otherwise appears to be philistinism of truly Goliath proportions. Bessie Smith was too black.

When, around 1920, the big recording companies began to grasp the commercial potential of black artists, especially those from the South, it looked for a while as though a similar rebuff was in store for Bessie. The very first blues record to appear in the lists was recorded in August 1920. The Okeh record company, having failed to contract Sophie Tucker, took a considerable chance on a little-known black vaudeville singer called Mamie Smith. Her first recordings, of undistinguished popular songs, did well enough to warrant a return visit to the studios. On this second session her manager, a persistent and energetic entrepreneur called Perry Bradford, persuaded the company to be even more reckless and allow her to sing a blues backed by a black band. 'Crazy Blues', sung in a manner indistinguishable from many white singers of the period, has little distinction other than that it was the first in the field. But half a blues was better than nothing for the huge audience which was ripe to receive it, and 'Crazy Blues' was a hit.

There can be little doubt that the success of 'Crazy Blues' took the record companies by surprise. Centred in New York as most of them were, such research as they might have done into the tastes of the black community would have been directed at the established Negro population which had settled in Harlem and which, as we have seen in the chapter on James P. Johnson, had high aspirations towards 'respectable' white culture. To them, the blues was the music of the rough, uneducated migrants from the rural South and, as such, definitely not nice to know. Once the record companies became aware that there was a much wider black audience to be tapped, they began to record more and more black artists for their newly established 'race' lists, aimed exclusively at the Negro market. In the fullness of time, many of these race records were to become the cherished possessions of avid jazz collectors from Stockholm to Sidney and Tokyo to Toronto. But in the early days it seems that the companies were paralysed with apprehension. In 1921 Bessie Smith auditioned for the Black Swan label which was newly founded by the erstwhile partner of composer W. C. Handy, Harry Pace. Despite their proud slogan, 'The Only Genuine Colored Record—Others Are Only Passing for Colored', Black Swan turned Bessie down, preferring to stay on safer ground with the more cultivated and lightweight style of Ethel Waters. News reports from the same year suggest that Bessie may have made some trial recordings for the Emerson Company, but if she did, they were never released. In January 1923, under the wing of the composer, pianist and entrepreneur Clarence Williams, she tried again for the Okeh label, but her style was once again adjudged too rough. 'Too black' might have been the exact comment of her judges in their private deliberation, for no other singer, least of all Mamie Smith, so characterised the essence of the blues with its subtle variations of pitch, sheer weight of melancholy and, above all, harsh and disturbing timbres.

It was Frank Walker, the man in charge of the Columbia

record company's 'race' lists, who eventually took the chance on recording Bessie Smith. The story that, having once heard her sing in the South, he sent Clarence Williams to find her and bring her to the studios loses some of its romantic gloss when it is noted that she was in New York two weeks earlier auditioning for Okeh. In fact, Clarence Williams had to go no further than South Philadelphia to summon Bessie to New York. It was on February 15, 1923 that Bessie Smith first went into the recording studios in earnest. 'She looked anything *but* a singer,' Walker recalled later, 'she looked about seventeen, tall and fat and scared to death—just awful.' A year or so later the sharp and superior musicians in Fletcher Henderson's Orchestra were to show the same blend of shock and amusement at the 'country boy' appearance of Louis Armstrong. New York considered itself to be the hub of the entertainment industry, and its denizens no doubt suffered some pain at the dawning awareness that these gauche bumpkins were giving them a lesson in musical sophistication. The bandleader Sam Wooding is quoted in the Albertson biography on the subject of Bessie's initial impact on them with her slow, drawn-out style. 'This is one reason she didn't go over too big with New York musicians . . . She would sing something like "Baby, I love you, love you mo' and mo' ''. I'd go to the bathroom, come back and catch the rest of the verse, "I hope you never leave me, 'cause I don't wanna see you go". She had dragged out each word so that I hadn't missed a thing.'

In the history of modern entertainment, there have been artists with a magnetic stage personality who have been unable to project it on to records. Bessie Smith was not one of them. It took two days to conquer nerves and unfamiliarity and produce a pair of marketable recordings, 'Downhearted Blues' and 'Gulf Coast Blues'. Once they were issued, Bessie experienced the same magical ascent to stardom that appears to have followed her teenage stage debut ten years or so earlier. She may have arrived in the studio looking like a frightened and clumsy teenager, but the singing that was transmitted to wax was, from the outset, mature, steeped in harsh experience and formidably commanding. Within six months, Bessie Smith's version of 'Downhearted Blues' sold 780,000 copies, obliterating all previous versions of the song. Discovering some 'irregularities' in her contract, Bessie and her husband Jack Gee severed relations with Clarence Williams in a brisk meeting which allegedly—and characteristically—left him in a dazed heap on his office floor. Frank Walker became her manager and, in the next five or six years, presided over a prolific recording career that ran to sales exceeding 8,000,000 and made her, within the limitations of black entertainment, a superstar.

It is this fact which confronts me at this point with a problem. Not all of Bessie Smith's recordings through the Twenties were 'classics'. Towards the end of the decade her turbulent lifestyle was reflected in a coarsening of the magnificent voice. The insatiable demands on her repertoire resulted in some numbers which conformed to a familiar pattern, others which did her little justice. But, like Louis Armstrong, Bessie Smith seemed artistically incapable of dispensing trash. From the most unworthy material, some trace of nobility can always be extracted. And, on top of the heap, there is the rich crust of widely acknowledged masterpieces. Having made the decision to deal with two recordings, the question remains 'Which two?' Can great performances such as 'Young Woman's Blues', 'Empty Bed Blues', the majestic 'Yellow Dog Blues' or the triumphant 'Cake Walkin' Babies' be left out? Each presents an important facet of her style. And when it comes to accompaniment, can I afford to neglect the great partnership with James P. Johnson, or the richly satisfying collaborations with her favourite cornet accompanist, Joe Smith? In the end, I have chosen two of her best-known recordings, confident that both are among her very best and mindful, too, that each puts her firmly in a jazz context.

The choice of 'St Louis Blues' makes it necessary to bring in one further character in the story of the blues. W. C. Handy will reappear later in this book, cast as a villain of the piece in one episode in the life of Jelly Roll Morton. He was a Memphis bandleader and cornetist, a trained musician who earned the Tin Pan Alley title of 'Father of the Blues' through a string of compositions which have since become standard material in the jazz and popular music repertoire. This soubriquet, often repeated and taken seriously in ill-informed jazz journalism, was the cause of much suspicion and obloquy directed at Handy as the 'authentic'

blues came to light. Jelly Roll Morton could hardly find words to
express his scorn at a radio announcer's suggestion that Handy
originated jazz and blues, and there are johnny-come-lately blues
pundits around today who recount with glee every instance of a
W. C. Handy lyric which turns up in pristine form in some
primitive blues from the common stock. It is perfectly true that
Handy, born into a self-made middle-class Negro family in
Florence, Tennessee in 1873, was not by any stretch of the
imagination a bluesman. The few examples of his cornet-playing
on record show him playing in a clipped, square ragtime manner
innocent of any blues or jazz inflections. But it is also true that,
when he came to write his autobiography, *Father of the Blues,* he
made no pretence to be other than what he was, a schooled
composer who heard and was intrigued by the rural blues on his
travels, and who incorporated their form, and sometimes snatches
of their words, in a series of blues compositions. When, in 1914, he
achieved both fame and a modest fortune with his 'St Louis
Blues', the time was ripe for just such a formal organisation of
blues material. Ma Rainey was in full spate, Bessie Smith was
just embarking on her career and the blues itself was making the
transition from a folk to a popular music. Anyone who has actually
read Handy's lyrics—the couplet ' I know the Yellow Dog District
like a book, Indeed I know the route that Rider took' from 'Yellow
Dog Blues' is a typical example—will find it hard to assert with
a straight face that he stole his material wholesale from folk
sources. And it would ill become a musician who has recorded, I
hope with love and affection, such Handy classics as 'St Louis
Blues', 'Memphis Blues', Beale Street Blues' and 'Yellow Dog
Blues' to add fuel to the canard that W. C. Handy was simply
a purloiner of other men's material. In the composed form in which
we know them, with their carefully-structured and contrasting
melodic themes, these pieces did not exist before Handy put them
down on paper.

'St Louis Blues' is a fine example. It was to Handy's advantage
that he was an active dance-band leader, to whom instantaneous
audience response was important. Once, when he was playing for a
vast audience at Dixie Park in Memphis, he noticed a curious
phenomenon. 'It was the odd response of the dancers to Will H.

Tyers' "Maori". When we played this number and came to the Habanera rhythm, containing the beat of the tango, I observed that there was a sudden proud and graceful reaction to the rhythm. Was it an accident, or could the response be traced to a real but hidden cause?' Handy experimented with the undiluted tango rhythm of 'La Paloma', and 'sure enough, there it was, that same calm yet ecstatic movement'. What he had stumbled upon was the rhythm, originally called *tangana*, which originated in African music, was the basis of Jelly Roll Morton's 'Spanish tinge' that underlay New Orleans music, and often emerged in the work of primitive blues players, notably the pianist Jimmy Yancey. This tango rhythm became something of a hallmark in Handy's compositions. The original piano copy of 'St Louis Blues' starts with the G minor theme in tango rhythm as an introduction, a deliberate and clever move of the composer's when one thinks of the suspicion that the blues aroused at first in audiences attuned to the conventional dance forms. 'I tricked the dancers by arranging a tango introduction, breaking abruptly then into a lowdown blues.' The ruse succeeded and 'St Louis Blues' was an instant hit.

When Bessie Smith came to record it, 'St Louis Blues' had already been popularised by other singers on the theatre circuits, one of whom, Ethel Waters, had made it her own speciality. As usual, Bessie ran over this obstacle like a steamroller. Her version became definitive, putting back into the song the essence of the real blues which had originally inspired Handy to write it. With her in the studio that day in January, 1925 was Fred Longshaw, a competent and diligent musician with no jazz pretensions who elected to play harmonium on the occasion, and young Louis Armstrong who had arrived in New York some four months before to join Fletcher Henderson's Orchestra. By this time, Bessie had been a recording star for a full two years, and there is little reason, in view of her temperament, to disbelieve the legend that she was far from pleased by the booking of Armstrong in place of her preferred Joe Smith who was out of New York at the time. Musical considerations apart, the prospect of sharing the limelight with a young and no doubt bumptious musician who was currently being hailed as a phenomenon was hardly likely to appeal to her.

In the event, Louis approached most of the numbers which they recorded at the session with great seriousness and restraint (the only dubious exception being some jokey, out-of-place playing in a vaudeville song called 'You've Been A Good Ole Wagon', which Bessie converts into a solemn blues). These were, after all, two already great artists with an instinctive awareness of their own transcendant artistry. Whatever was said on the surface—and Louis himself claimed to prefer the records he made with a much lesser singer called Maggie Jones—it would have been surprising if they had failed to find a common artistic meeting ground.

That common ground is located in the very opening bars of 'St Louis Blues', which they transposed into the key of E flat. It is easy to be derisive about the contribution of Fred Longshaw and his asthmatic harmonium. If the quality of swing belongs to the angels, then the devil must have invented the harmonium expressly to destroy it. And yet, like a great many odd noises from the primaeval days of recording, its sound has become woven into the very atmosphere of the piece to the extent that, were technology to find a way of expunging it and substituting a crisply-recorded rhythm section, I should be loth to see it go. What carefully-contrived arrangement could be better than the husky and sombre B flat major chord which replaces Handy's tango introduction and, as it were, opens the curtain on Bessie's performance?

Fresh in my memory is a conversation about Louis Armstrong with the British trombonist George Chisholm, a Louisphile of long-standing. He made the point that Louis was one of the very few musicians who possessed such innate swing that he could establish a tempo with the shortest of phrases—sometimes even with one note. Bessie Smith shared this faculty. While Fred Longshaw is hard at work trying to establish co-ordination between foot-pedals and keyboard, she makes plain within the span of the words 'I hate to see . . .' exactly the tempo which she intends to maintain. It is significant, in the light of Sam Wooding's comments earlier about her slow, drawn-out style, that this blues tempo is much slower than anything to be heard in instrumental jazz at that period. It was not until well into the Thirties that musicians started tackling this sort of slow-drag blues. If we

listen again to some of the famous instrumental blues that traditional jazz bands take at a crawling pace today—King Oliver's
'Riverside Blues', the Armstrong Hot Five's 'Savoy Blues', Jimmy
Noone's 'Apex Blues' or Ellington's 'Creole Love Call'—we find
that they trot along at what we now consider a medium tempo,
presumably to give the dancers what they wanted. Bessie, used to
singing to motionless or at any rate swaying audiences, could afford
to set her own dramatic tempo—and she was lucky in an accompanist for whom music held very few surprises to which he could
not instantly adapt.

No words about the rapport and musical understanding between
Bessie Smith and Louis Armstrong can do justice to the opening
chorus of 'St Louis Blues'. In a mood of experiment I once learnt
off by heart the vocal and cornet lines so that I could play them
on trumpet as one continuous melody. The result came as near to
a perfect *instrumental* blues chorus as one could conceive. It is
not just in inventive talent that the two principals were evenly
matched. Passion is an elusive quality in music, often impersonated
by a sort of spurious frenzy, a simulated hysteria that is all too
familiar in contemporary pop music that boasts a black gospel-
song influence. I have sometimes said that the great jazz giants
whom I have heard in person—Louis Armstrong, Sidney Bechet,
Coleman Hawkins, John Coltrane—have all made the same striking
impression that, were the instrument to be suddenly wrenched
from their lips, the music would continue to flow out of sheer
creative momentum. Such is the great wave of passion on which
'St Louis Blues' is carried that I am similarly rather surprised that
it doesn't continue to well out of the speakers when the amplifier
is suddenly switched off or the needle lifted.

Each one of Louis Armstrong's responses is worthy of analysis.
I will be content to pick out three. At the very beginning, in
answer to Bessie's opening line 'I hate to see that evenin' sun go
down', he reacts without hesitation to the dramatic mood which
she has set by starting a descending phrase with seven E flat notes
hammered out with great intensity. The whole phrase is imbued
with a beauty and melancholy that disguise the fact that all Louis
is doing in terms of structure is playing the straight five-note
scale from E flat down to A flat that ushers in the subdominant

chord of the second four bars. In this, he is bound by the meticulously correct but deadeningly unadventurous harmonies churned out by Fred Longshaw on the harmonium. Louis spent much of his musical career overcoming, and indeed glorifying, unimaginative backing, and this recording is a fine example. At the end of the first verse, Armstrong's feeling for harmony enables him to play a neat trick as he follows Longshaw's chord progression doggedly with a note pattern that changes only at the last moment, when it seems on the very verge of mockery. And then, in the very last verse of all, following a veritable clarion call to action by Bessie on the word 'Nowhere' that ends the minor tango section, Louis responds to the line 'I got the Saint Louis Blues just as blue as I can be' with a complex fill-in that almost comes a cropper. The snatch of melody that Louis plays, phrasing it recklessly across the beat, is one which crops up elsewhere in music related to New Orleans. It sounds as if its inspiration was the trio section of the famous march 'National Emblem' which, as we have already seen in the chapter on the ODJB, was always quoted by Louis Armstrong in his versions of 'Tiger Rag' and may possibly have had connections with that tune itself. In the tune 'Clarinet Lament' by Duke Ellington's Orchestra, featuring the New Orleans clarinettist Barney Bigard, the same phrase is elevated to the status of an introductory cadenza. Whatever its origins—and it is not inconceivable that Louis invented it himself—it fills the bill admirably in this instance, providing a fitting response to Bessie's stirring lament and showing, in passing, Louis Armstrong's uncanny, cat-like ability to recover from a bad mistake and continue on his way without the missing of a beat.

As for Bessie Smith herself, this is one of her masterpieces. Having said that, I shall not, to the reader's relief and certainly to mine, be following up with pages of detailed analysis. It was central to Bessie Smith's art that she simplified rather than elaborated her themes. In modern times the quality in black music popularly known as 'soul'—expressed in techniques directly borrowed from Negro church music—has been progressively exaggerated to the point where a simple blues becomes a positive firework display of shrieks and moans and wild vocal contortions. Neither the classic female singers nor the country bluesmen who preceded them went in for such antics. Bessie's way, taken up and carried forward right into the rock 'n' roll era by the great Kansas City blues singer Big Joe Turner, was to restrict the range of a song to no more than five or six notes and to construct her phrases so economically that a change in direction of just one note could have a startling dramatic or emotive effect. One example stands out in 'St Louis Blues'. The first two twelve-bar blues verses begin with identical phrases, sung to the words 'I hate to see that evenin' sun go down' and 'Feelin' tomorrow like I feel today' respectively. Bessie starts the second verse, as Handy intended, with a melody line that begins in exactly the same way as the first. But where the word 'see' in 'I hate to see . . .' descends to the E flat keynote as in Handy's original melody, the last two syllables of 'tomorrow' hover indeterminately in the 'blue note' area between the second and third notes in the scale, eventually making a little upward turn which creates an unimaginably desolate effect. Indeed, if I wanted examples to illustrate my earlier definition of 'blue notes' I need do no more than point to these two lines and to the words 'sun' in the first and 'feel' in the second.

There is another characteristic of Bessie Smith's style which goes a long way to explaining why many commentators, myself included, choose to regard her, not as the culmination of a tradition of blues singing, but as the beginning of a new tradition of jazz singing. Since a jazz critique developed a long time after the music itself had begun, we have had the luxury of making many of our definitions in retrospect. Thus the jazz singers to us are those who, like the musicians, have enhanced their chosen themes with a blend of insight, blues feeling and creative variation, whether improvised or not. A singer who sang 'St Louis Blues' note for note from the sheet music as Handy had written it down would not sound to us like a jazz singer, however sincere the interpretation. For one thing, much of Handy's phrasing is symmetrical, with matching phrases following hard on each other like flower patterns on a wallpaper. And this sort of tightly-knit symmetry is the very antithesis of the broadly-sweeping and imaginative composition which we recognise in the best of jazz. Bessie Smith shared with Louis Armstrong a sort of built-in musical radar which steered her unerringly away from approaching symmetry. Since the words of popular songs were often harnessed to fairly jerry-built construction, we find both Bessie and Louis often making a dog's breakfast of the the lyrics in the interests of improved musical architecture. A famous example of Bessie's cavalier treatment of the words occurs in the song 'Cake Walkin' Babies' where, in order to deliver a superbly rhythmic and swinging musical phrase, she sings 'The only way is to win is to cheat 'em'. Less extreme are the occasions in 'St Louis Blues' where, for purely structural ends, she inserts a breathing point right in the middle of a verbal phrase, knocking its grammar sideways. In the first verse, she sings 'It makes me think I'm / on my last go-round', emphasising the point by letting her voice fall off the syllable 'I'm' in a characteristic way. Likewise in the last verse, while Louis and Fred Longshaw faithfully reproduce Handy's repetitive melody to the words 'I've got the Saint Louis Blues just as blue as I can be', Bessie will have none of it. To turn the line into musical sense, she makes a dramatic pause on the second 'as', dropping off it in two steps in another of her striking mannerisms and cutting it off completely from the rest of the sentence. Paradoxically, this apparent sacrificing of the literary sense to musical construction actually deepens the emotional content of the song, a point to which I will return later.

The second Bessie Smith performance that I have chosen comes from a period, four years after the recording of 'St Louis Blues', when times had changed. Recording technique had made the giant stride into electrical reproduction, and singers no longer had to bellow into the cavernous mouth of a receiving horn as if aiming for the back row of the stalls. True, theatres continued to demand powerful voice projection—the era of whispering crooners was several years away. But the new recording methods could cope with subtler nuances now, and Bessie had plenty of these in her musical armoury. Unhappily, her career was moving rapidly towards a crisis. After almost a decade since Mamie Smith first opened up the blues market, the sales of blues records were beginning to decline. In an effort to boost sales, the managers of 'race' recordings began to stuff the lists with material in which 'blue' rather than blues was the operative word. Bessie Smith almost always managed to imbue the most relentless double entendres with a certain melancholy dignity, but neverthless it is a sad experience to play through her output of this period and hear the great voice, fraying somewhat at the edges under the stress of furious living, applied to a succession of songs in which the same old harmonic progressions—and sometimes the same melody—are trotted out to prop up a string of double meanings.

And then suddenly, a gem appears. In view of the imminent collapse of Bessie Smith's career, it is tempting to read some sort of autobiographical significance into her recording of 'Nobody Knows You When You're Down and Out'. She had recently been involved in a disastrous Broadway debut, and her records were not selling as briskly as they once did. But she was still very far from down and out. What is more, her uncertain and dangerous temperament had long put such tenuous friendships as she acquired at risk without applying the test of poverty. Bessie Smith rarely treated a song with anything less than total commitment, as witness the impassioned, almost tragic, overtones which she lent to songs such as 'Alexander's Ragtime Band' and 'There'll Be a Hot Time in the Old Town Tonight'. Written by an entertainer called Jimmy Cox, 'Nobody Knows You When You're Down and Out' teeters on the razor's edge that separates the lyrical from the maudlin, but with a firm embrace Bessie guides it on to safe ground. She has the assistance of a five-piece band led by Clarence Williams but dominated by the fine cornet-playing of Ed Allen, who backs her in a manner reminiscent of Joe Smith.

With benefit of greatly improved recording, we can hear in this performance more characteristics that stamp Bessie Smith as a supreme jazz singer. The manipulation of tone—or more accurately, timbre—is one attribute which distinguishes the jazz musician from his 'straight' dance-band colleague. A melody line will be given all kinds of contrasting nuances through a great repertoire of thin notes and thick notes, sweet notes and sour notes, clear notes and hoarse or 'growled' notes. These are used purely as materials in the musical construction, without particular reference to the theme or mood of the song that is being played. The fact that Bessie is singing words does not deter her from deploying her tonal resources in a manner quite independent of the general portent of the lyric. We have an example of this at the very outset of 'Nobody Knows You . . .'. The opening two lines—'Once I lived the life of a millionaire/Spending my money, I didn't care'—seem on paper to demand a wistful interpretation, tinged with regret. And no doubt from a 'straight' cabaret singer they would have got it, complete with a dollop of self-pity. Bessie is clearly not too concerned with a literal reading of the words. She takes her inspiration from the melody to which they are attached, treating those opening lines as two matching phrases, built on major and minor chord sequences respectively, which follow each other like great breakers on a sea shore. One can imagine Louis Armstrong or Sidney Bechet— or, much later on, Ben Webster—giving the second line the same majestic swell.

A few lines later, something equally unexpected happens. The words 'I carried my friends out for a good time . . .' are shouted like a full-blooded blues, with a poignant flattening of pitch on the word 'friends'. And then, with the phrase 'buying bootleg liquor', Bessie suddenly lets her voice drop away so that the words are virtually spoken, with a profoundly melancholy inflection. The moment brings vividly to life guitarist Danny Barker's recollection that, in performance, 'she was unconscious of her surroundings. She never paid anybody any mind.' Heaven knows what emotion prompted Bessie to lapse into soliloquy on those words. We learn from Chris Albertson that Bessie always preferred home-made liquor, maintaining that anything sealed made her sick. So far as we know, there was nothing in her often riotous relationship with bootleg liquor to prompt such sudden sadness. Once again, it transpires that there is a compelling *musical* reason for the device. For after building steadily for three lines, the melody suddenly collapses feebly on those words 'Buyin' bootleg liquor, champagne and wine'. It is the kind of weak, one-note phrase for which jazz players have become adept at improvising an alternative. Bessie's does not merely bridge the gap, it endows the line with great emotional strength. The point is made again most forcibly when, after the beautifully apt cornet solo by Ed Allen, Bessie returns to the chorus but, this time, hums the first bars of each line, in

the words of Chris Albertson, 'expressing the feeling behind the
song more effectively than any words do.' This is the standard
which Bessie Smith set for all jazz singers to follow, using improvisation in its fullest sense on the melody of a song to express a
deeper meaning than that of the words on their own. It was an
example which, a decade later, enabled Billie Holiday to make
remarkable music out of popular ditties of the calibre of 'I Cried
for You' and 'Back in Your Own Back Yard', not to mention
'Ooooooh, What a Little Moonlight Can Do'.

We cannot leave Bessie Smith without referring to the rhythmic
aspect of her music. Elsewhere in this book, I make the point that,
of all the musicians who recorded in the early Twenties, only three
—Louis Armstrong, Sidney Bechet and Bessie Smith—seemed
to possess the instinct to overcome and, indeed, change the
rhythmic conventions of the day. Of these three, I would put
Louis and Bessie together in the very top bracket. In some ways,
Bessie had the more difficult task, since she had to handle words
which were often harnessed to melodies conceived in the even
quaver, eight-to-a-bar rhythm which ragtime bequeathed. I have
already spoken of her habit of altering the words or the sentences
to conform to her rhythmic notions. 'Nobody Knows You . . .' is
full of such adjustments. For instance, Jimmy Cox's original
words in the song's second line are 'Spending all my money,
I didn't care' to match the syllables of 'Once I lived the life of a
millionaire'. Recoiling from symmetry as ever, Bessie drops the
word 'all', which enables her to sing the phrase across the beat,
stringing the words 'Spending my money I' into one phrase. In
several instances, her unerring rhythmic instinct, based like
Louis Armstrong's on an underlying rhythm of twelve eighth
notes (or four quaver triplets) to the bar, gets her out of difficulty
with the lyrics. The very opening line, for instance, is almost
impossible to sing in a 'straight' fashion without distorting the
word 'millionaire'. If an even-quaver style is used, giving the notes
of 'Once I lived the life . . .' equal value, then undue emphasis has
to be put on the last syllable—'million-*aire*' to make it scan. If
the quavers are dotted in more lilting style, then it is the first
syllable—'*mill*-ionaire'—that has to be stressed. Free of both tight
conventions, Bessie is able to drape the sentence loosely over the

two bars so that 'millionaire' comes out exactly as it is spoken.

I hope I have made the case for regarding Bessie Smith, not simply as an exalted blues singer, but as one of the greatest of all jazz performers. Unfortunately for her, technology inflicted upon singing styles in the Thirties the kind of radical changes which instrumental jazz was not to suffer until the arrival many years later of electronics. Bing Crosby, like most of his jazz associates a great fan of Bessie's, was to develop an intimate use of the newly-perfected microphone from which 'crooning' emerged. Bessie Smith's career had already suffered two setbacks by the end of the Jazz Decade. The blues on which her early triumphs had been built had lost their popularity and, with the dramatic slump of 1929, the bottom fell clean out of the recording industry. In 1933, at the instigation of John Hammond (a young enterpreneur endowed happily with both money and taste, who, three days later, was to introduce a newcomer called Billie Holiday to the studios), she made a recording comeback after two years' absence. At her own request, no blues were involved, but the rowdy vaudeville songs which she sang on this occasion seem to be a throwback to the rorty atmosphere of the Twenties rather than a presage of the new mood of the Thirties. Nevertheless, Bessie was in fine voice and apparently good spirits, and there has been much intriguing speculation as to how she would have fared had not her life come to its abrupt and violent end on a Mississippi road in 1937.

With the wisdom of hindsight we can understand why Hammond's courageous gamble with her in 1933 bore no immediate fruit. The singers who came to fame in the Thirties—among them Billie Holiday, Connee Boswell, Mildred Bailey, Ella Fitzgerald and, on the male side, a late-developing Louis Armstrong—all cultivated a light, confidential style well-suited to the improved sound techniques in both studios and theatres. Never in a million years could Bessie have trimmed her voice or her personality to the intimacy of the living-rooms into which rapidly developing coast-to-coast radio pumped popular music. But, in the very year of her death, the discovery of a legendary New Orleans musician called Bunk Johnson, who had played with Buddy Bolden at the beginning of the century and whom many believed to be long dead, instigated a revival of interest in early forms of both jazz and blues which was soon to grow into something of a craze. There is little doubt that Bessie Smith would have been sought after in the early stages of the New Orleans Revival. Whether her down-to-earth nature, deeply suspicious of anything smacking of the phoney, would have put up for long with the movement's inherent nostalgia and sentimentality, is another matter. Sidney Bechet's awful verdict makes such speculation appear trivial. 'It was like she had that hurt inside her all the time, and she was just bound to find it.'

Jelly Roll Morton

OF ALL THE SELECTIONS made in this book, that of a Jelly Roll Morton 'masterpiece' is likely to be the most arbitrary and controversial. To call him the Chopin of early jazz is no more absurd than these analogies usually are. Taken with a pinch of salt, it sums him up quite usefully. His reputation—a controversial one even to this day—rests on the cumulative effect of scores of piano compositions, many of which he himself adapted for small, New Orleans-style band, and some of which he lived to see converted into rabble-rousing swing band fodder in the Thirties.

Here's a paradox. The man who, in forty itinerant years, frequently neglected music to earn a living as gambler, pimp, vaudeville comedian or pool-room hustler, later poured angry scorn on the successful swing musicians whose arrangements of numbers such as 'King Porter Stomp' and 'Milenberg Joys' gave his music an extended lease of life. One assumes that the royalties which recordings by Fletcher Henderson, Bob Crosby and, more especially, Benny Goodman attracted made a vital contribution to his livelihood in the late Thirties when he himself was without a recording contract and, indeed, lapsing into complete obscurity. And yet here was this figure, according to contemporary reports, standing around on Harlem Street corners dressed in sharp, if rather out-dated style, and flashing the diamond inlaid in his front tooth as he held forth on the shortcomings of the younger musicians around him and proclaimed the elementary principles of jazz as he had 'invented' it in 1902. As he himself pronounced in an interview, 'Not until 1926 did they get a faint idea of real jazz, when I decided to live in New York . . . very often you could hear the New York (supposed to be) jazz bands have twelve, fifteen men; they would blaze away with all the volume they had. Sometimes customers would have to hold their ears to protect their eardrums from a forced collision with their brains.'

To savour the full audacity of this claim, I refer the reader back to the chapter on James P. Johnson, which describes the rivalry and competitiveness that existed within the 'Harlem school' of piano-players even before the outrageous loudmouth from the West stalked vociferously into their midst. Reactions were predictable. Years later Duke Ellington, usually generous or discreet about fellow-musicians, gave his unforgiving judgement: 'He played piano like one of those high school teachers in Washington; as a matter of fact, high school teachers played better jazz.' The Duke's own idol, Willie 'The Lion' Smith, was more respectful. Indeed, he wrote in his autobiography, 'It used to make me mad to hear the New York cats who hadn't been out of Harlem making fun of Morton. Like myself, Jelly Roll had played in all kinds of places and that was the way you learned about life—playing in all the different back rooms.' But the pianist's fraternal sentiments had a sting in the tail . . . 'Jelly was a guy who always talked a lot. He used to be around the Rhythm Club every day and stand out on the corner and he used to bull and con all those fellows . . . I used to come around especially on Friday and Saturday looking for Jelly. I went round this one Friday and he was standing on the corner. "Look, Mister One-Hand," I said, "let's go inside and let me give you your lessons in cutting." So Jelly and I would go inside by the piano. I was the only one he would stand and listen to and then he didn't open his mouth. I must have played nearly everything you could name and when I got through, I said, "Well, Jelly, you'll keep quiet now." And true as I'm sitting here, Jelly would be quiet.'

But not for long. Jelly kept at it through thick and thin. And in the spring of 1938, exiled by circumstances to a tiny club in Washington, Jelly Roll Morton was finding times exceedingly thin when, suddenly, his persistent street-corner oratory achieved a kind of apotheosis. A chain of events that was to prove vastly important to the understanding of jazz history was set in motion when Morton chanced to hear a reference, on Robert Ripley's 'Believe It or Not' radio programme, to W. C. Handy as 'the originator of jazz and the blues'. It was the kind of sloppy, ill-informed comment that lay journalists have made ever since the word jazz was coined, for Handy, as bandleader and cornetist, was not a jazz performer at all, while his famous pieces such as 'St Louis Blues', 'Memphis Blues' and many others were formal compositions based on the blues rather than intrinsic blues material. But Ripley's gaffe hit Morton on a nerve excoriated by neglect, and he exploded. In a letter to 'Dear Mr Ripley' re-produced in the jazz magazine *Downbeat*, he unleashed the kind of extravagant polemic that his street-corner audiences had endured down the years. 'It is evidently known, beyond contra-diction, that New Orleans is the cradle of jazz and I, myself, happened to be the creator in 1902.' And later ... 'Mr Ripley, these untruthful statements Mr Handy has made, or caused you to make, will maybe cause him to be branded the most dastardly imposter in the history of music.'

It may well have been this eruption in the columns of *Downbeat* and the subsequent controversy that prompted Alan Lomax, the curator of the Library of Congress Archive of American Folksong, to invite Jelly Roll Morton to record his reminiscences for the archives. Be that as it may, the whole incident had certainly primed Jelly with such a mountainous sense of injustice and outrage that his story, rich in almost Biblical cadences, developed into a manifesto on behalf of New Orleans in general and Jelly Roll Morton in particular.

Fate could not have chosen a better time for him to make public all his bottled-up indignation. A movement to find out more about the origins of jazz had already begun to stir among jazz writers in the States. A year or so earlier Bunk Johnson, who once played in Buddy Bolden's prototype jazz band, had been dis-covered working in the Southern rice-fields and was all set to provide the New Orleans Revival, as it came to be called, with a legendary figurehead. In the ensuing years, Jelly Roll Morton's story, eventually transcribed and amplified by Alan Lomax in a definitive biography called *Mister Jelly Roll*, proved despite all the absurd bragging to be the most perceptive analysis of the nature and significance of New Orleans jazz ever expounded. The more one probes the thought behind the grandiloquent speech, the more one agrees with the clarinettist Omer Simeon that Jelly 'would back up anything he *said* by what he could *do*'.

And up pops another paradox. Jazz music's first intellectual, the man whose lifelong preaching for the cause of New Orleans roused generations of musicians to derisive fury, was a 'loner' if ever there was one. As one who achieved the status of a 'house pianist' in the red-light Storyville district in the early years of the century, his New Orleans was not the permanent carnival of street parades, bandwagons and rough cabarets that horn-men like Louis Armstrong and Sidney Bechet have described. As Morton was quick to point out, it was the piano-players—all-round entertainers with a repertoire of ragtime, classical and original music—who were the élite amongst New Orleans musicians. Their undisputed territory was in the lavish and expensive 'sporting houses' where, performing the function of one-man pit orchestras to the orgiastic goings-on, they had a certain standing and were no doubt regarded with some envy by the lowlier musicians who played in the 'joints' and on the streets. Jelly Roll asserted that he was about seventeen years old when he achieved the rank of a piano 'professor' in the District. As such, he remained somewhat aloof from the horn-blowers whose names crop up in fraternal terms whenever reminiscences of New Orleans have been evoked. In one of jazz critic Leonard Feather's 'Blindfold Tests' for *Metronome* Magazine in America, Louis Armstrong could only recall Morton as 'that boy who went to California in the early days'.

Indeed, by the time young Louis had begun to take an active part in New Orleans music, Jelly Roll Morton had long left the city, travelling, often in hobo style, through the South and mid-West in pursuit of easy money and a variety of ambitions that included recognition as 'the pool champion of all the world'. His activities as a pimp—a profession adopted without shame by many musicians as a 'filler' when the music business was slack—had him run out of more than one town, and his wanderings eventually led him as far afield as California where he settled for five years, making money in all sorts of ways, legitimate and otherwise, and spending it as fast.

The high peak of Jelly Roll Morton's career came in the 1920s when, like every other New Orleans musician with a nose for 'the action', he drifted into Chicago for a protracted stay. Even then, when the black South Side ghetto was crowded with bands and musicians with a New Orleans reputation, Jelly remained curiously aloof. He toured extensively, mainly as a bandleader. But unlike such compatriots as Joe Oliver, Louis Armstrong, Johnny Dodds and Jimmy Noone, he never became associated with any of the famous Chicago jazz haunts. It is more than likely that his proud insistence on his superior Creole caste deterred him from becoming too closely involved in the black ghetto with its dense population of migrant workers from the South. He clearly liked to think that he belonged elsewhere. One of his earliest recording sessions in Chicago finds him as a guest in the select company of the white New Orleans Rhythm Kings. And apart from his tours and his recordings, he earned his living working for the publishing firm of the white Melrose brothers.

Alan Lomax's research into the relationship between the tough, not unduly scrupulous members of the publishing family and the proudly independent itinerant pianist and composer whose work they published makes poignant reading even in the face of Jelly Roll's aggressive personality. Morton's business card at this time read 'Jelly Roll Morton, composer and arranger for Melrose Music Company', and he obviously regarded Lester and Walter Melrose as business partners *and* friends—probably the only friends he had. They, on the other hand, were cool in their recollections of him. 'Oh no,' said Walter, 'of course he didn't work for us. He used to come around sometimes to talk about numbers. That's all.' One doesn't need to be a profound student of the racial climate of Chicago in the early Twenties to appreciate the impact of Jelly's not altogether diplomatic arrival at the Melrose office that day in 1923, which Lester Melrose recalled twenty-five years later. 'A fellow walked into our store with a big red bandana around his neck and a ten-gallon cowboy hat on his head and hollered "Listen everybody, I'm Jelly Roll Morton from New Orleans, the originator of jazz!" He talked for an hour without stopping about how good he was and then he sat down at the piano and showed that he was every bit as good as he said he was, and better.'

The Memphis-born pianist Lil Hardin had been equally impressed when, on one of his earlier visits to Chicago, Jelly Roll Morton had dropped into a music store where she was hired to demonstrate the newly-published numbers and, as he had done to a hundred other piano-players across the States during his peregrinations, elbowed her off the piano stool to teach her a lesson in every sense. 'So one day Jelly Roll Morton came in. He sat down and he started playing. Oooh, gee, he had such long fingers and, oh, in no time at all he had the piano rockin' and he played so heavy and all goose-pimples were stickin' out all over me. I said, ooooh, gee, what piano-playin'! So I sat there and I listened and I stood up and I walked . . . I was so thrilled. So when he got up from the piano he did something like this as if to say "Let that be a lesson to you!"—and it was a lesson because, after that, I played just as hard as I could just like Jelly Roll did, and till today I'm still a heavy piano-player and I attribute it to my hearing Jelly Roll.'

Jelly Roll Morton's piano style remained remarkably constant and unaffected by fashion during his lifetime, so reference to any of the scores of piano solos which he recorded will give an idea of the playing that so impressed both Lil Hardin and Lester Melrose. It will also give us an insight into why players brought up in the 'Eastern', Harlem school of piano-playing—I have already quoted Duke Ellington and Willie 'The Lion' Smith—invariably put him down. James P. Johnson was politer than most. He heard Morton in 1911 when 'he came through New York playing that "Jelly Roll Blues" of his . . . Of course, Jelly Roll wasn't a piano-player like some of us down here. We bordered more on the classical theory of music.' No doubt Jelly's long, disdainful nostrils would have twitched at this comparison for, although he admitted that he was not a fast sight-reader, he prided himself on being able to rattle off by ear such classical standards as the 'Miserere' from *Il Trovatore*, the Anvil Chorus, the Overture from *Martha* and so on. But the fact remains that Jelly Roll Morton's style was quite different from that of James P.'s Harlem school. And yet both styles stemmed directly from ragtime, sharing some of its conventions—namely, the 'striding' left hand that sustained the beat, and the use, in composition, of two or three related themes. Wherein lies the difference?

The answer is, in New Orleans. Another of the paradoxes which seem to cluster like angry wasps around the person of Jelly Roll Morton is that the born 'loner', the aloof figure who virtually turned his back on New Orleans in 1907 and was never a close associate of any of the other New Orleans giants, nevertheless represents for us a one-man piano-playing encyclopedia of the New Orleans musical tradition. As he intoned into Alan Lomax's microphone in a characteristically resonant phrase, 'Jazz music came from New Orleans and New Orleans was inhabited with maybe every race on the face of the globe.' This in itself would not have produced the jazz of which Jelly Roll was so proud. Jelly's own family history encapsulates the process through which jazz emerged. His family were Creoles, once an elite amongst the officially-termed 'coloured' population. Alan Lomax sums up the Creoles' position in a paragraph: 'Under tolerant Spanish and French rule in Louisiana, mulatto children were sent to school, taught trades and given professional jobs. Freedmen of colour helped to win the Battle of New Orleans under Andy Jackson. Before 1861, these coloured Creoles accumulated fifteen million dollars-worth of property, much of it in slaves; they organised literary societies and musicales and published their own news-papers, while the craftsmen amongst them built lovely churches and homes in New Orleans and cast the lacy ironwork for its balconies and doorways.'

Ironically, it was the Civil War and emancipation which under-mined this cultured community's position in the world. When all 'coloureds' were free, social distinctions became blurred. The Creoles were drawn inexorably downwards until, by the end of the nineteenth century, they had little left but their pride and the remnants of a culture. Near the very bottom of their descent, in the prosperous and volatile city of New Orleans, they met the black descendants of freed African slaves on the way up. These were musicians who had no practical experience of overtures or operatic arias from the European tradition. Their musical heritage was the self-taught, raw and intensely vigorous music of the rural South—notably the blues, that musical form (described in the

Bessie Smith.

JELLY ROLL MORTON'S
RED HOT PEPPERS. *Left
to right, Andrew Hilaire,
Kid Ory, George Mitchell,
John Lindsay, Jelly Roll
Morton, Johnny St Cyr,
Omer Simeon.*

Fletcher Henderson.

LOUIS ARMSTRONG'S
HOT FIVE. *Left to right,
Louis Armstrong, Johnny
St Cyr, Johnny Dodds,
Kid Ory, Lil Hardin
Armstrong.*

chapter on Bessie Smith) of childishly simple structure which nonetheless was to prove capable of expanding to encompass an almost limitless expressive content.

In recent times, some commentators on the popular music scene have aspired to a sort of instant punditry by excitedly challenging the long-established proposition that jazz began in New Orleans. They have pointed to other regions in America where, co-existent with New Orleans jazz, syncopated improvised music with jazz characteristics was to be found. To be sure, jazz historians have acknowledged for a long time that New Orleans at the start of the century had no monopoly of bluesmen, Creole orchestras, street bands, brothel pianists, gospel choirs or any other of the basic ingredients that went into early jazz. Yet the fact remains that it was from New Orleans that the first masters came, scattering the seeds of a vital new music wherever they went. One need only point to the 'growling' trumpets and trombones in Duke Ellington's music that are descended from King Oliver, to the soaring clarinets of the Swing Era that were inspired by Jimmy Noone and Johnny Dodds, to a whole school of alto-saxophone players who can be tracked back through Johnny Hodges to Sidney Bechet —everywhere the New Orleans influence. And it was exerted not only through the great virtuosi. The 'collective improvisation' of so-called Dixieland or traditional jazz, whether it speaks with a Chicago, New York, West Coast, European, British or Australian accent, follows, however ineptly in Jelly Roll Morton's view, a model established in New Orleans.

In all of this activity, we find Morton, once again, a lone figure. He did not have the immediate influence on his contemporaries and successors that men like Armstrong and Noone exerted. Most piano styles in jazz derive from a combination of primitive blues piano and the sophisticated Harlem 'stride' school, with a substantial dollop of the ubiquitous Louis Armstrong influence thrown in. When Morton recorded his band masterpieces, most of them huddled together in two or three sessions by his Red Hot Peppers in 1926, the strictly disciplined New Orleans band style was already on its way out of fashion. Attention had begun to focus on Louis Armstrong whose 'Hot Five' recordings showed a break away from the bandmasterly approach of both

Oliver and Morton towards an altogether freer approach with emphasis on the soloist. So we can say that the recordings by Jelly Roll Morton demonstrated the very epitome of the New Orleans style at a time when that style had already begun to disintegrate. When, in the years after Jelly's Library of Congress exposition, a new generation of musicians set about reviving and reconstructing the New Orleans music, few of them pursued Jelly's line for very long, if at all. In the face of the loud and frantic Trad Jazz of today, not to mention the pop music that surrounds it, Jelly Roll Morton would undoubtedly have concluded that his strictures upon the New York (supposed to be) jazz bands of the Twenties had remained unheeded too long and that, among the customers, eardrums and brains were now inextricably entangled.

I have chosen the 'Original Jelly Roll Blues' for discussion not only because it is a favourite of mine, but because it is the complete demonstration, a text-book exercise if you like, of Morton's teaching. Fortunately, that teaching is available for all to read and hear. The recordings for the Library of Congress Archive of American Folksong have been issued on commercial disc in their entirety, and they also form the basis of Alan Lomax's Morton biography. Indeed, Morton's dictum that 'Jazz is to be played sweet, soft, plenty rhythm' has been quoted so often that it has become a rather quaint cliché, like the Victorian adage that 'Children should be seen and not heard'! But Morton said very much more than that, enough to surround the bed-head of any aspiring New Orleans-style bandleader with embroidered mottoes. Here are a few to start with: 'Always have a melody going some way against a background of perfect harmony.' 'Without breaks and without clean breaks and without beautiful ideas in breaks, you don't even need to think about doing anything else, you haven't got a jazz band and you can't play jazz.' 'If a glass of water is full, you can't fill it any more; but if you have half a glass, you have the opportunity to put more water in it. Jazz music is based on the same principles, because jazz is based on strictly music.' 'If you can't manage to put tinges of Spanish in your tunes, you will never be able to get the right seasoning, I call it, for jazz.' Most of these principles are self-explanatory, calling for such basic musical ingredients as melody, variety and dynamics. But the reference (another often-quoted one) to the Spanish tinge needs some explanation. What Morton spoke of as a tinge of Spanish was the range of rhythmic variations which Spanish music acquired from African sources and which form the basis for what we loosely describe as Latin-American music. The simplest of these variations—and the one most often found in jazz—is the *tangana* rhythm from which the Tango derived and to which, as we have seen, the composer W. C. Handy was drawn. Count a couple of bars of eight-to-a-bar and emphasise the first, fourth and seventh beats—*one*-two-three-*four*-five-six-*seven*-eight—*one*-two-three-*four*-five-six-*seven*-eight—and you have the basic rhythm. Superimposed on a straightforward four crotchets or quarter notes to the bar in a way that comes naturally to guitar or banjo players, it provides a certain respite from the regular beat and underlies in a subtle way many good New Orleans jazz performances. In his 'Jelly Roll Blues', Jelly Roll Morton decided to state it unequivocally by bringing in castanets at a strategic moment.

The first thing to be said about the performance itself is that it is based throughout on the twelve-bar blues. In accounts of Jelly's modus operandi in rehearsing a band for a performance such as this, there is at first sight a contradiction. According to his wife Mabel, whom he married in 1928, 'He used to tell his band "You'd please me if you'd just play those little black dots . . . you don't have to make a lot of noise and ad lib. All I want you to play is what's written." ' But according to the clarinettist Omer Simeon and guitarist Johnny St Cyr, both of whom were in on the classic Red Hot Peppers sessions, Morton allowed them a considerable freedom. Said Simeon, 'He was exact with us. Very jolly, very full of life all the time, but serious. We used to spend maybe three hours rehearsing four sides and in that time he'd give us the effects he wanted, like the background behind a solo . . . The solos, they were ad lib. We played according to how we felt.' Johnny St Cyr confirms this: 'Reason his records are so full of tricks and changes is the liberty he gave his men . . . he was always open for suggestions.' What we have to remember here is that on the greatest Red Hot Pepper sessions in 1926, Morton was surrounded mainly by New Orleans men who had been brought up on the same precepts. In Kid Ory he had not only the king of ensemble trombonists but a musician of vast experience. At the time that Mabel Morton recalled—that is, from 1928 onwards—he was increasingly having to drill musicians from a different background, which would explain his strictness.

The 'tricks and changes' to which St Cyr referred are what elevate 'Jelly Roll Blues' from a string of blues choruses to a composition of enormous grace and style. Morton's chime-like introduction establishes a fine, stately tempo and then immediately the fun begins. The guitar makes a statement which is answered by cornet and trombone in succession, and then we are off into a lilting New Orleans ensemble with its Crescent City sound established by John Lindsay's resonant string bass. (One important legacy of the operatic and orchestral tradition in New Orleans creole music is the high standard of double-bass playing. Some of the most primitive examples of New Orleans jazz recorded in the Twenties—by Sam Morgan's Band, for instance— are distinguished by accurate and peculiarly sonorous bass work.) The cornetist George Mitchell was not a New Orleans man— he came from Louisville, Kentucky, but had moved into Chicago early in his career and had clearly been influenced by King Oliver. Throughout this record he plays with a mute in Oliver style, using it to give additional bite to an incisive lead that must have delighted his leader. Many bandleaders would have been content to follow this effective first chorus with the mixture as before, but Morton has other ideas. A trill on the clarinet introduces a variation on the first four bars of the blues harmonies, and one which is to play an important part later in the composition. In this, the normal progression from B flat through B flat seventh to E flat takes another route, namely B flat, D seventh, G minor, B flat seventh, E flat. This progression, smacked out in the form of 'stop chords' by the band, leads into another ensemble, but this time punctuated by a clarinet break—another refinement which most bands would have overlooked. The third of these choruses in B flat has yet another change. The first four bars revert to the standard progression, but feature piano breaks in which a chromatic figure repeats itself in descending octaves before turning over on its back and surfacing into a third joyful blues ensemble.

'You have the finest ideas from the greatest operas, symphonies and overtures in jazz music,' preached Jelly Roll. 'There is nothing finer than jazz music because it comes from everything of the finest class music.' Certainly, the dignified and measured modulation which now follows is of impeccable pedigree, so redolent is it of those nineteenth-century European drawing-rooms in which quadrilles, mazurkas and stately waltzes were played. It leads into the key of E flat and to a series of choruses in which the variation used in the second chorus of the piece, suitably transposed into the new key, becomes a permanent feature of the rest of the composition. In the first of these choruses the castanets come into play behind George Mitchell's cornet lead, emphasising the Spanish tinge. Even this chorus, appearing at first hearing to be a cornet solo, is thoughtfully enhanced by some counter-melody from Omer Simeon's low-register clarinet.

The danger arises now that, if I continue to detail the variations which Morton explores—the piano figure behind the first clarinet solo, the unusually-placed stop chords behind the second and so on—the impression might be given that the piece stops and starts with a superfluity of tricks and devices. But Morton was too cunning a composer for that. Anyone who has ever played traditional jazz for dancers will have discovered that to contrast broken or legato passages with forthright New Orleans-style ensemble is a sure way to elevate the spirit and lighten the feet. (Boogie woogie piano-players who broke into the pounding rhythm with across-the-beat breaks were up to the same trick, if in a less subtle way than Morton.) Thus, Jelly Roll Morton gets his men to come back into the ensemble in the seventh bar of each chorus using identical phrasing each time so that, amidst the variation, familiarity keeps returning. Musical psychology plays a large part in the arranger's art, and Morton was a master of it. The same effect was used even more effectively in his 'Sidewalk Blues', made a few months earlier, when he brought in two extra saxophone players so as to contrast the legato 'Liebestraum' theme with the ensuing bars of jaunty New Orleans ensemble.

At the beginning of this chapter I referred, in what might have been a careless generalisation, to Morton's compositions being piano pieces, many of which he adapted for New Orleans-style ensemble. In fact, we have here a chicken-and-egg enigma. 'No jazz piano player can really play good jazz unless they try to give an imitation of a band, that is, by providing a basis of riffs.' As with most of Morton's rules, a queue of notable exceptions forms instantly in the mind. With Jelly Roll Morton's own music, it doesn't much matter how the ideas took shape, whether the gracefully melodic phrases were expressed through George Mitchell's cornet or by Jelly's hands on the keyboard. What does matter is that in Jelly Roll Morton, jazz found its first—and New Orleans jazz its only—thoroughgoing, fully-fledged composer.

Fletcher Henderson

IN THE PERIOD between 1910 and 1920, America went dance crazy. Up until then, popular song and music for dancing had been two separate commodities, the only link between them being that the majority of sentimental songs were written in waltz time. Otherwise, the music for the gallops, polkas and schottisches of dancing America were instrumental, custom-built pieces. It was the emergence of the Fox Trot—originally one of a whole series of dance steps in 4/4 or 2/4 time that included the Turkey Trot, the Bunny Hug, the Grizzly Bear and the Kangaroo Dip—that wrought the change. The main reason for the Fox Trot's survival through the ages is that it is a basic step (some killjoy once described it sourly as 'walking backwards through a crowded room encumbered by a member of the opposite sex') capable of sophisticated variation, which it received in the period immediately before World War I from a new breed of professional dancers headed by Vernon and Irene Castle. In response to the demand for popular music, the publishers begin to insist that new songs should have danceable rhythms or at least be capable of adaptation to the new dance steps.

The activities of the Castles was absolutely crucial to the development of modern dance music. For one thing, they lifted the social status of the dance-hall, which had hitherto been considered in respectable society to be a low-class sort of place in which it was not proper to be seen except, possibly, on the occasional reckless 'slumming' party. With the establishment of larger and larger ballrooms, it followed that the bands that provided the music began to grow. It has never been satisfactorily established who formed the first dance-band in the modern form. Vernon and Irene Castle took on as their musical director James Reece Europe, a black musician with formal training who, by 1910, had established himself in New York as an honoured representative of Harlem music at the respectable, white-orientated end of the spectrum. We can judge the measure of dignity which he attained and the style of presentation which he favoured, from a concert which he presented in 1914 at the Carnegie Hall which featured 125 musicians and singers. Apart from ten pianos, seven cornets and eight trombones, the bulk of the huge orchestra seems to have been made up of banjos, mandolins and such contemporary oddities as the bandolin and the banjophone. The saxophonist Garvin Bushell, who arrived in New York in 1919, recalls that elephantine orchestras were not confined to the concert platform. 'The Negro dance-bands I heard were often from thirty to fifty pieces . . . there were sometimes twenty men playing bandolins, a combination of the banjo and violin [mandolin, surely] that was plucked. They played pop and show tunes. The saxophone was not very prominent as a solo instrument, but the trumpet, clarinet and trombone were. The soloists, especially the trumpet players, improvised, and those trumpet players used a whole series of buckets and cuspidors for effects' (*Jazz Panorama*).

Garvin Bushell's reminiscence takes us forward from the era of Jim Europe (and other rivals of his, leaders like John C. Smith, Allie Ross and Ford Dabney) to a point at which the 'gutbucket' element began to infiltrate into the most respectable black orchestra. We have seen in the chapter on James P. Johnson how migrants from the South, moving into New York in increasing numbers during the second decade of the century, created a demand for the sort of vigorous, improvised music, well aquainted with the blues, that had been the basis of their country music back home. So many conflicting definitions of the term 'gutbucket' have been put forward that I will say no more than that it is handed down as an appropriate-sounding term for this rough music and the sort of dives in which it was to be found in its raw state. Buckets and cuspidors, part of the home-made tradition in poor country music that also involved washboard percussion and cigarbox fiddles and guitars, no doubt found a ready acceptance among a dancing public that was hungry for novelty. And 'hot' improvisation was clearly given a hefty boost when the Original Dixieland Band arrived in 1917 to spread jazz mania into the upper strata of New York society.

Once the battalions of banjos and bandolins had become redundant and were dismissed, there remained the prototype dance-band, with two or three brass instruments and a clarinet to give excitement and brilliance while a couple of saxophones added to the required volume and provided tonal ballast. In the rhythm section, the piano derived importance through its role as accompanist for singers and dancers as well as its close historic connection with the ragtime from which the dance music of the early Twenties still drew rhythmic inspiration. From the plethora of catgut or steel wire that had once surrounded this nucleus, a solitary banjoist remained, and it was usually a tuba, otherwise known as a brass bass, that supplied the foundation.

Of course, not all of these early dance-bands employed improvisation. It would have been during the formative years before 1920 that the great river of popular dance music began to divide into two streams, the one carrying 'straight' or 'sweet' music that stuck faithfully to written arrangements, the other heading off towards more improvised 'hot' music that gave scope to jazz soloists. How near did those first New York improvisers come to jazz as it has since been defined? In Garvin Bushell's judgement of the music he heard on his arrival in 1919, 'New York "jazz" then was nearer the ragtime style and had less blues. There wasn't an Eastern performer who could really play the blues. We later absorbed how from the southern musicians we heard, but it wasn't original with us. We didn't put that quarter-tone pitch in the music the way the Southerners did. Up North we leaned to ragtime conception—a lot of notes.'

By the start of the Twenties, there were good players active in the Harlem area. The New Orleans notion of jazz had been implanted by visitors such as the Original Creole Band led by Freddie Keppard and the itinerant Sidney Bechet. The success of Mamie Smith's prototype classic blues recording of 'Crazy Blues', which hit the music shops early in 1921, led to an increase

in blues activity around New York. Mamie herself stepped up
her touring schedule, and it is hard to find one musician associated
with the Harlem scene at that time (and they include Bubber
Miley, Joe Smith, Garvin Bushell, Johnny Dunn and Coleman
Hawkins) whose potted biography does not include a stint with
Mamie Smith's Jazz Hounds. As we saw in the story of Bessie
Smith, other more accomplished and deep-dyed exponents of
the blues soon converged upon New York to give an object lesson
in how to imbue an improvisation with jazz feeling. Furthermore,
the touring itinerary took most of the musicians through Chicago
where, according to all their reminiscences, they took a crash
course in jazz playing at the feet of King Oliver and his Creole
Jazz Band. Garvin Bushell recalled having heard that band in 1921,
before Louis Armstrong joined Oliver. 'Bubber Miley and I went
to hear King Oliver at the Dreamland every night. It was the
first time I'd heard New Orleans jazz to any advantage and I
studied them every night for the entire week we were in town. I
was very much impressed with their blues and their sound. The
trumpets and clarinets in the East had a better "legitimate" quality,
but their [Oliver's] sound touched you more. It was less cultivated
but more expressive of how the people felt. Bubber and I sat there
with our mouths open.'

It was in the small, 'gutbucket' cabarets in Harlem that the
young musicians were able to exercise the skills in jazz-making
which they were rapidly acquiring. It appears that the first local
star that they produced, one as imposing in his 'attitude' as any of
the great piano-ticklers of James P. Johnson's circle, was the
Memphis-born trumpeter, Johnny Dunn. The saxophonist and
composer Don Redman, who will make a significant appearance
later in this chapter, remembered him in an interview reproduced
in *Jazz Panorama*: 'When I first came to New York, Johnny Dunn
was *the* trumpet player. He was a terrific salesman for himself and
he was the first one I knew to use any kind of mute. He'd set
himself up in a show with just himself and dancers. His valet
would come followed by all sorts of trunks, and I used to wonder
if they were all for one man. The valet would set them up against
the wall, and in them would be all kinds of pots and pans, flower-
pots, cans, anything to get a different sound out of his horn.

I think he was an influence on Duke [Ellington] because he really did get a lot of sounds out of his horn.' The examples we have of Dunn on record show a player full of drive but prone to over-use the effects and rather wooden and inflexible in his phrasing. It can be little surprise to us that, though he stayed around New York for most of the Twenties, he was soon outstripped as a manipulator of mutes by Ellington's star cornetist, Bubber Miley, and was left standing as an improviser and showman by Louis Armstrong and the formidable trumpet-men who followed in his wake.

This was the pattern of jazz development in New York in the early Twenties. With admirable objectivity, Garvin Bushell constantly returns in his reminiscences to the same theme. Johnny Dunn 'played the blues so it moved you, but not as soulfully as those blues players out of Louisiana.' Harlem was catching on, but there was much to learn. One musician who seems to have arrived in New York with a fully-fledged and quite independent style was the cornetist Joe Smith. He was born into a musical family in Cincinnatti, Ohio, and having been taught cornet by his father, left home in his teens to work in travelling shows. He arrived in New York in 1920, still only eighteen years of age. In some ways his development was very similar to that of Bix Beiderbecke in that he appears to have conjured out of his own head a calm, relaxed and rhythmically free style, coupled with a ravishingly beautiful tone on both open and plunger-muted cornet, that ran contrary to all those influences which other Harlem-based musicians were eagerly absorbing from the South—or the West, as the whole area from New Orleans up to Chicago was sometimes called by New Yorkers. 'To my mind,' recalled trumpeter Louis Metcalf, 'the controversy about the two different styles of playing, Eastern and Western, came to a head when Louis Armstrong joined Fletcher Henderson, taking Joe Smith's chair. It was a real jazz feud with all the musicians taking sides. Louis represented the Western style of jazz, while Joe Smith was the Eastern.' As we shall see when we come to discuss Bix Beiderbecke, New York jazz throughout the Twenties was to polarise into what, in later parlance, came to be identified as 'hot' and 'cool' jazz styles. No doubt other musicians of that period played with a legitimate rather than a dirty tone, used vibrato sparingly and couched their solos in an unhurried, reflective manner. They would have been classed by Garvin Bushell as technically proficient but lacking in feeling. Joe Smith qualifies as the first of the 'cool' jazzmen in that, through what at that time were unorthodox means, he achieved the vocalised sound, the blues spirit and the swing which makes for convincing jazz performance—convincing enough for him to become, upon their first meeting, the favourite accompanist of that most exacting judge of 'blues feeling', Bessie Smith.

Indeed, it is as members of the backing bands for blues singers that Joe Smith and the other budding musicians in New York first got a fair hearing on record. I must stress here that the recognition of them as important jazz musicians is retrospective. In New York after the arrival and departure (on a European tour) of the Original Dixieland Jazz Band, the furious argument about jazz or jass centred upon the rackety, novelty-ridden music of the ODJB's imitators and the syncopated dance music of Jim Europe and his rivals. The jazz craze sparked off by the ODJB even brought a reaction among respectable Harlemites against Europe, whose orchestra was now billed as a jazz band and advertised as 'Fifty Joy Whooping Sultans of High Speed Syncopation'. In his book *Early Jazz*, Gunther Schuller sums up the situation as we now look back on it. 'In the midst of all this wrangling over true jazz and Negro music, a new generation of Negro musicians, unheralded and practically unnoticed, was quietly slipping into New York. They were men like the trumpet player Johnny Dunn, who came to New York with W. C. Handy's Orchestra from Memphis; trumpet player Joe Smith and clarinettist Garvin Bushell, both from Ohio; Fletcher Henderson and Wilbur Sweatman; while other men like Bubber Miley, June Clark and Perry Bradford had either grown up in New York or had already been there for some time before the jazz craze really burst on to the scene.'

Schuller goes on to make a significant point. These temporarily displaced jazz persons, who were kept in work by the craze for blues recordings, were for the most part literate musicians. Several of them—Coleman Hawkins, Bushell and Don Redman—had studied music at college and were well versed in reading and theory. Fletcher Henderson had a university degree in chemistry to add to musical qualifications acquired since the age of six. He moved to New York from Atlanta University intending to do post-graduate research, but became instead the song demonstrator for the publishing company that W. C. Handy and Harry Pace set up. When this company spawned Black Swan Records, specialising in black artists, Henderson became its musical director. It was in this role that he was established when the blues craze erupted.

The alert reader will have spotted by now that, in New York in the very early Twenties, a situation had developed which is fascinatingly similar to the explosive events that had brought jazz into being in New Orleans twenty-odd years earlier, and had created in New York itself the fruitful strain of Harlem stride piano. A schooled, sophisticated culture with no particular place to go was set on a collision course with a virile folk tradition on its way up in the world. As usual, the actual birth of big band jazz was a casual, accidental affair. Don Redman, who had come into New York with a short-lived band from Pittsburgh, told the story. 'I wasn't in town but a few days after that when I got a phone call to come and make a record date for Emerson. I went down to the studio and found Fletcher Henderson on the date. There was a band there, but it wasn't his band. He didn't have a band then, but was kind of house pianist for Emerson ... On this date Florence Mills was singing.' The session led to others, in the course of which the ad hoc or, in contemporary terms, 'pick-up' band, was augmented. One session led to a successful audition for the Club Alabam'—'that was the Cotton Club of that era. When we went into the Club ... we decided to make Fletcher the leader because he was a college graduate and presented a nice appearance.' There were also, of course, the not-inconsiderable connections that Henderson had built up in the recording and publishing world, which ensured that the band made prolific recordings from the very outset. An incident at the Club Alabam' throws light on the close, almost family bond that was characteristic of Henderson and his men throughout the Twenties and beyond. Redman again: 'Edith Wilson was on the bill with us and she wanted Hawk [Coleman Hawkins] to come out on stage and play blues behind her. He didn't mind but he wanted to get paid for it. George White was the manager of the club and he told Fletcher to fire Hawk. Since we were doing terrific business and had gotten other offers from the Roseland and other places, we decided we'd give notice to a man if Hawk was fired. We moved over to Roseland and from then on we were the top band in New York. No one rivalled us then.'

Top band or not, the first big jazz band in the modern sense did not spring fully mature into the world. Just as in the collision between Creole and folk-music in New Orleans, and again in the meeting of schooled ragtime and country influences in the Harlem piano haunts, an uneasy hybrid existed for a while before proper fusion was effected. The Fletcher Henderson Orchestra's early recordings in 1923 suggest that the ambitions of the leader and his arranger, Don Redman, lay in the direction of creating a new-style of dance-band. Redman claimed that the Pittsburg band, Billy Paige's Broadway Syncopators, with which he came to New York, was the first band in that city to play arrangements. Certainly the recordings we have of Jim Europe's bands find all the melody instruments playing in unison, with thin harmony provided by piano and one or more banjo-type instruments. Redman's arrangements deployed the 'blowing' instruments in vertical harmony, in the manner which today is commonplace in bands both big and small. This differed from the method not only of Jim Europe but of Armand J. Piron's New Orleans Orchestra which came to New York in 1922 and 1923, on the second occasion preceding Henderson into the Roseland Ballroom. It was the custom of New Orleans bands of whatever size to play in the loose, polyphonic manner which is familiar to us through the jazz bands as 'New Orleans style'. Indeed, the only difference (if we forget about the leader's violin, which he often did himself!) between Piron's dance-band and the jazz bands from the same city is that Piron's men repeated their themes over and over in the same way, without the heated variations which the jazzmen would give them.

It is doubtful if Fletcher Henderson's band regarded itself as a *jazz* band in those early days. We have to remember that, among musicians with the pride in their calling that strict technical training had engendered, the word 'jazz' was, in the early Twenties, given a bad name by the crude excesses of the ODJB's imitators. The efforts of the young white bandleader Paul Whiteman to make jazz respectable by dressing it up in symphonic guise (described briefly in the ODJB chapter) were almost certainly inspired more by the example of the huge Negro bands of Jim Europe's generation, with a possible nod in the direction of John Phillip Sousa, than by the brief sensation that the ODJB caused. Jim Europe's bands seem to have spawned two separate traditions, one of elephantine dance-bands with a concert potential (remember that Europe preceded Whiteman into the Carnegie Hall by a margin of ten years), the other of exciting black dance music with strong ragtime links, a 'hot' music in terms of vigour and syncopation if not of improvisation. Whiteman took up the challenge of the former, Henderson of the latter, only deigning to swap ideas much later in the decade. There is one piece of glaring circumstantial evidence to support this assumption. 'The soloists, especially the trumpet players, improvised,' recalled Garvin Bushell about the dance-bands that he heard in New York when he arrived there in 1919. In regularly hiring the elusive Joe Smith for his early recording sessions and in wooing, and eventually winning, Louis Armstrong away from Chicago to join him, Henderson clearly attached a special significance to the role of a good 'hot' trumpet-player who could beat all-comers in this department.

'I decided that the youthful trumpet-player would be great in our act.' This was Fletcher Henderson's somewhat phlegmatic recollection of hearing Louis Armstrong for the first time in 1922, when Louis was still in New Orleans and Henderson was on tour with Ethel Waters. His words, which must qualify as the greatest understatement in the history of jazz commentary, convey an impression which Henderson's subsequent handling of Louis in the orchestra bears out—that is, that Fletcher Henderson never at any time realised the full significance of Armstrong's impact on his band. Contemporary evidence abounds that he himself preferred the mellower style of Joe Smith, whom he no doubt found more 'musianly'. And when, after fourteen months, Louis returned to Chicago, there is no hint in the history books of the kind of trauma on both sides that such a parting should have caused.

There are plenty of recordings available which show us how

Fletcher Henderson's band played before Louis Armstrong's arrival. They do not inspire the jazz lover with enthusiasm. Of the team which Henderson gathered around him, only one musician, Coleman Hawkins, had any potential as an improvising jazz musician—in the absence, that is, of Joe Smith, who does not appear on every recording. And with Hawkins, the word 'potential' needs stressing. Aged only nineteen when the Henderson band began recording in earnest, Coleman Hawkins was nevertheless a fully experienced musician, having previously toured for two years with Mamie Smith's Band. To say that he stood head and shoulders above contemporary exponents of the tenor saxophone is to claim no more than that he was a giant among pygmies. The clarinettist Buster Bailey, who joined Henderson shortly after Louis, remembers Louis's comment on Hawkins—'Man, he swings! He swings out of this world!' Hawkins himself recalled: 'I was aware of jazz right from the start as a kid. I used to sit up and practise all day—all day long. Then when I was through with my lessons I would play jazz all the rest of the day.' Since he then goes on to recollect hearing Armstrong and Earl Hines in Chicago when he was fourteen—that is, in 1918, some four or five years before either musician arrived in the city—it seems that his dates were a bit confused. Be that as it may, the truth is that the recorded examples of his work before and during the period when Armstrong was in the band reveal a musician who neither swung nor played convincing jazz. The tone which was to become legendary in later years was undoubtedly big, but cumbersome as well. Melodically, his solos did little more than run up and down the chords in the manner of an ensemble part, and rhythmically, he played in the clipped, jerky manner—as different from the relaxed phrasing of the New Orleans bands as a facial twitch is from a broad smile—in which Redman and Henderson between them wrote for the band.

Clearly, the lessons being slowly absorbed from the South by New York musicians were not enough to effect a magic transformation upon the Henderson Band. Even when, at the time of Louis Armstrong's arrival, it was further reinforced by a powerful trombonist from the rather unpromising area of Nebraska, Charlie Green, and by the Memphis-born clarinettist Buster Bailey, fresh from King Oliver's band, it still suffered from one central problem. Don Redman did not know how to translate the essential elements of swing, blues feeling and 'hotness' into written arrangements, even if he fully comprehended them in the first place. If the Fletcher Henderson band had ended its career suddenly in August, 1924, the recordings handed down to us would have revealed no more than a competent dance-band bogged down in the mannerisms and rhythmic conventions of its time. To bring about any sort of explosive metamorphosis, it required an injection of the raw essence of jazz administered sharply in its ossified rump.

It received it in good measure on September 29, 1924, when Louis Armstrong arrived from Chicago. From the Louis Armstrong biography by Max Jones and John Chilton (*Louis*), we glean that the hip Harlem men in Henderson's band did not exactly greet Louis as a Messiah come to show them the error of their ways. First of all, Louis Armstrong's unfashionable appearance hardly impressed them. The drummer, Kaiser Marshall, recalled: 'I remember the day Louis showed up for rehearsal . . . the band was up on the stand waiting when he got there, and Louis walked across the floor. He had on big thick-soled shoes, the kind policemen wear, and he came walking across the floor, clump-clump, and grinned and said hello to all the boys.' Henderson, according to Max Jones, found Louis 'pretty much a down-home boy in the big city' who took a ribbing from the band and endured it good-naturedly. Don Redman summed it up elsewhere. 'He was big and fat and wore high-top shoes with hooks in them and long underwear down to his socks. When I got a load of that, I said to myself, who in the hell is this guy? It can't be Louis Armstrong. But when he got on the bandstand it was a different story . . . in fact, Louis, his style and his feeling, changed our whole idea about the band musically.'

Most of the Henderson men have since testified, with varying degrees of warmth, to the effect that Louis had on their music. The qualities which he showed, fresh from King Oliver's band, covered every aspect of the playing of jazz. His tone, even filtered through the straight fibre mute which frail recording machines then demanded, was full and commanding. Furthermore, he hit each note with an attack and a varied use of pulse or vibrato which gave it a life of its own, in striking contrast to the dead sounds that fell from the horns of his colleagues in the trumpet section. Every solo that Louis recorded with Henderson springs from its surroundings with such leaping energy that one might believe, had such a thing been possible in those days, that it had been 'edited' in from recordings of a later era. The flat-footed fox-trot rhythm that pervades the written ensembles is suddenly galvanised into something approaching swing, largely due to Armstrong's facility in placing accents all around the beat in an ever-changing rhythmic pattern.

I have to confess at this point that, with a few exceptions such as the masterly exposition of 'Everybody Loves My Baby' and the explosive 'TNT Blues', Louis Armstrong's solos within the context of the full Henderson orchestra are not among my favourites. It always sounds to me, especially in the earlier recordings, as if he had been typecast as a sort of cheer-leader for the band, to provide a virtuoso 'spot' and generally whoop up the proceedings. Had Fletcher Henderson or Don Redman possessed the musical acumen to tap the vein in Armstrong's playing that manifests itself in, say, 'St Louis Blues' with Bessie Smith or, indeed, in some of the relaxed records made with Clarence William's Blue Five or the Red Onion Jazz Babies, who knows how much sooner his influence would have shown itself in the recorded work of Henderson's own band?

As it is, there was a time lag. Through the thirteen months of Armstrong's presence, there was steady improvement. The most successful overall of the early recordings, 'Copenhagen', achieved a sort of unity by letting Louis rip in the ensembles, where he can be heard elbowing the whole thing along in a way that is reminiscent of the Oliver band's two-cornet power-section. And 'TNT Blues', made about a year later, has not altogether derisory written passages, despite a twittering clarinet trio (one of Henderson's trade marks initiated by Don Redman) and occasional pompous use of the tuba. For all these advances, it was not until Louis had left the band that his lessons seemed to bear full fruit.

'The Stampede', recorded four months or so after Armstrong's departure, shows a band totally revitalised. The tune was one which Fats Waller, whose legendary appetite for food was not matched by comparable monetary greed, allegedly sold to Fletcher Henderson in a job lot of nine compositions for the price of a dozen hamburgers. It has some of the characteristics of a piano 'shout' in the riffy first theme which matches simple figures from the trombone with answering phrases by trumpets and saxophones. And all the way through there is strong emphasis on rhythmic development rather than melody, which is left almost entirely for the soloists to provide. It takes no great effort to imagine the introductory passage, with its procession of little skipping phrases in the treble followed by a burst of improvisation over heavy oom-chah bass, played entirely on piano by Fats Waller himself. In the event, piano, saxes and brass handle the opening figures, and Rex Stewart, seemingly on the verge of explosion with eagerness, rips off the solo passage.

Rex Stewart, then only nineteen years of age, had been an ardent admirer of Louis Armstrong from the moment Louis set foot in New York. 'I went mad with the rest of the town. I tried to walk like him, talk like him, eat like him, sleep like him. I even bought a pair of big policeman shoes like he used to wear and stood outside his apartment waiting for him to come out so I could look at him.' When, after some persuasion, a shy and reluctant Rex Stewart was finally persuaded to follow Louis into Henderson's trumpet section, the idolatry still showed itself in every eager solo. It may have been this excessive reliance on the Armstrong model that prompted Henderson to send him away after a few months to do some more studying at Wilberforce College, where Fletcher's brother Horace led a student band. Stewart returned to Henderson after two years, contributed much fine work with the band and then found his own niche in jazz history as one of the most original voices in the Duke Ellington orchestra. Until he died in 1967, he remained faithful to that first love by continuing to play the short cornet when all other, including Louis himself, had long since changed to trumpet.

If Rex Stewart was still immature by Henderson's exacting standards—and there's no doubt that he lacked Louis Armstrong's poise and rhythmic sure-footedness in the heat of battle—he nevertheless suits the mood of this 'new' Fletcher Henderson band admirably. Everything about the opening passage has a

forward thrust, a feeling of urgency, which had been entirely
lacking in earlier Henderson performances except when Louis
Armstrong took over the reins. Someone once described swing as
the quality which not only makes people want to dance but would
also cause them to fall over in a heap if the music stopped unexpectedly. By this definition, 'The Stampede' swings.

The opening 32-bar theme enables one to be more specific.
There was one characteristic which so dominated Louis Armstrong's contributions to the Henderson records that it amounted
to a cliché Indeed, it may have arisen from Armstrong's frustrated
efforts to get the band's pedestrian phrasing off the ground, since
he never overdid it in other surroundings. The best way to grasp
it is to count four crotchets or quarter notes in a bar—one-two-
three-four—then omit the first beat and move the other three
back half a beat, so that, in fact, they fall on the three hyphens
between one-two-three-four. In the chapter on Bix Beiderbecke,
I refer to this three-note, before-the-beat phrase as being the
springboard from which Louis launches into his solo in 'Potato
Head Blues'. These anticipated beats have the effect of creating a
forward momentum. Count several bars of them in a row and
you will find yourself propelled forward as if you were leaping
down a steep flight of steps, with the danger of falling flat on your
face. Balanced against notes played strictly on the beat, they form
the basis of the advanced syncopation which in the Thirties was to
earn that decade the title of the Swing Era.

Louis Armstrong did not invent this syncopation, even though
he was apparently born with a natural ability to handle it. One
of the characteristics of Harlem stride piano, as demonstrated in
James P. Johnson's 'Carolina Shout', was that the right-hand
figures were phrased in advance of the metronomic oom-chah
bass. Thus Fats Waller's tune, sensitively arranged by Don
Redman and interpreted by the soloists in the swinging Armstrong
manner, may justly be cited as a bridge linking the advanced
rhythmic notions of Louis Armstrong and James P. Johnson on
the one hand with the big band music of the Swing Era on the
other. The first full chorus in 'The Stampede' has the delighted,
faintly surprised air of a full orchestra, with its arranger on hand,
suddenly discovering how to do it! While the banjo plays a steady

four-in-the-bar, the phrases thrown to and fro between trombone and the rest of the front line anticipate the beat in a relaxed, 'hot' and faintly disreputable way which is not recognisable as being by the same po-faced Fletcher Henderson band of old.

Perhaps the most startling revelation of Louis Armstrong's liberating influence comes when Coleman Hawkins leaps out of the ensemble for his solo. Here for the first time is a glimpse of the tenor saxophone player from whom all rivals were to stand back in awe for the next decade. Not only is his solo couched in terms strikingly similar to Armstrong's up-tempo contributions, but the actual notes themselves have a vibrant life of their own. There are two notes at the beginning of the ninth bar which show how Hawkins had learnt from Louis the vitalising properties of a tiny pulse or vibrato in even the shortest note. It is an interesting historical point that the trumpeter Roy Eldridge, whose fast and furious playing in fluent 'saxophone' style revolutionised the jazz trumpet in the immediate post-Armstrong period of the late Thirties, has always claimed it was this thrusting Hawkins solo, which he learnt by heart, that sowed the seeds of his own style.

After Hawkins and a short modulation, another theme, starting in the minor, is introduced. It was a stroke of brilliance on Don Redman's part to bring in Joe Smith to elaborate upon it. After the scorching eagerness of Rex Stewart and Coleman Hawkins, Smith's uncannily placid chorus offers a cool oasis. I say 'uncannily' because there is mystery inherent in Joe Smith's playing. He uses no fewer notes, and only marginally less rhythmic impetus than his predecessors in the solo order, and yet the whole solo is pervaded by a feeling of calm. Towards the end of the passage, Fats (or Redman) provides him with a long phrase of rippling eighth notes which he plays in a singing, crystal clear way which is absolutely ravishing.

Trio passages for three clarinets were, throughout its life, a trade mark of the Fletcher Henderson Band. If not invented by Don Redman, they were certainly exploited by him from the outset, in a manner which, when harnessed to the jerky, rhythmically unsubtle style of his early writing, gave a silly, twittering effect which I have already remarked upon. In this department, as in all others, 'The Stampede' shows a dramatic improvement. After Joe Smith's solo, the clarinets come in wailing, anticipating by a year or so the eerie use to which Duke Ellington was to put them in some of his most sombre compositions. Previous appearances of what has come to be called the Henderson 'clarinet choir' were not marked by any great ambition or expertise, but here it plays a positive role, establishing a contrasting atmosphere to the jolly romp that surrounds it, and, in a break in mid-chorus that is reminiscent of one of Louis Armstrong's reckless leaps into space, a flash of technical brilliance, too.

It took musicians in general, and orchestrated bands in particular, many years to acquire the sort of rhythmic freedom which Louis Armstrong demonstrated. In the chapter on Luis Russell, I make what I hope is a convincing case on behalf of the Russell Band as a major forerunner in the advance into the Swing Era, with Pops Foster's New Orleans-style, four-in-the-bar bass playing pointing the way. Fletcher Henderson's Band, not only in 'The Stampede' but for some years to come, leaned heavily on the two-beat base given by the use of a powerful tuba-player alternating with the lighter beats of the banjo. For all the thrusting energy of Armstrong-inspired solos and arrangement, there is still something faintly inhibited about the ensemble that follows another fine Rex Stewart solo and rounds off the piece. It neither lopes to a blithe climax in New Orleans style nor builds up the massive tension and excitement of which Luis Russell's Band was capable.

But in introducing this qualification to the claim often made by jazz historians that Fletcher Henderson's band was the sole progenitor of the big bands which were to dominate the Swing Era, I have been guilty of criticism's most heinous crime—that is, of taking a performance to task for failing to achieve what it did not set out to do in the first place. We sometimes forget that many of the early bands—and some later ones, too—were engaged not for their contribution to high art, but to provide music for dancing. The Roseland Ballroom was a whites-only establishment whose customers would have required the band to accompany the Fox Trot and its sundry derivatives. Not for Henderson the luxury enjoyed by King Oliver with his black audience in Chicago's

South Side ghetto, or by James P. Johnson catering for the eccentric hoofers fresh from Carolina or the Georgia sea-islands. At the Roseland, Henderson played opposite the best white bands of the day, and in terms of the music which he offered the dancers, he had to conform to their standards. Seen in this light, 'The Stampede' stands out as a final triumph of art over expediency, of jazz over respectability. And in showing, under Redman's direction, how to handle to its richest effect instrumentation handed down by a random process of evolution from street bands and circus outfits, it set the pattern which all big bands, sweet or swing, would follow to the present day.

Louis Armstrong

THE 'HOT FIVES', a term invariably uttered in tones of deep reverence by students of jazz history, represent a towering peak in Louis Armstrong's career. Indeed, such is the collective impact of these recordings of the middle and late Twenties that they have sometimes distorted the picture of Armstrong the professional musician and performer.

'It's not like the old Hot Five days' was a sentiment quite commonly overheard, from the Forties onwards, as devotees of Louis on record came away from one of his 'live' performances in a state of mild shock at the manifestations of commercial 'showmanship' which they had just witnessed. In the forefront of their minds was a picture of a quite different Louis Armstrong of bygone days, a musician dedicated to pure art who created masterpieces of improvised jazz in defiance of commercial pressures.

In the interests of truth as well as critical fairness, it has to be stressed that, in this sense, 'the old Hot Five days' never happened. Louis Armstrong's Hot Five—sometimes augmented to the Hot Seven—was a band that existed, apart from one or two charity appearances, in the recording studio alone. And even there, its existence was sporadic. In three years from 1925 to 1928, the inspired music-making that profoundly affected the whole course of jazz occupied just twenty-two scattered days. For Louis, 'the Hot Five days' were no more than interruptions in a professional career that involved every facet of showmanship from featured solo spots to accompanying floor shows and, for a while, silent movies.

The Chicago to which Louis Armstrong returned in the winter of 1925 from his stay with Fletcher Henderson in New York had blossomed into a hotbed of jazz. In the so-called Black Belt that ran through the city's South Side, clubs, cafés, dance-halls and music stores had proliferated. History is confused as to whether it was Lil Hardin Armstrong or Joe Glaser, the manager of the Sunset Café who was to take control of Louis Armstrong's career ten years later, who first had him billed, on a banner across a club front, as The World's Greatest Trumpet-Player. It was to be some time before the world was to recognise Louis' talent. But in Chicago, he returned to find himself a star, so much in demand that he was able, at one period, to commute between three different jobs on the same night.

Many of the romantic notions about 'the old Hot Five days' stem from the belief that 'clubs' in the Chicago of the Twenties resembled the kind of informal, free-and-easy jazz clubs which in the post-war years have become familiar the world over. A reminiscence by the Chicagoan tenor-saxist Bud Freeman (*You Don't Look Like a Musician*) might help to dispel such misconceptions: 'In the middle Twenties Joe Glaser (who later became Louis Armstrong's manager) owned a night-club on the south side of Chicago. It was called the "Sunset Café." It featured the Carroll Dickerson Orchestra and a floor show. The show had the usual master of ceremonies who told a few jokes and ended his routine with a tap-dance. There was a chorus of girls who could *really* dance and sing and there were very funny comedians most of whom were to become famous in the Amos 'n' Andy television show ... A little man (by the name of Percy Venable) produced and directed the floor show. If he had lived longer (he died at an early age) he would have become one of the greats; his shows were way ahead of their time ... with all this talent, the most talented of them all was a not-too-well-known trumpet-player by the name of Louis Armstrong ... No one used the word 'Jazz' to define Louie's playing; everybody knew he was hearing a true master. After the floor show the band would play a short dance set. They would take a stock arrangement of some Broadway show tune that Louie loved to play (one in particular was Noël Coward's "Poor Little Rich Girl") and play the introduction, verse and chorus as it was written, down to the coda, and then Louie would play twenty or more improvised choruses, always to an exciting climax! I have *never* heard anything like it, nor do I expect I shall ever hear anything to equal it again.'

It was during the dance set that touches of informality, more compatible with the jazz image, would creep in. Then it was that the marauding trumpet-players, intent upon cutting Louis Armstrong down to size, would converge to sit in with the band. Earl Hines, who was musical director for Louis Armstrong's own band when it took over from Carroll Dickerson, tells a hilarious story concerning these episodes. Many of the sitters-in were 'hot' men, not too strong in the reading department. Sometimes a composer with a new tune to try out would come into the club and distribute the lead sheets around the band to be read at sight. On one occasion Fats Waller came in with one such arrangement, and sat in himself on piano. The bandstand was at the time overloaded with visiting musicians, who made heavy weather of the written parts. At one stage, says Earl, Fats lent over from his seat at the piano which was raised above the rest of the band, and shouted: 'What key are you guys *strugglin'* in?'

This sort of cabaret club was only one facet of Armstrong's activity. At the same time, he also played in the trumpet section of Erskine Tate's Orchestra which was resident at the Vendome Theatre. This was a movie theatre in which the band was expected not only to accompany the silent movies but also to provide an hour-long show several times a day in between showings. It was under Tate's leadership that Louis' talents as a showman were discovered and given some encouragement. From time to time he was allowed to come forward to solo in a 'classical' speciality—his favourite was a popular excerpt from 'Cavalleria Rusticana'—and also to air his talent for comedy, presenting a mock sermon under the name of the Reverend Dippermouth.

This is the musical context into which the Hot Five and Hot Seven recordings were periodically inserted. Had it not been for the strict segregation which then, and for many years, governed the appearance of black artists on records, it is in fact unlikely that the Hot Fives would ever have been made. They were commissioned, so to speak, for the Okeh recording company's 'race' catalogue, the sphere of recording activity aimed at the Negro market which the blues boom of the early Twenties had opened up. For those who constantly hold up the Hot Five recordings as the zenith of Louis Armstrong's recording career, it should be a sobering thought that, had a more liberal attitude prevailed in the recording studios, they would almost certainly not have happened at all, and it would have been 'Poor Little Rich Girl' and 'Cavalleria Rusticana' by which we would have come to judge Louis!

According to the musicians who took part, the Hot Five sessions themselves fell far short of solemnity. 'We'd work the tunes out in the studio, no trouble,' Louis recalled. 'Good atmosphere, so good that a trombonist, not Kid Ory, forgot himself and started blowing like hell into the wall instead of into the recording. A lot of those comments on the records were just as though we were talking to one another on a club date—real natural.' Kid Ory, too, remembered that 'the records I made with the Hot Five were the easiest I ever made. We spoiled very few records, only sometimes when one of us would forget the routine or the frame-up, and didn't come in when he was supposed to. Even then, we'd try and cover up.' From all accounts, it was not unusual for one of these precarious takes to end with these great men of jazz clinging to each other and bent double with painfully suppressed giggles like naughty schoolboys.

None of this, of course, detracts from the great historical and artistic importance of the Hot Five recordings. Indeed, the total absence of pressure, the blissful ignorance among the participants of the significance of what they were doing, almost certainly enhanced the music. Outside the studios, there were already a host of demanding fans who flocked to the Vendome Theatre or the Sunset Café to hear the man billed as 'The World's Greatest Trumpet-Player' hit the high notes. Lil Hardin Armstrong, Louis' wife at this time and a strong influence on his career, once told of his horror at discovering that people were coming to the theatre just to hear him play—or miss—high F. She gave him practical advice: 'C'mon and make some G's at home—if you can get a G at home, you won't worry about an F in the theatre!'

There is no evidence that anyone, not even the persuasive Lil, exerted any such pressure on Louis in the recording studios even though, with the Hot Five, he was feeling for the first time the responsibility of leadership. From first to last, a festive, off-duty atmosphere pervades the Hot Five sessions. Armstrong's development as a virtuoso performer is reflected in the music, but only in the most oblique way. In this respect, the carpers of later years were right. Nothing in Louis Armstrong's career, not even the work that he was doing at the time that the recordings were made, was quite like 'the Hot Five days'. For about the only time in his career, these recordings offer a picture of Louis Armstrong musically on vacation. The jazz history books, taking as they often do a simplistic view, have been pretty well unanimous in pointing to the Hot Fives as examples of Louis gradually bursting the established New Orleans ensemble style at the seams. But by the time the quintet first went into the recording studios in Chicago on November 12, 1925, the loose-knit New Orleans ensemble was already out of fashion. Even Louis' old mentor, King Oliver, had succumbed to the pressure for a saxophone section, and Louis himself had waved goodbye to the New Orleans ambience when he joined Fletcher Henderson's big dance orchestra in 1924. As Armstrong's diligent biographers, Max Jones and John Chilton, have pointed out, the frenzied, scorching trumpet heard on recordings with Erskine Tate's Vendome Orchestra in 1926 probably reflects Louis' 'public' style more accurately than anything from the Hot Five sessions of that time. By reverting to the relaxed collective improvisation of the New Orleans style for his recording sessions, and by retaining that basic style in the Hot Five's music for the full three years of its existence, Louis provided us with the opportunity of hearing his talent developing, as it were, in laboratory conditions.

'Potato Head Blues' was recorded almost exactly at the halfway point in the group's life. Stylistically, it represents a culmination. While the title (an uncomplimentary but jovial reference to some person unknown) reveals the light-heartedness of the occasion, the music shows a powerful cohesion throughout. Holes can be picked in the ensemble work. The trombonist who replaced Kid Ory (the same enthusiast who serenaded the brickwork in his abandonment?) does little but moo harmoniously, and Johnny

Dodds is not altogether at home with the harmonies that composer Louis—or more probably Lil—Armstrong specified. But somehow the blistering energy of Louis' trumpet carries everything along with it. Comparing the work of Johnny Dodds in the Hot Five and Seven setting of this period with contemporary recordings with his own little band (to be discussed later), some critics have noted a certain strain, as if Dodds were striving to match Louis Armstrong's virtuosity with an uncharacteristically florid style. As a soloist, Dodds was undoubtedly more at home with the simple blues and march harmonies of the New Orleans repertoire than with the rather more sophisticated chord progressions that crop up in 'Potato Head Blues'. But he bears down on his solo with a heroic determination and swing that commands respect.

Louis Armstrong has two solo spots, and in each he lays down unequivocally what will be demanded of the generations of jazz soloists who follow in his wake. After the first ensemble, he rips out an unaccompanied 'break' that leads into what, in popular music parlance, would be called the 'verse'—that is, a short secondary theme which returns, by way of an imperfect cadence, to the main theme. The verse in 'Potato Head Blues' starts with four authoritative notes, the first two firmly implanted on the beat. It would make simple, if not very exciting, sense if the rhythmic pattern of those first four notes were repeated symmetrically in bars 5 and 6 and again in bars 9 and 10. If the tune was ever committed to paper, that is almost certainly how it was laid out.

Jazz solo improvisation has been described as 'spontaneous composition', and Louis Armstrong's innate instinct for composition made him discard dull symmetry in favour of elegant, and exciting, variation. So, in the fifth and sixth bars, he alters the four-note phrase entirely, stretching the first note over three beats, squeezing notes two and three together to make room for it, and holding back the fourth so that it becomes, in effect, the first note of the ensuing phrase. Then again, in bars 9 and 10, notes from the underlying chord are borrowed to elaborate the original four notes with short arpeggios in yet another variation. 'Phrasing' is the term given to this sort of balanced construction, and Louis had a remarkable flair for it. It enabled him, on many occasions before and after 'Potato Head Blues', to bestow nobility upon undistinguished themes.

Exciting as it is, the verse in 'Potato Head Blues' is a mere prelude to the central Armstrong performance. At the end of the clarinet solo, Johnny St Cyr strums a short linking passage on banjo and then Louis literally launches himself into an improvisation against 'stop chords' by the band. Four years earlier, when Louis was with King Oliver's band, he recorded a tune of his own called 'Tears' in which, for one whole chorus, he improvised unaccompanied two-bar responses to the band's statement of the tune. At the time this was a pretty daring feat. It is hard to think of any musician (with Bechet and Beiderbecke as possible exceptions) who had the melodic and harmonic sense to maintain the music's impetus over the unbridged gaps. A certain similarity in the two tunes—the mingling of major and minor harmonies, for instance—leads Louis to repeat, in 'Potato Head Blues', the very phrase that, in bars 15 and 16, links the two halves of 'Tears'.

But if 'Tears' was daring, 'Potato Head Blues' is positively reckless. Here are no solid chunks of melody against which to pitch the responses, but single chords on the first beat of alternate bars which are there to help the listener rather than inspire or guide the soloist. Louis treats these staging posts with a certain amount of arrogant disdain, sometimes using them as launching pads from which to project a rhythmic phrase, at other times careering straight over them as if they were not there.

Anyone who listens again and again to this superbly constructed solo will discover his own magic moments in it. It might be the phrase that stalks majestically across the beat in bar 3, perhaps, or the augmented chord that is implied in bar 6 in place of the tune's more conventional dominant 7th, or again, the surprising but absolutely scintillating D flat against a D seventh chord which distinguishes bar 12. Apart from these technical niceties, there is the glory of that searing, burnished tone and the triumphant joie de vivre with which Louis emerges from the solo and rejoins his colleagues for the finishing straight. And above all, for anyone with a feeling for jazz history, there is the awareness that, after this, jazz would never be the same again. For better or worse—and surely only the most crabbed purist would say that it was for worse —the way was opened for a whole era of fruitful solo exploration.

Bix Beiderbecke

SOME TIME IN THE YEAR 1910, the *Davenport Daily Democrat*, a smalltown newspaper in Iowa, ran a feature article which began 'SEVEN-YEAR-OLD BOY MUSICAL WONDER, little Bickie Beiderbecke plays any selection he hears! Leon Bix Beiderbecke, aged seven years, is the most unusual and the most remarkably talented child in music that there is in this city. He has never taken a music lesson and does not know one key from another, but he can play in completeness any selection, the air or tune of which he knows.'

The happy concatenation of circumstances which converted a boy musical wonder into a jazz genius are laid out in the admirable biography of Bix by Richard Sudhalter and Philip Evans from which the above quotation is taken. For our purposes they can be summed up in a few pages. Davenport stands on the Mississippi river at a point where the excursion steamers from New Orleans, Cape Girardeau and St Louis moored and turned around. As a small boy, Bix was drawn to the music, from small bands and from the steam organs called calliopes, which poured from these pleasure boats and, on clear evenings, wafted up as far as the Beiderbecke home on Grand Avenue. At the same time, he was driving a piano teacher to distraction by using a prodigious musical ear and memory to circumvent the tedious business of sight-reading—and sticking to—the written notes.

A new, strange and exciting outlet for this inventive talent presented itself when Bix's elder brother Charles, home from the war, brought into the house a new wind-up gramophone and a batch of records which, among an assortment of operatic arias and overtures, included two freshly recorded numbers—'Tiger Rag' and 'Skeleton Jangle'—by the Original Dixieland Jazz Band.

To the precocious and at the same time anarchic Bix, the free and unfettered sounds of this early jazz were a revelation. It was not long before he borrowed a cornet and began tentatively to pick out the clear, incisive notes with which Nick La Rocca led the ODJB into action.

From this point onwards, the story falls into a familiar pattern. There is the formation of a schoolboy band, the sitting-in with local and visiting musicians, the taking-in of sundry influences. In 1919, Bix heard, and probably struck up a fleeting acquaintance with, nineteen-year-old Louis Armstrong, who pulled into Davenport aboard the SS Capitol as a member of Fate Marable's band. There is no aural evidence that Bix became a sudden convert to the Armstrong style. By all accounts Louis was already something of a virtuoso, and it is likely, that, as a learner still, Bix stayed with the more approachable music of the ODJB and Nick La Rocca whose example could be studied at leisure on gramophone records. A few years later, in Chicago, Bix was able to listen to Louis more consistently, but by this time he had already acquired a strong style of his own. Where from? Setting aside, as the main factor, his own innate originality, it is probable that the most impressive music that Bix could hear in the flesh during his formative years was provided by two young New Orleans musicians who worked in and around Davenport in 1921. One was Leon Roppolo, whose clarinet solos subsequently recorded with the New Orleans Rhythm Kings have a plaintive, legato quality which is shared by Bix's earliest work on record. The influence of Emmett Hardy—a few months younger than Bix but clearly a more experienced and accomplished player at that time—must be taken on trust, since he died of TB in 1925 without making his mark on record. When I first began to read the jazz magazines in the mid-Thirties, Hardy was painted as a romantic, almost Keatsian figure given to playing compulsively until his lips bled. Of such nonsense is jazz legend compounded. In this present context, we must be content with the comparatively boring conclusion that Emmet Hardy, a good player according to those who remember him, probably had some influence on Bix's style.

Coleman Hawkins.

Bix Beiderbecke (l) and
Frankie Trumbauer.

Bix Beiderbecke.

Duke Ellington.

Eddie Condon.

The first band of note with which Bix Beiderbecke played was a youthful group which took shape in the last weeks of 1923. It is alleged that they chose to call themselves The Wolverine Orchestra after Jelly Roll Morton's composition 'Wolverine Blues' which in the early days was a popular item in their repertoire. What is more certain, listening to the recordings which they made throughout 1924, is that The Wolverine Orchestra was a band of note solely because Bix was playing in it. Rhythmically, it played in the jerky, 'vo-de-o-do' style of the typical dance-bands of the time, but against this framework, Bix's clear and already distinctive cornet sound reveals some of the subtlety which, long before the wider record-buying public had ever taken note of his name, earned him the admiration of his fellow musicians.

It was an admiration which had, at first, to surmount Bix's unpromising appearance. His eyes and 'silly little mouth' were what first struck the pianist and songwriter Hoagy Carmichael. The young Eddie Condon also found Bix's eyes noteworthy, though it was the overall apparition that inspired some characteristically laconic Condon prose. He took in Beiderbecke as 'a kid in a cap with the peak broken. He had on a green overcoat from the walk-up-one-and-save-ten district; the collar was off his neck. He had a round face and eyes that had no desire to focus on what was in front of him.' Eddie Condon was not exactly enthralled at the prospect of working with Bix. 'I've made a mistake, I thought. I'm stuck with this clam digger for two months . . . how can a guy in a cap and a green overcoat play anything civilised?' The clarinettist Mezz Mezzrow's recollection of young Beiderbecke is perhaps the most surprising, contrasting with the pudgy, whey-faced, sleeked impression that the familiar photographs convey: 'Bix was a rawboned, husky, farmboy kind of kid, a little above average height and still growing. [Mezz's musical perception is clearly stronger than his human biology—Bix was over twenty-one when they met and presumably had reached full height.] His frog-eyes popped out of a ruddy face and he had light brown hair that always looked like it was trying to go some place else . . .'

Both Carmichael and Condon were reporting impressions received before they had heard Bix blow a note, and even Mezzrow had only heard the indistinct sounds emanating from records by the Wolverines. Musicians, and especially those of the tough jazz school, are not usually prone to attacks of the vapours, but nothing else will adequately describe the effect which the first notes from Bix Beiderbecke's cornet had on our three witnesses. 'Just four notes,' recalled Hoagy Carmichael, 'but he didn't blow them—he hit them like a mallet hits a chime. And his *tone*—the richness . . . He ruined me. I got up from the piano and staggered over and fell exhausted on the davenport.' Eddie Condon was on the train en route to an engagement when he first heard Bix actually play. 'With nothing to do but sit and stare at the scenery from there [Cleveland] to Buffalo, I began to wonder again about the cornet. I got out my banjo. Eberhardt [another colleague] dug up his saxophone and doodled along with me. Finally Beiderbecke took out a silver cornet. He put it to his lips and blew a phrase. The sound came out like a girl saying yes. Eberhardt smiled at me. "How about 'Panama'?" he said. I was still shivering and licking my insides, tasting the last of the phrase. "All right," Beiderbecke said, " 'Panama'." By itself, so it seemed, my banjo took up the rhythm. At last I was playing music; so far as I was concerned, it could go on for ever.'

Strangely enough it was Mezz Mezzrow, whose slangy literary style normally sagged beneath the weight of colourful hyperbole, who produced the clearest analysis of Bix's style. 'I have never heard a tone like he got before or since. He played mostly open horn, every note full, big, rich and round, standing out like a pearl, loud but never irritating or jangling, with a powerful drive that few white musicians had in those days. Bix was too young for the soulful tone, full of oppression and misery, that the great Negro trumpeters get—too young and, maybe, too disciplined. His attack was more on the militaristic side, powerful and energetic, every note packing a solid punch, with his head always in control over his heart. That attack was as sure-footed as a mountain goat; every note was sharp as a rifle's crack, incisive as a bite. Bix was a natural-born leader. He set the pace and the idiom, defined the style, wherever he played, and the other musicians just naturally fell into step.' This is fascinating stuff, seeming to contradict almost wilfully the picture which legend has built up—

the picture of an eccentric and weak-willed genius, the stereotype
of the misunderstood artist driven by self-doubt and false friends
into alcoholic self-destruction, with a musical persona that was
correspondingly introspective and 'cool'. But if we forget altogether
the Young Man With A Horn of Dorothy Baker's novel (allegedly
inspired by Bix) and concentrate on the music, it is not hard to
recognise the musician whom Mezz is describing, even if some of
the magic is lost in the inhibiting atmosphere of the recording
studio.

That the magic was potent is confirmed by the swift ascent
which Bix, without any formal musical qualifications, made into
the first league of the popular music business. With the Wolverines
he went to New York towards the end of 1924. A reviewer for
the showbiz magazine *Variety* found the band 'a torrid unit that
need doff the mythical chapeau to no one'. More important for
Bix, the celebrated and influential bandleader Paul Whiteman
heard the band and filed away in his memory a highly favourable
impression of the young cornet-player. But it was a bandleader
from Detroit, Jean Goldkette, who was the first to tempt Bix away
from the Wolverines. With Goldkette at the end of 1924, Bix's
musical illiteracy brought problems, not least of which was the
necessity, on recording sessions, for an extra trumpet-player to
play the written parts while Bix stood by for the hot solos which
the ever-conservative recording executives did not always want.
Jean Goldkette had to let Bix go, but added 'I don't want to let
him out of my sight. He's going to be very good indeed, mark my
words.'

Sure enough, Bix Beiderbecke was back in the Jean Goldkette
fold within eighteen months. But by this time he had renewed
contact with a musician with whom, for the rest of his short life,
he was to form a close musical partnership. In many ways, Frank
Trumbauer was the perfect foil for Bix—an accomplished and
forward-looking musician, but sober, disciplined and businesslike where the other was erratic, unbridled and an increasingly
heavy drinker. Their somewhat Laurel and Hardyesque career
together (there would be many occasions when Trumbauer would
have cause to say 'Another fine mess . . .') began in the autumn of
1925 when Bix joined Trumbauer's band for a season. From it,

they went together into the Goldkette Orchestra, Bix having by this time marginally improved his reading but greatly enhanced his reputation as a 'hot' man. Jean Goldkette, though a well-schooled musician, was always a non-playing leader and, as he turned his attention to the business side of things, Frank Trumbauer took charge of the band in the field. It is relevant to the huge influence which Bix had on his contemporaries, both white and black, to record that the Goldkette band was good enough to challenge—and rout—Fletcher Henderson's famous orchestra in the Roseland Ballroom in New York, Henderson's own home ground. Despite this, it was only a matter of eighteen months or so after Bix rejoined before Goldkette disbanded.

From the band which had adopted—and earned—the title of 'The Paul Whiteman of the West', Bix Beiderbecke and Frank Trumbauer moved on together into the Paul Whiteman Orchestra proper. In terms of professional success, they could go no higher. Although Whiteman's organisation was nothing if not commercial, it was willing and able to draw on the finest talent in what was then called the 'hot' field—assuming, of course, that the talent was encased in a white skin. Integration on the bandstand was not to come for another decade or so. Jazz legend for years indulged itself in the simplistic theory—'cornfed' would have been Bix's own word for it—that it was the restriction and sheer boredom of big band work that drove Beiderbecke, the great artist, into alcoholism and a premature and spectacular death. It was the British jazz critic and musician Benny Green, in a perceptive essay on Bix, who first propounded the belief, which Sudhalter and Evans confirm in their detailed biography, that Bix's self-destructive urge was fuelled by a deep sense of inadequacy. The musicality which once drew little Bickie Beiderbecke to the attention of the *Davenport Daily Democrat* had a strong conventional facet. He was reared in a middle-class home with the strongest possible links with European culture. It would take a full chapter, with a psychiatrist in attendance, to plumb the complex causes of jazz music's yearning for respectability. The symptoms are everywhere and extend from Paul Whiteman's guying of 'crude jazz' in 1924 to the carefully-contrived concert-hall image of the Modern Jazz Quartet in the Fifties. With Bix, we can assume that upbringing, family environment, education and, perhaps, ancestry exerted a magnetic pull. It was reinforced by the genuine musical interest which he and many of his contemporaries had in the twentieth-century European composers. Bud Freeman has said to me, 'Apart from going to hear all the greats like Louis and King Oliver and Bessie, we didn't listen to *that* much jazz—it was more the classical composers for us.'

Some jazz historians with a 'New Orleans or bust' approach have called in Bix's involvement with European music as evidence to disqualify him as a 'jazz musician'. For anyone wishing to enter into a debate that leads straight into a quagmire of definitions and semantics, it can just as reasonably be used to prove the exact opposite—namely, that Bix, unlike some contemporaries whose use of the whole tone scale and advanced harmonies sounded like mere trickery, was able to absorb these diverse ingredients into an integrated style just *because* he was a great jazzman. Be that as it may, Bix Beiderbecke's fan-worship of Maurice Ravel and the like strengthens the proposition that he admired Paul Whiteman's Orchestra and that his frustration, which manifested itself in increasingly frequent and prolonged absences from the bandstand, arose from his belief that he could not live up to it. It has become fashionable to deride Whiteman's elephantine 'symphonic jazz' and to scoff at the title 'King of Jazz' which a Hollywood movie bestowed on him in 1930. The term 'jazz' had less sophisticated connotations in those days, and we should now be able to accept without rancour that, while offering no competition to true jazz artists of the calibre of Louis Armstrong, Duke Ellington, Jelly Roll Morton or Bix himself, Paul Whiteman did preside over an organisation which set itself a high standard of musicianship, from which jazz talent was not excluded. By the standards of a dance-band, a concert light orchestra or a show band (and his orchestra combined all three) he did not purvey tripe. The men who arranged for him—Bill Challis, Tommy Satterfield, Ferde Grofé—were friends of Bix and shared his musical aspirations. That he felt pride, rather than shame, in playing what they wrote is shown by the story, told by Sudhalter and Evans, that he sent home to his parents copies of every record he made with Whiteman, and was bitterly hurt when, on one of his leaves-of-absence from the band, he found all the packages unopened.

It was the story of Bix's last years, with their decline into alcoholism and broken health punctuated by sometimes violent breakdowns, that provided fuel for the legend, rather than anything which he consigned to gramophone records. Indeed, to some who, like myself, were first gripped by the more spectacular music of Louis Armstrong, the initial exposure to Bix's recordings was something of an anti-climax. I suppose we expected to hear music deeply imbued with tragic melancholy, lapsing into pathos as physical and mental deterioration progressed. What sprang from the grooves, however, was a joyous, clean-cut, extrovert sound, as clear as a bell and endowing every tune, however banal, with almost boyish enthusiasm.

After Louis, Bix's solo flights were, at first hearing, unadventurous. It was only after patient and persistent listening that the truth became apparent. Starting from the same point in the development of jazz playing, Louis and Bix moved in diametrically opposite directions. Louis Armstrong's music expanded outwards, as if violently impelled by centrifugal force. It was not only the New Orleans conventions which he 'burst at the seams', to use the popular cliché. Melodically, harmonically, rhythmically and emotionally, he took off on an exploration into the unknown. Bix, seemingly more cautious by temperament, took the opposite course, staying within the musical conventions of his time but digging deeply into them and upturning little gems of subtlety and fresh discovery every inch along the way. One specific instance underlines the contrast. In a piece called 'Ory's Creole Trombone' by the Hot Five, Louis Armstrong, with a rush of imaginative zeal to the head, attempts a 'break' which, while recognisable as a musical thought, cannot technically be played on the trumpet at all. In a triumph of mind over matter, the idea comes through to us, but musically it is a very strange sound indeed. It is quite inconceivable that Bix would ever have allowed invention and execution to come unstuck in this way. When, in a series of famous encounters, he bandied spontaneous phrases with Frank Trumbauer, there are few, if any, moments when one literally gasps at the sheer recklessness of it all. What astounds here is the cool-headed, even laconic way in which phrases that seem set on some well-worn path suddenly dart off at a tangent or double back on themselves in a totally unexpected way.

The moment has come to broach the tricky subject of the terms 'hot' and 'cool' as they are used in jazz discussion. The trickiness arises from the fact that 'hot' has performed more than one role over the decades. At the time when Bix was establishing his reputation with the Goldkette and Trumbauer bands, he would have been known as a 'hot' man, a musician adept at improvising as distinct from a 'straight' man who was restricted to playing the notes put in front of him. Likewise, at the end of the Twenties when the word 'jazz' became temporarily unfashionable, the music which employed a large degree of improvisation was generally known as 'hot style'. Even when it became respectable in trendy circles to talk about 'jazz' again, the word 'hot' persisted. In France, where their devotion to the art was always rather more impassioned than among the phlegmatic Anglo-Saxons, 'le jazz hot' was what they enthused about. But nobody at that time talked about 'le jazz cool'. Hot jazz was simply a term to distinguish the real thing from all the novelty music and syncopated dance tunes which the uninformed media insisted on calling 'jazz'.

The distinction between 'hot' and 'cool' as an approach to jazz improvisation did not really start to be made until the arrival of the Modern Jazz Era immediately after World War II. This was a period when many long-established jazz notions were being overthrown. One belief, propagated more by jazz writers and fans than by musicians themselves, was that the type of musician who fired off passionate improvisations straight at an audience's gut sensibilities was part of a vanishing past. The new image of the jazzman depicted a musican withdrawn behind dark glasses who communicated, if at all, in monosyllables, regarded an audience as an intrusive but necessary evil and approached his music-making with a certain clinical detachment. Being wise after the event, the adherents of the 'Cool School' would point to two of the great heroes of the Swing Era, tenor-saxists Coleman Hawkins and Lester Young, as epitomising the old and the new.

Coleman Hawkins, who played with a huge tone encrusted with overtones and enriched by a breathy vibrato, was the 'hot' musician par excellence. By contrast Lester Young, with his light airy sound and soft, almost flabby, articulation, was taken to represent coolness.

Of course, the whole discussion, bound up as it was with fashionable attitudes, produced a lot of fatuous nonsense. Dizzy Gillespie, who inaugurated the craze for dark glasses, and Charlie Parker, from whom emanated the cliché of the modern musician turning his back on the audience, both rarely forged a solo at anything less than white heat. The modern musicians or beboppers were hardly more detached and cultish than the marihuana-smoking 'vipers' in Harlem in the Thirties, for example, who numbered Louis Armstrong among their founder-members and who assumed all the elements of a secret society from the language they spoke to the way they walked. And theory took a bad beating when Coleman Hawkins and Lester Young appeared onstage together in Norman Granz's gladiatorial show, 'Jazz At The Philharmonic' in 1946. For in that rabble-rousing arena, the apotheosis of Le Jazz Hot, it was the extrovert Hawkins who played blithely on his own sweet way without any special concessions to the audience, while the introverted, 'cool' Lester honked and riffed them into a frenzy.

To pour scorn on the trendy concept of 'cool jazz' is not to deny the existence of 'hot' and 'cool' elements in jazz. But they have nothing whatever to do with any one period or movement, whether fashionable or artistic. Nor indeed are they confined to music—when that passionate British political orator Aneurin Bevan called Labour Party leader Hugh Gaitskell a 'dessicated calculating machine', he was expressing in different words exactly what Eddie Condon, the ringleader of the tough but deeply sentimental Chicago jazz fraternity, thought of the modern alto-saxophonist Paul Desmond. Objective criticism cannot afford to take sides, especially when the core of the argument—'hot' versus 'cool', heart versus head, passion versus calm reflection—turns out to be no more than a whopping great human platitude.

But there is one way in which the word 'hot' and 'cool' can be endowed with some useful and constructive meaning. It lies in the contrast I have already made between the directions in which Louis Armstrong and Bix Beiderbecke travelled in their musical progress. There was Louis pushing into unknown areas which he *felt* rather than actually perceived, while Bix stayed within the conventional forms but explored them more deeply than anyone had yet done. It would not be far-fetched to link that break of Armstrong's in 'Ory's Creole Trombone', which in the heat of creation tried to transcend the trumpet's limitations and very nearly succeeded, with the eldritch shrieking of avant garde saxophonists no longer able to express themselves within the instrument's normal range. An arbitrary list of these flyers into space, the jazz astronauts, takes us from Louis on to Henry Allen and Rex Stewart, Roy Eldridge, Dizzy Gillespie (and here the baton passes to saxophone players), Charlie Parker, John Coltrane and the avant gardists. These, and other musicians through the whole range of instruments, pushed the boundaries of jazz further and further outwards, the cumulative effect of their key recordings giving the impression of men impelled by demons. If we label them the 'hot' men, this is not to elevate their role above all others —indeed, it could well be argued that the almost frenetic pushing outwards of jazz boundaries over the short space of five or six decades has not altogether been to the music's advantage. Fortunately for the richness of jazz, there is the creative direction, exemplified by Bix Beiderbecke, which has led musicians of equal genius to dwell upon, explore, refine and illuminate each new extension to the idiom. For all the influence which he had on the young modernists of the late Forties, Lester Young did not, in fact, make any major harmonic innovations. He worked as much within the musical conventions of the Thirties as did Bix within the established style of the Twenties. Miles Davis, in the early phase that culminated in his 'Sketches of Spain' collaboration with Gil Evans, likewise set to work on the new worlds which Charlie Parker and Dizzy Gillespie had opened up, burrowing into them when others were content to keep running round the surface. If we call them the 'cool' men, it implies no lack of warmth or intensity in their music, simply that they seem to us to have sought tranquillity rather than turbulence.

Of course, we are dealing here with crude over-simplifications.

Like male and female hormones, hot and cool elements exist, in varying proportions, within every musician. Lester Young, for instance, favoured the surging four-beat rhythm that distinguishes most 'hot' styles, and the taxi-horn honks and deliberate variations of pitch which he occasionally used, while in no way central to his style, nevertheless revealed occasionally the 'hot' man's urge to push outwards into unorthodoxy. Conversely, Louis Armstrong made in the mid-Thirties an artistic decision to abandon his explorer's role. His conscious explanation was characteristically mundane, since profound self-analysis was not in his line. He said: 'I stopped all that playin' for musicians, guys who'd come around the stand just to see what you could do. They never paid you a thing, but you could mess your lip up real good doin' all that!' But when we listen to his records of that period, many of them made with sloppy and poorly-arranged big band backing, what we actually hear is Louis taking a cooler, more reflective look at the idiom which he himself had been largely responsible for fashioning ten years earlier. Gone are the breathtaking imaginative flights and the fluffed notes and slightly tense articulation which went with them. Instead, we have relatively spare phrases, selected with majestic poise and a masterly sense of structure—and, incidentally, performed with an instrumental control that has rarely been equalled. I believe it was this cooler facet of Armstrong that has led Miles Davis to say in recent years: 'You know, you can't play anything on a horn that Louis hasn't played—I mean even modern.' Dig out the recording which Louis made of 'I Can't Give You Anything But Love' on June 24, 1938 and you will hear a solo which, within a firmly Louis-esque context, harks straight back to Bix Beiderbecke and 'Singin' the Blues'.

I have noted in the chapter on Fletcher Henderson that New York in the late Twenties was a city of musical extremes. Hot and cool existed side by side. To forestall any suggestion that there was a clear racial division between the two, it is worth making the point that, by offsetting the high and wild contributions of trumpeters Louis Armstrong and Tommy Ladnier with the more lyrical and placid solos of cornetist Joe Smith, Fletcher Henderson made in the trumpet department the same musically effective 'hot and cool' distinction that Count Basie was to make, a decade later, when he pitted such muscular tenor-saxists as Herschel Evans and Buddy Tate against Lester Young. Nevertheless, it is true that most of the white New Yorkers with whom Bix associated favoured the cool approach that had been established in popularity by such leaders as Red Nichols and Miff Mole.

Nowhere is this coolness more obvious than in the rhythm department. The opening bars of 'Singin' the Blues' provide a sharp contrast with the New Orleans style and its immediate derivatives that flourished in Chicago in the Twenties. Compared with records by Louis Armstrong's Hot Five and the McKenzie Condon Chicagoans—and they were different enough from each other, as we shall soon see—this music sounds almost lethargic. Contrary to superficial belief, the New Orleans jazz recorded in the early Twenties was not 'two beat' music. In the King Oliver and early Hot Five recordings, the rhythmic pulse was an even four beats to the bar. Even when Louis Armstrong employed a tuba-player to grunt away on the first and third beats, the underlying rhythm was still a pushing four-four. Here is an answer for those who, relying for a definition of 'hot' jazz on such blowing characteristics as the weight of tone or intensity of vibrato, have stumbled over piano or vibraphone players whose tone is built unalterably into the instrument. 'Hotness', according to the 'centrifugal' analogy that I have used, is very much a rhythmic thing. Listen again to 'Potato Head Blues' and, in the famous stop chorus without benefit of rhythm section, hear how Louis Armstrong seems increasingly to be straining at the leash towards the end of the chorus and beyond into the final ensemble. Such is the momentum that is built up that to lift the needle or turn down the volume sharply would invite an almost physical shock.

Cool deliberation does not thrive under such a momentum, which is why adherents to the reflective style of improvisation often lean instinctively towards the more measured pace that two-in-a-bar provides. In the fastest numbers that, say, Frankie Trumbauer's band essayed—and 'Clarinet Marmalade' from the Bix period is a good example—fidgety arrangement tends to disguise the fact that the playing is basically in the 2/4 style of a military march. In slower tempo, the choice of a side-to-side two-beat, in deliberate preference to the thrusting 12/8 rhythm that Louis Armstrong demonstrated, is even more marked. The introduction to 'Singin' the Blues' is the old-time dancing-master's '*one*-and-*two*' set to music!

About Frankie Trumbauer, who opens the proceedings with an elegant variation on the theme, strong subjective feelings have always been aroused. When the record came out, his solo attracted as much attention and praise from musicians and aficionados as that of Bix Beiderbecke. We know that the flat, polished tone that he got from the now obsolete C melody saxophone (pitched between the alto and the tenor) had a big influence on the light and airy sound that Lester Young was to bring to the tenor-saxophone a few years later. Today, the solo, while still admired for the gracefulness of its melodic line, is generally rated below that of Bix. Somehow, in Trumbauer's work, there is the feeling that an essential jazz element is missing. 'Some of you guys are all belly,' Lester Young is alleged to have told his great rival, Herschel Evans. By the same token, it could be said that Trumbauer was 'all head', with little sign of the raw spirit of jazz that Bix derived from his devotions at the feet of King Oliver, Louis and Bessie Smith. In music, the pulse or throb in a note that is called vibrato is not simply a device for prettifying a tone. As both Bix and Louis Armstrong showed in their own different ways, it performs an essential rhythmic function, even when, as with Bix, it is barely perceptible. Trumbauer's slack vibrato, no more than a faint quaver, does nothing to give his phrases buoyancy, and one or two otherwise interesting runs sound flat-footed as a result.

For contrast, we need only hear Bix Beiderbecke's opening note in the solo that follows. There is a learned thesis waiting to be written on the way jazz improvisers use opening notes to, as it were, 'tee up' a solo. Lester Young would often open with a single note followed by a gap of three or four beats, rather in the way that a speaker about to make an important point concentrates his listeners' attention with the word 'Now . . .' If we go back once again to 'Potato Head Blues' and the Armstrong stop-chorus, we hear that characteristic opening which Louis bequeathed to a host of imitators—three repeated notes played across the beat followed by a short one a third below. Apart from their actual rhythmic placings, there is a vibrancy in each note that somehow primes the ensuing solo with energy. To use another sporting metaphor, it's like the little hop and skip that a high-jumper gives before embarking on his run. Coincidentally, Bix Beiderbecke's two introductory notes are identically placed in the scale, but instead of Armstrong's three stabbing notes, Bix plays one, a gentle but taut note that puts him in perfect balance for the ensuing solo.

There is one thing further to be said about Bix and vibrato. Because he eschewed the broad, throbbing vibrato of New Orleans players in general and Louis in particular, many jazz commentators have used loose phrases like 'vibrato-less' or 'virtually no vibrato' in describing Bix's sound. Most people nowadays are sufficiently acquainted with the guitar to know how flat and lifeless is a plucked note that is absolutely devoid of vibrato. Yet I have been able to quote earlier a string of witnesses to the almost uncannily vibrant and ringing quality of Bix Beiderbecke's cornet tone. The singing effect that we can pick up on recordings such as 'Singin' the Blues' reminds me of nothing more than the poignant note that a master guitarist, be it Segovia or Django Reinhardt, will send winging on its way with an incisive attack and a subtle and well-timed vibrato. Ringing, singing or winging, Bix Beiderbecke's vibrato was not negligible, it was at the very heart of his magical sound.

In probing some of the secrets of Bix's 'Singin' the Blues' solo, I find it useful to remind myself that, when I first heard it, I was not greatly impressed. I have confessed earlier that the Bix legend had prepared me for something more emotionally charged. By comparison with the slurring and sliding and quivering music of Armstrong, Bix sounded at first like a man picking his way rather meticulously through a prepared script. The structure, with its shifting symmetry seemed, unlike Wordsworth's *Perfect Woman*, 'too good for human nature's daily food'. But familiarity, in this instance, bred a deepening respect. Hard as it is to believe, the testimony of Bix's friends and colleagues adds up to overwhelming evidence that 'Singin' the Blues', like every other Bix solo, was a spontaneous improvisation. He was simply not interested in repeating himself as long as the opportunity was there for further exploration. It may be that on that first occasion

I heard no further than the symmetry of the first four bars which, taken out of context, sound like a stanza of rather stilted verse. But of course, one must not stop there, for this formality is then beautifully counterbalanced by an asymmetric phrase of more complexity spread over the next four bars to make beautiful sense. And so it goes on—a perfect construction of balanced phrases, some of them a melancholy or seductive legato, some a triumphant, even dictatorial staccato. Within a single phrase there are notes that fall rigidly on the beat and notes that run ahead as if anticipating the next turn of melody.

I will content myself with one further point of detail. In rhythmic style, 'Singin' the Blues' belongs to the pre-Armstrong era. Had the same record been made by the same musicians ten years later, when Louis Armstrong's rhythmic freedom had been generally assimilated, the stilted two-beat would have been discarded as 'corny' and the piece would have loped along more loosely in a 12/8 time. Bix Beiderbecke personified the musical truth that rhythms do not in themselves go in and out of fashion or supersede each other in the advance of 'progress'. They simply exist, to be used or misused. As a 'cool' thinker according to my definition, it suited him quite well to stay within the two-beat conventions of the time and place. To see how restricting these could be if handled inexpertly, we need only move forward to the short solo by Jimmy Dorsey in the final chorus. He is so inhibited by the rigid framework that, before the eight bars are out, he practically expires from asphyxia. Bix on the other hand gloried in the opportunity for subtle variation which the framework provides. For one example, listen to the four bars that follow the fluent, tumbling break in mid-chorus. There is an explosive whip-up which is typical of many of Bix's excursions into the high register (it was another aspect of the inward direction of his exploration that he was usually quite happy to stay within the natural one-and-a-half octave range of the human voice). Descending from it with measured steps, he puts together another of his neat and logical couplets which most trumpet-players who know the chorus by heart (this writer included) interpret in an even-note style which underlines the meticulous construction of the musical sentence. But Bix's phrases were never so predictable, and close listening reveals that he does not play it like that. His first two bars use dotted notes in an almost jerky fashion—one-a-two-a-three—reminiscent of the 'vo-de-o-do' dance rhythms that the Wolverines used. In the second, answering phrase, the notes even out. Indeed, they so narrowly miss being straightforward even quavers or eighth notes that they would be almost impossible to describe accurately through musical notation. These extremely subtle rhythmic contrasts—between jerky and smooth, staccato and flowing, strictly on-the-beat and lazily across it—seemed to occur naturally and spontaneously in Bix Beiderbecke's improvisations, and it is through them that his solos have retained vitality over the years while those of his contemporaries have tended to sound increasingly mannered.

It would be blatantly unjust to leave the impression that 'Singin' the Blues' owes its peculiar magic solely to Bix's contribution. Fate played an important part in assigning to the session a recording engineer who was either a genius or an incompetent blessed with astonishingly good luck. Faced with a seven-piece band with a rhythm section weak in both numbers and efficiency, he cleared the airways effectively by consigning two of them to the limbo of inaudibility. In those days, drummers were encouraged to bring no more than one cymbal into the studio out of consideration for the recording equipment's sensitivity. So all we hear of Chauncey Moorhouse is an occasional splash of sound. As for Itzy Riskin, he can be detected vamping away manfully on the outer perimeter of the action, but it takes careful listening and I do not recommend it. For the virtual absence of these two warriors leaves the field clear for Eddie Lang, the only man in the rhythm section to match Bix and Trumbauer in stature. Born Salvatore Massaro, Lang inherited from his Italian background a schooled, 'classical' approach to the guitar. Compared with the fluent, wide-ranging work of successors such as Django Reinhardt or Charlie Christian whose melody lines, played on single strings, emulated those of trumpet and saxophone, Lang's rare solos in this vein sound rather laboured and pedestrian. His finest solos were just that—unaccompanied guitar solos in which he supplied both melody and chordal background in classical style, but with a rhythmic sense that belonged to a born jazzman. In the company of other musicians, he became a superb accompanist, and his reputation among jazz buffs to this day rests largely on great partnerships which he formed —with blues guitarist Lonnie Johnson (when Lang used the pseudonym Blind Willie Dunn) and, more especially, with his boyhood friend and fellow Italian, violinist Joe Venuti.

It is as accompanist, virtually single-handed, to the solos of Trumbauer and Bix that Eddie Lang shines on 'Singin' the Blues', contributing beyond measure to its quality and continuity. I will just pull out one plum—the silvery cascade of notes behind the twentieth bar of Trumbauer's solo which must have caused a few delighted smiles in the studio. Lang's virtues were negative, too. Having turned the Trumbauer and Bix solos into effective duets, he takes a back seat in the rather complex ensemble which follows Bix, leaving cornet and saxophone to decide, in a brief moment of confusion, who shall take the lead. The outcome is eminently satisfactory for the listener, for Trumbauer captures the melody line and leaves Bix to play a second part for eight bars which amounts to a continuation of the mood of his solo. After Jimmy Dorsey, there is no doubt who shall lead, for Bix assumes control in his most positive manner, giving the melody of Con Conrad and J. Russell Robinson its first unequivocal statement. Even here, the Bixian sense of rhythmic contrast prompts him to link the emphatic phrases of the tune with a beautifully-timed and nonchalant upward run that seems to pre-echo the break that Eddie Lang delivers a few bars later.

The reader may have begun to suspect, by this time, that there is no end to the refinements that I am capable of finding in 'Singin' the Blues'. Indeed, this is almost the definitive Desert Island Disc, three minutes of music with enough hidden treasures to keep a castaway digging away for years. Historically, it serves to pinpoint the effect which Bix—and his colleagues—had upon their contemporaries, both black and white. Their 'cool' style impressed that hotbed of burgeoning talents, the Fletcher Henderson Orchestra, who actually recorded a 'cover' of 'Singin' the Blues' with cornetist Rex Stewart playing Bix's solo note for note. The black arranger and saxist Don Redman was strongly influenced by the white New York school and the band known as McKinney's

Cotton Pickers (booked, incidentally, by Jean Goldkette) bristled with Bixian and Trumbaueresque touches while Redman was its leader. Through Redman, this influence reached its most unlikely source, right in the heart of Louis Armstrong's band in 1928 when the Hot Five in its later form was augmented by Don Redman's alto saxophone. True, it was subverted almost instantaneously by the resolutely four-beat, thrusting style of Armstrong, Earl Hines and drummer Zutty Singleton. But there are moments in such Redman arrangements as 'Heah Me Talkin' To Ya' and 'No One Else But You' when one can hear a New York two-beat feeling struggling to get out!

The influence of Bix himself was more widespread than most jazz historians acknowledge. I have been content to list such players as Jimmy McPartland and Bobby Hackett, who followed Bix's gentle and lyrical side. But fine as these players are in their own right, there was more to Bix than that, and others have found inspiration in the facet that Mezz Mezzrow stressed—the 'militaristic' attack, the 'solid punch', the notes 'sharp as a rifle's crack', which remind us more of such superficially unlikely Bix disciples as the rumbustious Wild Bill Davison, the terse Max Kaminsky, and the voluble Ruby Braff. It is not far-fetched to suggest that, through Rex Stewart, some Beiderbecke influence found its way into the formative styles of such black exponents as Clark Terry and Miles Davis. Certainly, a positive line of influence extended back to the New Yorkers when, in the first modern jazz era of the late Forties, 'cool' was promoted from a creative process to a way of life. Lester Young always insisted that he was attracted, as a learner, to the light, tranquil sound that Trumbauer achieved on C melody saxophone. When Lester's own influence affected the thinking of a whole generation of musicians in every branch of the saxophone family, it became easier still to hear Trumbauer —and perhaps, by association, Bix himself—in the sound of Paul Desmond, Lee Konitz and Stan Getz.

And so the ripples go on, transferring from 'cool' to 'hot' and back again. Ever since Bix Beiderbecke died, in 1931, at the age of 28, jazz enthusiasts have speculated as to the course he would have taken had he lived. Would his style have continued to develop until it reached the point from which the Cool School started in the late Forties? It's an attractive notion, but highly improbable. So much depends upon his own aspirations. Had they led him successfully in the direction which both Benny Green and Sudhalter and Evans have suggested, then the recording studios of Hollywood seem a more likely destination than the small and short-lived associations through which jazz innovators move most freely. But this is pedestrian, earthbound speculation, hardly worthy of a musical genius. For like many other geniuses in the creative universe, he flashed like a comet across the sky, leaving in his recordings some material evidence of the brilliance and magnificence of his passage.

Duke Ellington

THE YEAR 1923 IS to jazz history what 1066 is to the schoolboy's table of dates. In that year, King Oliver's Creole Jazz Band made the batch of recordings which are generally taken as the starting-point in the development of jazz on record. In them, the fully-fledged cornet of young Louis Armstrong was heard on record for the first time. Elsewhere, Bessie Smith, too, was making her first records, defying the technical shortcomings of the medium with the voice that literally elbowed its way out of the grooves to deliver the message of the blues.

In that same fateful year, Duke Ellington, after one false start, finally arrived, aged twenty-four, to find his fortune in New York. He was born on April 29, 1899, in Washington DC, and grew up in an environment which was, in the context of black America, middle class. His father, James E. Ellington, was a draughtsman in government employ, by Duke's account a fine fellow with a line in grandiloquent and outrageous flattery which he passed on to his son. (On tour with the Duke in Canada, he startled one of the local ladies by pronouncing: 'The millions of beautiful snowflakes are a celebration in honour of your beauty!') Duke Ellington's mother, to whom he was deeply devoted, appears in rare photographs to have been a lady of Edwardian style, beauty and elegance. Indeed, Edward Kennedy Ellington seems to have inherited a certain aristocratic stylishness long before a school friend of gregarious disposition dubbed him 'Duke' to enhance his own social status.

With the benefit of a solid education, Duke Ellington had earned a scholarship to art college before he left high school, but he never took it up. By this time, he was already earning 'a lot of money' by playing piano and by booking bands for dances. His art training was not entirely useless: 'When customers came for posters to advertise a dance, I would ask them what they were doing about their music. When they wanted to hire a band, I would ask them who's painting their signs.' In piano-playing, Duke had had early lessons from a formal music teacher called, incredibly, Mrs Clinkscales. When her pupils gave their recital in the local church, young Ellington was the only one who didn't know his part. 'So Mrs Clinkscales had to play the treble and I just played the umpy-dump bottom! The umpy-dump bottom was, of course, the foundation and understanding of that part of piano-playing I later learned to like.' The style of piano-playing which attracted the Duke flourished in places like Frank Holliday's poolroom, which appears to have satisfied Ellington's gracious standards by boasting lawyers, doctors and college graduates among its otherwise raffish clientele. The masters here were players like Doc Perry, Les Dishman, Clarence Bowser, Sticky Mack and Blind Johnny, some musically literate, some non-readers who nonetheless made their own original contribution.

Ragtime, with its florid, fulsome right hand and 'umpy-dump bottom', was without doubt the foundation of the solo piano style which these men practised. But it's probable that under the influence of the player-piano rolls which spread the new pianistic fashions emanating from New York as effectively as the gramophone was to do later, they were moving away from ragtime's almost militaristic 2/4 rhythm towards the more fluent, jazz-like style discussed in the chapter on James P. Johnson. Duke drank it all in. 'I was always a terrific listener. I'm taller on one side than the other from leaning over the piano, listening.'

And he went on listening when, already quite experienced as solo pianist, bandleader and entrepreneur, he and his close friends Sonny Greer and Otto 'Toby' Hardwick followed up a tip-off from Fats Waller and made the move to New York. Harlem was already a veritable university of advanced piano-playing and, as I have described apropos James P. Johnson, the lessons took the form of open contests. The 'professor' whom Duke admired most of all and who had the greatest influence on his own piano style, was the formidable Willie 'The Lion' Smith, scourge of any upstart with inflated ideas of his prowess. 'This was the big thing about The Lion: a gladiator at heart. Anybody who had a reputation as a piano-player had to prove it right there and then by sitting down to the piano and displaying his artistic wares. And when a cat thought that he was something special, he usually fell into that trap (or, you might say, into the jaws of The Lion) and he always came out with his reputation all skinned up, covered with the lacerations of humiliation, because before he got through too many stanzas The Lion was standing over him, cigar blazing.'

However, unlike Willie The Lion, James P. or Fats Waller, Duke Ellington did not graduate from this Harlem school to become a featured piano-player. Many early critics were led into underrating his abilities at the keyboard simply because he featured himself so sparingly. It is almost as if the 'terrific listener' was so preoccupied with listening to the musicians whom he gathered around him that he scorned his own contribution. Certainly, listening to, and utilising to the best advantage, the idiosyncrasies of his side-men proved to be one of Duke's great talents once the band which he formed in 1924 flowered into the Ellington Orchestra, ten or eleven strong, that took up residency first at the Kentucky Club and then in Harlem's most glittering entertainment showcase, the Cotton Club. Recordings by Ellington bands began late in 1924 and, significantly, acquired distinction only when soloists of real calibre joined the ranks. Even then, the characteristic which made Duke Ellington's music unique and the first example of 'jazz composition' within the big band meaning of the term was what, to anyone versed in straight composition, must appear to be an eccentric method of composing. Whatever inhibition it was that deterred him from becoming just another pianist-leader in the egotistical mould, also restrained him from imposing his will on the band in the manner of a composer-leader like, say, Jelly Roll Morton. The Ellington method entailed first of all gathering together musicians each of whom had a distinctive improvising style and tonal 'voice'. From that point on, it was a matter of using those voices to the full—and that meant taking suggestions from the musicians, altering preconceived ideas to suit them and coming as close as possible to 'improvising' through them.

Billy Strayhorn, the arranger who joined Duke in 1939 and thereafter became his compositional alter ego, described the process well: 'Ellington plays the piano, but his real instrument is his band. Each member of his band is to him a distinctive tone colour and set of emotions, which he mixes with others equally distinctive to produce a third thing, which I like to call the "Ellington Effect".

'Sometimes this fixing happens on paper and frequently right on the bandstand. I have often seen him exchange parts in the middle of a piece because the man and part weren't the same character.

'Ellington's concern is with the individual musician, and what happens when they put their musical characters together. Watching him on the bandstand, the listener might think that his movements are stock ones used by everyone in front of a band. However, the extremely observant may well detect the flick of the finger that may draw the sound he wants from a musician.

'By letting his men play naturally and relaxed, Ellington is able to probe the intimate recesses of their minds and find things that not even the musicians thought were there.'

I was once present in a hotel room when a group of rather earnest students were interviewing the Duke for a university magazine. One of them remarked on what he saw as the divergence of technical prowess within the ranks of the Ellington orchestra of the late Fifties. 'Let's be like the businessmen and talk percentages,' said the Duke, 'Nobody plays 100% of an instrument. Some guys like Clark [Terry] play 90% of their instrument. Someone like Ray Nance maybe plays 45% of the instrument—but he plays that 45% in a way that no one else on earth can play it!'

The first Ellingtonian of this calibre and stature was the cornetist Leroy 'Bubber' Miley. Born in South Carolina in 1903, Miley had been raised from the age of six in New York where, by the time he met Ellington in 1924, he had become a master of a style of playing that was prevalent—and extremely popular—in Harlem. 'Gutbucket' is what the musicians called it, and the word is certainly apt for the earthy, slightly ribald music that made much use of wah-wah mutes and 'growl' techniques. Jazz historians have discovered over the years the dangers that await anyone who attempts to deduce a chronological order of events by listening to gramophone records alone. It is all too easy to say that, because Joe Oliver recorded effective 'wah-wah' solos in 1923 and Bubber Miley is heard in similar vein in 1927, therefore Miley was influenced exclusively by Oliver. Another legendary master of the plunger mute was the Memphis cornetist Johnny Dunn, and both he and Bubber Miley were members of blues-singer Mamie Smith's band during the early Twenties. Miley also played and recorded in the band of cornetist Tom Morris, who did not enjoy Dunn's enormous popularity in New York, but who can be heard wielding a deft plunger on recordings made before any of the famous Oliver solos went into circulation.

This does not rule out Oliver as a direct influence upon Miley. Indeed, we have the evidence of Garvin Bushell (in *Jazz Panorama*), who travelled with Bubber Miley in Mamie Smith's Jazz Hounds, that Oliver did indeed make a great impression on the young cornetist. 'When we were in Chicago, Bubber and I would go to the Dreamland and hear King Oliver every night. Bubber got his growling from Oliver. Before hearing Oliver, he never growled. That's where Bubber changed his style and began using his hand over the tin mute that used to come with all cornets. It was hearing Oliver that did it.'

Let us, for the fun of it, assume that Oliver begat Bubber. This leads us to another intriguing facet of Duke Ellington the composer, and that is his eclecticism. I have already noted that, with considerable geographical licence, the music which came up to New York from New Orleans via Chicago was known as 'Western style'. The Eastern musicians—those operating on the Washington-Philadelphia-New York axis—were prone to look down on the Westerners. Louis Armstrong recalled encountering a cool breeze when he first moved up from Chicago to join Fletcher Henderson's band in New York. 'They simply ignored me to an extent, and so I don't say nothin' to them. But I'm saying to myself "This bunch of old stuck-up . . . !" ' Henderson saw Louis as 'pretty much a down-home boy in the big city'. And when Duke Ellington himself first encountered Willie The 'Lion' Smith, the latter invited him straight up to play. 'One of those Western piano plonkers just fell in—I want him to take the stool so I can crush him later.' Duke's account doesn't record who the piano plonker was—nor how he himself felt about being used as a decoy!

Contrary to the current trend, then, Duke Ellington showed no reserve towards Western style when he began to write his own music. He admired Sidney Bechet—'one of the truly great originals'—without stint, and even managed to pin down that notoriously unclubbable 'loner' in his band for a few months in 1926. (Indeed, the Bechet sound, to some degree domesticated, became an almost lifelong colour on the Ellington palette through the alto-playing of Johnny Hodges.) Further New Orleans colouring was deliberately added with the later inclusion of clarinettist Barney Bigard and bassist Wellman Braud. Duke seems to have been particularly receptive to ideas emanating from the King Oliver band of earlier years. The clarinettist who preceded Bigard was Rudy Jackson, who had played (though not recorded) in the famous band that included Louis Armstrong. In the long-defunct magazine *Jazz Music*, the writer and broadcaster Charles Chilton wrote of a conversation he had enjoyed with Jackson in Ceylon in 1945 in which the clarinettist recalled having enthused to Duke Ellington about Oliver's work, especially in the area of the blues. One piece which Rudy Jackson played over to the Duke was Oliver's 'Camp Meeting Blues' whose themes, filled out with fat harmonies and a liberal injection of the Ellington Effect, re-emerged there and then as 'Creole Love Call'. We may fairly assume that the Oliver-Armstrong 'break' from 'Snake Rag' which finds its way intact into Duke's 'The Creeper' owed its new lease of life also to Jackson's suggestion.

One further 'coincidence' brings us abruptly from the general to the particular. 'Black and Tan Fantasy' was written by Duke Ellington and Bubber Miley. It is generally accepted that the sombre opening theme was contributed by Miley, who is said to have based it on a church song that his sister used to sing. With a little acute listening we can go further than this, for the first eight bars of the theme are no more nor less than 'The Holy City' ('Jerusalem, Jerusalem') transposed into a minor key. This borrowing from 'The Holy City' has made quite frequent appearances in New Orleans jazz through the years and, more intriguingly still in the present context, it was used by King Oliver as a central theme for his piece 'Chimes Blues'! Fun though it is, this sort of amateur detection, which is open to anyone with a record-player and a pair of ears in good working order, is no mere self-indulgence. It gives an insight into the sort of mind—alert, inquisitive and unusually receptive—which recognised and drew in all the basic ingredients of jazz and then put them through the subtle culinary process that results in what Billy Strayhorn called the Ellington Effect.

In 'Black and Tan Fantasy' the Effect was pronounced and, as we shall see in a moment, controversial. Before going into the details of it, it is necessary to introduce one more distinctive and important Ellington 'voice'. Trombonist Joe 'Tricky Sam' Nanton was a prime subject for Duke's percentage calculations. He was born in New York in 1904, and was playing his own brand of 'gutbucket' in Harlem clubs when Duke hired him in 1926. He was brought in to replace Charlie Irvis, who had matched Bubber Miley in his experiments with the plunger mute. Between 1926 and 1948 when he died, Tricky Sam had virtually no musical existence outside the Ellington Band. As a straight trombonist, playing open horn, he was inclined to be staid and pedestrian and would scarcely have qualified for more than a passing mention in the history books. But when he put a cone-shaped metal mute in the bell of the instrument and manipulated a large rubber plunger in front of it, he became a poet. It was not a style that called more than ten per cent of the instrument into play—indeed, as Duke Ellington discovered when he wrote for him, there were no more than a handful of notes that could be pitched accurately under such a burden of mutes. But no one, before or since, ever produced such evocative sounds out of that ten per cent. I have already established that 'wah-wah' is the common onomatopoeic term for the kind of plunger work in which both Nanton and Miley specialised, but there are trombonists of my acquaintance who have almost worried themselves into a nursing-home trying to discover how Nanton's trombone seemed to say 'yah-yah'!

Duke Ellington subsequently referred to the opening minor-key theme of 'Black and Tan Fantasy' as the funeral-march section, and clearly Bubber Miley and Tricky Sam Nanton, plungers flapping lugubriously, are cast in the role of mourners. We do not know who it was who put the 'jungle music tag' on Ellington's music of this period—I would guess that it was someone on the publicity rather than the musical side of the fence. It was a label that came in handy when the Duke was called on to write music for the lavish and exotic productions at the Cotton Club, but to me it has always seemed a clumsy and obvious term to describe the eerie, nocturnal and *open-air* effect which muted horns, clanking banjo and a strangely reverberative studio acoustic produced. If I say that it evokes for me an impression of the American South rather than the African jungle, I have to confess that I have seen neither. But nor, as far as I know, had Duke Ellington!

In his book *Early Jazz*, Gunther Schuller pours some scorn on the second strain of 'Black and Tan Fantasy' as compared with those sections in which Bubber Miley clearly made a strong contribution. Indeed, in comparing, to the Duke's disadvantage, the difference in artistic levels at that time between Miley and Ellington, he says: 'Whereas Miley's theme, his solos—and to a lesser degree Nanton's—again reflect an unadorned pure classicism, Ellington's two contributions derive from the world of slick, trying-to-be-modern show music.' This is stern, schoolmasterly stuff, but in the end the quality that has made 'Black and Tan Fantasy' an acknowledged classic for fifty years has more to do with the Ellington Effect than with 'unadorned pure classicism'. And it would be unreasonable to expect that effect to exclude the Ellington personality altogether. From the start Duke revealed many musical facets, and they were often flatly contradictory. As a composer, he often revelled in fast and furious stomping, and in the early days he developed a brass section which was unbeatable in that genre. The opposite side of his nature showed itself fully from the mid-Thirties onwards in luxurious, almost sybaritic, melodies such as 'Sophisticated Lady', 'Prelude to a Kiss' and 'In a Sentimental Mood'. The second strain of 'Black and Tan Fantasy', which Otto Hardwick plays here on alto saxophone, is an early manifestation of this leaning. Until I read Schuller's condemnation I had always accepted it as an attractive snatch of melody and a typical Ellingtonian touch. Trying to be modern? Well, there is a chunk of whole-tone scale at the beginning of each eight-bar section, but it falls into place quite naturally and without pretension. Out of keeping with the rest of the record? At the risk of sounding truculent, one is tempted to ask 'Whose record is it anyway?' Duke chose to call the piece a fantasy, no doubt acknowledging a certain dreamlike cross-fading of images and impressions. Fifty years and innumerable performances later, that alto-sax interpolation is inextricably enmeshed in the fabric of the piece, and there is nothing much that any musicologist can do about it. Its very lushness seems to give added point to what follows.

At this stage in his career, Duke Ellington showed a cavalier attitude towards his contract with Victor Records and took his band from studio to studio under a variety of transparent pseudonyms—The Washingtonians, the Harlem Footwarmers, the Jungle Band and so on. As a result, 'Black and Tan Fantasy' was recorded no less than five times in eight months in 1927. Each version has its own character. Trumpeter Jabbo Smith replaced Miley in two 'takes' made on the same day, and on one recording the first solo after the alto-sax passage is played by Nanton on trombone. The version from an October session which I have chosen to discuss has, I believe, the best Bubber Miley solo. But each of these interpretations, and, indeed, all subsequent performances of the piece, retain, as though it were written into the score, the device with which Bubber Miley made his solo entry in the very first recording—a long sustained high note, tightly muted, that is held up like an arresting forefinger to drag the listener's attention back from sentimental fantasies to a fervent oration on the theme of the blues. Bubber Miley's solo in the version under review is absolutely superb. It is a passionate harangue in which everything that has ever been written about the influence of the vocal blues on instrumental jazz—the infinite variations in timbre, the bending of tones into 'blue notes', the use of throat sounds or 'growls'—is exemplified. Like King Oliver's solo in 'Dippermouth Blues', this is 'preaching trumpet' and the description cannot be bettered.

No piano style of the period could have sustained Miley's mood, and Duke's jaunty solo, couched in the two-fisted 'stride' style of the Harlem school from which he graduated, does little more than relieve the tension before Tricky Sam Nanton comes in with another oration. This solo is not by any means his most impressive, but in the last four bars he bursts into a macabre lamentation which shows the way in which his style was to develop. Bubber Miley's final solo, this time exhorting and scolding the congregation even more passionately, has again provided all subsequent interpreters with a model to which they have adhered more or less faithfully. It reaches a climax in the eighth bar with a surprising G seventh chord (Duke's inspiration rather than Miley's, perhaps) that gives a suitably dramatic lead into the quotation from Chopin's 'Funeral March' which forms an apt coda to a piece that breathes atmosphere.

The Chicagoans

THE NUCLEUS OF McKenzie and Condon's Chicagoans was a group of young musicians—Jimmy 'McPartland, Bud Freeman, Jim Lannigan and Frank Teschmacher—who had become hooked on jazz in the early Twenties while they were still at the Austin High School in Chicago. They learnt to play, like scores of embryo jazzmen since, by putting on records by their favourite bands (with them, the New Orleans Rhythm Kings topped the list) and stopping the turntable every few minutes while they learned the music off, bar by bar. According to Jimmy McPartland, 'In three or four weeks we could finally play one tune all the way through—"Farewell Blues". Boy, that was our tune!' Hearing these musicians reminisce, one is struck by their resemblance, in eagerness and enthusiasm, to the 'revivalist' bands which sprang up all over the world in the years immediately after World War II.

But the Austin High School Gang, as they came to be called, were no revivalists. For one thing, they were Chicagoans, at a time when Chicago was the hub of contemporary and forward-looking jazz. They had only to hop on a streetcar to hear, night in and night out, the very finest jazz that could be heard anywhere, from musicians such as King Oliver, Louis Armstrong, Johnny and Baby Dodds and Jimmy Noone. More important still, they were Americans, and it was no part of the mood of young Americans in the early Twenties simply to emulate the great jazz masters from a respectful distance. It would be unrealistic to evade the fact that they were white, too, and had access while they were still learning to avenues of employment from which their 'teachers' were barred. All of these factors served to give them and the associates whom they gathered round them the sort of brash confidence that was needed to establish them as stylists in their own right.

A wide range of critical views have been expressed about the Chicagoans and the so-called 'Chicago style' with which they have been accredited. A common verdict among those purists who accept the New Orleans style of collective improvisation as Holy Writ is that they tried to copy New Orleans jazz and simply got it wrong. All the evidence contradicts this rather lofty view. The listening habits of the Austin High School Gang seem to have been catholic if not downright indiscriminate. Jimmy McPartland has recalled: 'We sometimes went down to a Chinese restaurant, The Golden Pheasant, where there was a band by the name of Al Haid. They played pretty good, a semi-commercial brand of jazz, so we used to go down and eat chop suey and listen to the orchestra. It wasn't as good as the New Orleans Rhythm Kings— but we listened.' They listened also—and closely identified with— The Wolverine Orchestra which featured the brilliant young cornetist Bix Beiderbecke. Apart from his shining musical quality, Bix had other attractions for the young Chicagoans. I do not go along with the view that has sometimes been voiced that Bix Beiderbecke's reputation was inflated by his contemporaries in some sort of anti-black propaganda move. The frequent forays which the white musicians made into the black area on Chicago's South Side to hear their idols—and Bix himself often accompanied them—discounts any such racial bias. On the other hand, it was clearly encouraging for the young hopefuls in Chicago to have a hero who was not separated from them by age (he was only two or three years their senior) nor by any racial or social barriers. Bix was 'one of them' and his influence was enormous. To say that the style revealed by the young Chicagoans in their early records is simply a bad attempt at New Orleans style is to turn a deaf ear to the Bix influence in every bar.

Whether or not the early enthusiasms and explorations of the Austin High School Gang and their friends amounted to a definable 'style' is another matter. Certainly the musicians shared an attitude of mind about their music, a thrusting aggressiveness that seems to permeate the music of the McKenzie-Condon sessions and set them apart from the recordings of that period by New Orleans men. Jazz historians recognised this trait years ago and groped around for the cause. The city of Chicago itself—'tough, cynical, gangster-ridden'—took much of the blame or praise, according to the critical point of view. I should like to throw into the pool another theory which is, at least, more closely connected to the process of making music.

Let us first see how the McKenzie-Condon session actually came about. The principals who gave their names to the band were not from Austin High School. Indeed, they were not even Chicagoans by birth. Red McKenzie, from St Louis, Missouri, was an ex-jockey, a compulsive singer, an instrumentalist *manqué* who made good the deficiency by making quite convincing jazz noises through comb and paper, and an energetic entrepreneur with useful connections, in which role he appears on this record label. Eddie Condon, born in Indiana, had moved to within striking distance of Chicago with his family in 1914 and, almost as soon as he was old enough to hold a banjo in a band, threw himself into a one-man crusade on behalf of jazz in general and his Chicagoan friends and associates in particular. Condon knew the musicians, McKenzie knew Tommy Rockwell, the powerful head of Okeh Records. The result was a record session at the outset of which, according to Condon, Rockwell was 'polite but dubious'.

Eddie Condon shared the Austin High School Gang's fanatical devotion to jazz. Indeed, it is in his reminiscences of that period (*We Called It Music*) that we see the first glimpse of jazz and 'the public'—that is to say audiences, bookers, recording chiefs and anyone else who paid the piper—drifting apart. He recalls playing for a dance at the unpromising-sounding Gedney Farms Country Club in Westchester in 1928: 'There were three generations of Westchesterites present: the kids wanted "Tiger Rag", the middle-aged group wanted "Alice Blue Gown", the old folks asked for Strauss waltzes. The entertainment chairman came up and said, "I used to play drums at Yale. Trouble with your man is he doesn't syncopate enough." "He didn't go to Yale," I said.

'Nothing pleased anybody—the music was too fast, too loud,

too slow, and where was the melody? Finally we decided to turn our backs on the audience and enjoy ourselves. We took off on "Jazz Me Blues", "I Wish I Could Shimmy Like My Sister Kate", "I Ain't Gonna Give You None Of My Jelly Roll", "Royal Garden Blues", and "Clarinet Marmalade". Now and then I took a quick look at the dancers; they were shocked, disgusted, irritated, bored, and mad.'

Half-a-century later, musicians trying to earn a living in jazz will recognise almost identical symptoms of sales resistance, reading 'rock' for 'Tiger Rag' and 'Glenn Miller' for 'Alice Blue Gown'. They will find it surprising, if not comforting, to learn that it happened to Eddie Condon as early as 1928. True, the Original Dixieland Band had frightened New York to death when they first unleashed their 'jass' in 1917. And in the early Twenties, controversy over the new music raged in both musical journals and the lay press. But it's equally true to say that the originators of the music, the great black exponents such as Oliver, Armstrong, the Dodds brothers, Kid Ory and Jimmy Noone, felt no draught from the outside world. Their music had grown up freely in New Orleans without pressure from either commercial or artistic quarters. In Chicago, for a while at least, the same free and unselfconscious growth was able to continue. Themselves migrants from the South, the black musicians played to audiences who had come up the same way and shared the same culture. Furthermore, most of them had been active in music long before the term 'jazz' was coined, so they claimed no special identity for their wares. Faced with a situation comparable to Eddie Condon's Westchester débacle, they would have obliged with 'Alice Blue Gown' and even a Strauss waltz—and since they knew no other way to play than in their warm New Orleans style, it would have sounded wonderful!

Eddie Condon's problem was one which has beset jazzmen of every race and persuasion ever since jazz spread across the world —namely, how to 'sell' the music to people who were not culturally predisposed to accept it. It seems to me quite feasible that at any rate some of the nervous anxiety that is discernible in the Chicagoans' music, the fact that it lacked the freewheeling joy of the best New Orleans music and often sounded more feverish than

Johnny Dodds.

Jimmy Noone.

Earl Hines.

LUIS RUSSELL'S ORCHESTRA, *early Thirties. Henry Allen, third trumpet from the left, Albert Nicholas, third saxophone from the right, George 'Pops' Foster, bass, Paul Barbarin, drums.*

'hot', may have derived not so much from the character and environment of the musicians as from the defensive attitude of mind which they found themselves having to adopt. The recording session that produced 'Nobody's Sweetheart' bristled with it. Eddie Condon had booked the Austin High School team en bloc. The drummer Dave Tough, who had been playing regularly with them, had just taken off on a working trip to France, and Condon replaced him by general consent with an eager nineteen-year-old called Gene Krupa. The band was completed by pianist Joe Sullivan, a player who blended the styles of Earl Hines and Fats Waller with a rollicking Irish pugnacity that was all his own.

In his book, Condon recalled that, as the musicians set up for the session, an already nervous Tommy Rockwell observed Gene Krupa building up his drums: ' "What are you going to do with those?" Rockwell asked, "Play them," Krupa said simply. Rockwell shook his head. "You can't do that," he said. "You'll ruin our equipment. All we've ever used on records are snare drums and cymbals." Krupa, who had been practising every day at home, looked crushed. "How about letting us try them?" I asked. "The drums are the backbone of the band. They hold us up." I could see that Rockwell was leery of the whole business; drums or no drums, I figured, we are probably going to get tossed out. "Let the kids try it," McKenzie said. "If they go wrong I'll take the rap." "All right," Rockwell said, "but I'm afraid the bass drum and those tom-toms will knock the needle off the wax and out into the street." '

Well, the recording equipment survived and 'Nobody's Sweetheart' was passed on to posterity as an important piece of jazz history, a minor classic and, so it has always been said, the epitome of 'Chicago style'. Can the performance of a hastily assembled and notoriously unruly bunch of musicians, some of them musically immature, really be called a 'style'? Jimmy McPartland has shown himself doubtful. 'They say we got our particular style down well on that session. Of course, we didn't have a name for it or anything—it was simply the way we used to play.' And the way they played was extremely diverse. Jimmy McPartland himself had shaped his early playing in the Bix Beiderbecke mould, with such success that in 1924 he had gone to New York to take

Bix's place in the Wolverine Orchestra. As his lead playing and solo in 'Nobody's Sweetheart' reveal, he didn't possess Bix's striking clarity of thought, tone or execution. Indeed, in view of the widely-accepted image of Chicago jazz as hard-boiled and tough, McPartland's cornet playing is surprisingly soft-centred. Its main attraction, clearly absorbed from Bix, is its unpredictability. One is never quite sure in which direction the phrases, hemmed in by the tune's rather slow-moving harmonic structure, are going to make a dash for freedom.

Frank Teschmacher, who precedes McPartland in the solo order, was a musician of a different order. It is a source of great frustration to the jazz historian that a fatal car accident in 1929 deprived us of the chance to see how his talent would have developed. All that comes down to us now is the bespectacled, studious face in the photographs, some rather colourless recollections by his associates of a man deeply absorbed in music both jazz and 'classical', and some fervent, wildly expressive solos that ignited controversy almost as soon as they were committed to wax.

Analysis of his solo in 'Nobody's Sweetheart' isolates, without too much difficulty, three distinct elements in his style. We have a clue to one of them in the opening ensemble chorus of the piece. It was Teschmacher, we are given to understand, who designed the routines of these McKenzie-Condon recordings, setting out the order of events and writing out the occasional scored passages. The pattern that he used here, with a legato—and fairly 'straight' —statement of the theme in which the clarinet harmonises soulfully, followed at once by a contrasting 'hot' chorus with clarinet again playing a leading part, is, as we shall see, one which was used almost invariably by the New Orleans clarinettist Jimmy Noone in his small-group recordings of the period. It is known that Teschmacher was an ardent admirer of Noone's, and if that had been his only influence we might have expected him, in his solo chorus, to have set off, Noone-like, on a series of fluent but bustling runs over the whole range of the instrument, interspersed with stabbing high notes and wailing slurs. But with Tesch there was another clear influence, and one that worked in the opposite direction. I am referring, if you had not already guessed, to the ubiquitous Bix. Leaving aside the style in which it is delivered, the actual melody line of Teschmacher's half-chorus could be described as a Bix-style cornet passage transcribed to clarinet. Indeed, Tesch captures rather better than McPartland the commanding, parade-ground side of Beiderbecke's style. The Bix influence, calling for lines that were convoluted rather than wide-ranging, staccato rather than flowing, clashed with, and overcame, the Noone influence in Teschmacher's playing.

And yet it is clear, from every solo that he recorded, that Frank Teschmacher aspired to the passion, the intensity, the 'hotness' that he heard in the black musicians' work. This third element, emanating from the man himself, is the one which aroused all the controversy over his playing. Jazz commentators can be found, past and present, who dismiss Teschmacher's recordings on the grounds of their technical inadequancy. Compared with either Noone or Bix, whose actual instrumental sounds shared a certain schooled purity, Teschmacher played 'out of tune', used a 'squawky' tone and often let fly carelessly-articulated phrases. It is tempting to say, glibly, that he was not the first jazz musician deliberately to distort his instrument's natural sound and capability in the interests of self-expression. But on reflection he probably *was* the first. Throughout subsequent jazz history one can think of many musicians—from clarinettist Pee Wee Russell, trumpeter Henry Allen, cornetist Rex Stewart and trombonist Dicky Wells right through to 'moderns' like saxists Sonny Rollins and Roland Kirk—who have exploited 'wrong' playing to convey their individual message. Here was a musician who, according to fellow clarinettist Joe Marsala, had 'terrific technique,' who had studied violin at the Austin High School and who, like several of his associates, had a passion for music that extended to Ravel and Gustav Holst. It seems grotesquely unlikely that, after so much absorption in music, he would not have known how to tune a clarinet! No, what I hear in Frank Teschmacher is the assertion, albeit unformed and probably largely unconscious, of an alternative way of playing jazz, a freely-expressed, romantic, 'anything goes' approach which ignored the unwritten laws and precepts of New Orleans style.

In some ways, the same judgement applies to Lawrence 'Bud'

Freeman, although when 'Nobody's Sweetheart' was recorded, he was probably lagging behind his contemporaries in musical development. He was the only one of the Austin High School Gang who had undergone no musical training before taking up jazz. Eddie Condon described his first meeting with Bud, when he was sent to play a gig in a small-time cabaret in Chicago. 'When I got there the other musicians had arrived. One of them, Squeak Buhl, was setting up drums. A good-looking kid was trying to get notes from a tenor saxophone which was green with corrosion. It sounded the way it looked. A blond, solidly-built boy was watching him; he had a cornet. I introduced myself; the saxophone player shook hands with me. "My name is Bud Freeman," he said. "This is Jimmy McPartland." We sat down and began to play. Freeman seemed to know only one tune; everything sounded vaguely like "China Boy". McPartland had a strong rugged tone; he knew where he was going and enjoyed the journey. Buhl set a good beat and we all pushed it a little. Now and then Freeman hit a note that sounded like music.' Jimmy McPartland has also put down his recollections of Bud's earliest work with the Austin Gang. It was so bad that Teschmacher would say, 'Let's throw that bum out!' But McPartland stood up for him. 'There was one thing I could recognise in Bud then—he had a terrific beat. He still has. He began by just playing rhythm, getting on one note and holding it; I mean swinging on it, just that one note. He didn't change the harmony or anything, and we used to get so mad at him, you know. We'd yell at him "Change the note!" Still, as I remember, he had a great beat.'

By the time 'Nobody's Sweetheart' came to be recorded, Bud had found a few more notes and he swung them, in his short half-chorus, with a great beat. A short time before this session, Bud Freeman had heard the Fletcher Henderson Orchestra and had been floored by the playing of Coleman Hawkins, whom he had previously heard only on record. The inspiration of Hawkins was no doubt there in this performance, but Bud had little technique to express it except in the most skeletal way. And, as with Tesch, there was always the more insistent influence of Bix Beiderbecke, revealed chiefly in the rhythmic approach, that brought Bud's contribution in line with those of Teschmacher and McPartland. Excluding hindsight, there's nothing much in 'Nobody's Sweetheart' to suggest that, within three years, Bud Freeman would be fluent enough—and sufficiently his own man—to present fully-fledged to the world an alternative tenor-sax style to that of Coleman Hawkins.

In their solos, the work of these young Chicagoans seems to have been not so much a style, more schizophrenia set to music! Likewise, the ensembles show the tug of conflicting influences. Once again there is the model of Beiderbecke. In the second half of the final ensemble Teschmacher, have thrown off a Noone-type run, plays a legato phrase across the beat which is pure Bix. The rhythm combination of Sullivan, Condon and Krupa, however, lays down a pushing beat which is much closer to the steady four-four of the New Orleans bands than the rocking two-beat which usually accompanied Bix at this period. The juxtaposition of these two rhythmic notions—the one-two-three-four of the rhythm section and the variations on *one*-and-*two*-and from the front-line—gives the music an agitated feeling which is accentuated by the little tricks (the self-explanatory 'shuffle', 'flare' and 'explosion') which the lads thought up. I have left bassist Jim Lannigan out account since he produced an idiosyncratic style on the string bass which no subsequent jazz style preserved—a tuneless hunker-dunker which leads one to think that he must have overhauled his technique drastically before graduating to the Chicago Symphony Orchestra a few years later!

How do we assess the music of these Chicagoans? In his book *Really the Blues*, the clarinettist Mezz Mezzrow, a Chicagoan himself and one of the cronies of the musicians under discussion, analysed their early recordings—at which, incidentally, he was present and on some of which he played the tenor saxophone. Despite mutual compliments which passed between Mezzrow and Bud Freeman in later years, I sense that little love was lost between Mezz on the one side and Eddie Condon and the Austin High School graduates on the other. Mezzrow identified himself closely with the black race. When he went to jail in the Thirties on a narcotics charge, he actually declared himself a Negro and served his sentence in the black section. He was a brash, opinionated and, in some aspects of his posing, aburd man and it must have infuriated the keen and conscientious members of the McKenzie-Condon band to have him constantly around lecturing them on the error of their ways in departing from the principles of black New Orleans music. Mezzrow's stern judgement on his fellow Chicagoans was that, instead of sticking close to the New Orleans pattern and working to perfect it, they got too big for their boots. 'Trying to show how good they were, they got too fancy, sometimes, too ornate and over-elaborate, full of uncalled-for frills and ruffles.' It is sometimes difficult to ascertain whether Mezz's displeasure arose because they listened to him and got it wrong, or because, as seems probable as time went on, they ceased to listen to him at all.

Whitney Balliett, the distinguished jazz critic of the *New Yorker*, has taken up a position at the other extreme: '. . . a number of white musicians from the Chicago area suddenly coalesced and produced a new ensemble-solo music that is generally known as Chicago jazz . . . it seemed . . . very snappy, very modern . . . the white Chicagoans had the new-broom quality that bebop offered fifteen years later.'

Was Mezzrow right, or does Whitney hit the nail on the head? Or again, does the truth lie somewhere in between? The conclusion to which the thoughts in this chapter seem to have led is that the most significant thing about 'Chicago style' as exemplified in 'Nobody's Sweetheart' is that it was not a style at all.

Johnny Dodds and Jimmy Noone

I HAVE CHOSEN TO DISCUSS recordings by Johnny Dodds and Jimmy Noone in a single chapter for two reasons. One is that neither musician demands—or indeed offers—the sort of background information that I have given for, say, Jelly Roll Morton or Sidney Bechet. We know surprisingly little about them. They were not 'characters' with colourful careers nor, so far as we know, did they go in for much theorising about their music. They died within a few years of each other in the early Forties, before the great tidal wave of research and literature that accompanied the New Orleans Revival had got fully under way. And in the recollection of their surviving colleagues, it is their music rather than their personalities that looms largest.

The other reason for putting them together is that they are literally poles apart. I have gone into some detail in earlier chapters about what we might call the Explosion Theory of the creation of jazz which, in simplified terms, I have described as the result of a collision between Creole culture on the way down and 'slave' culture on the way up. In the schooled, classically-based music of the Creole families, the clarinet played an important role alongside the stringed instruments of the small, salon orhecstras. When, with the decline in social status that followed Emancipation, those orchestras became bands and the salon gave way to the dance-hall, the honky-tonk and the open street, the clarinet had the robustness and the versatility to survive. Furthermore, in the hands of the Creole musicians, it retained a high degree of its classical purity of tone and fluency of execution even when it found itself outnumbered by brass instruments of a rougher background.

One Creole musician proved the exception to the rule. He was Sidney Bechet, whose maverick personality drew him towards the more expressive, rough-and-ready music of the blues. In his reminiscences, he speculates modestly on the influence which he might have had on his contemporaries in New Orleans. 'There was Johnny Dodds about that time, he was with Kid Ory when I was with the Eagle Orchestra. Johnny, he's said I influenced him, that he got a lot of inspiration from me. Well, I'm proud to be told that. There was Jimmy Noone there too, I influenced him— that's what people who have written books have said he told them.'

If Bechet was one great influence upon young New Orleans clarinettists in the second decade of the century, there was another who is less well-known but equally important. Lorenzo Tio, Jnr., was a Creole whose father and uncle were both distinguished clarinettists. The few recordings which we have that show his work—he travelled and recorded in the early Twenties with Armand Piron's New Orleans Orchestra—impress more with the smoothness of his technique and the purity of his tone than with his creativity as a jazz player. His significance in our story is that he appears, from a glance through the biographies of early jazz, to have taught every single New Orleans musician who ever picked up a clarinet, from Bechet himself through Johnny Dodds and Jimmy Noone to the younger generation of Albert Nicholas and Barney Bigard. By his own admission Bechet proved a recalcitrant pupil: 'It's a funny thing about teaching, about all those lessons. They didn't really do for me. They weren't doing what had to be done. I guess you come right down to it, a musicianer has to learn for himself, just by playing and listening.' In his references to another of his teachers, the Creole George Bacquet, Sidney Bechet clearly defined the difference between the schooled Creole approach and the self-taught, intuitive method of music making that stemmed from the blues. 'What he played, it wasn't really jazz . . . he stuck real close to the line in a way. He played things more classic-like, straight out how it was written. And he played it very serious . . . there wasn't none of those growls and buzzes which is part of ragtime music, which is a way the musicianer has of replacing different feelings he finds inside the music and inside himself . . . all those interpreting moans and groans and happy sounds.'

It is not too fanciful to regard Sidney Bechet and Lorenzo Tio as the 'father and mother' of New Orleans jazz clarinet. The family that they raised was as diverse as any human family, inheriting in differing degrees the characteristics of each parent. Thus we can hear, in the blues-playing of Jimmy Noone, a fair measure of Bechet's 'interpreting moans and groans', although in the purity of his tone and the flamboyance of his technique he favoured the Creole style of Tio. Likewise in the work of Johnny Dodds, it is the close likeness to Bechet's throbbing, rough-edged blues sound that first strikes us as exclusive until we listen to some of his most fluent ensemble work, especially with King Oliver's Creole Jazz Band, and hear plenty of the decorative, liquid clarinet which was Tio's Creole heritage. So when I say that Dodds and Noone were poles apart, it means no more than that they represented the extreme differences in character that can exist within one family.

Choosing a Johnny Dodds 'masterpiece' presented the problem that has occurred elsewhere in this book. We know him more from an accumulation of varied recordings than from any one revealing work. It is with not so much regret as positive anguish that I have passed over two superb sides—'Gatemouth' and 'Perdido Street Blues'—recorded in 1926 under the name of the New Orleans Wanderers. My reason was that I wanted to find something as far removed as possible from the atmosphere of the Louis Armstrong Hot Five and Seven sessions which I have already touched upon in the context of 'Potato Head Blues', and the Wanderers did include four-fifths of the Hot Five. Some jazz critics of recent years have dismissed Dodds's work with the Hot Five, especially in the later years, on the grounds that he could not keep up with the great strides that Louis was making in the direction of more rhythmic and harmonic freedom. In agreeing with them to a large extent, I do not go on, as some have done, to deride Dodds's musicianship. In transforming his little five-piece recording band from a tight New Orleans-style ensemble into an

arena for improvisational fireworks on the grand scale, it was
Louis, not his colleagues, who was out of step. Johnny Dodds
produced some fine solos, notably in 'Wild Man Blues', 'SOL
Blues' and 'Potato Head'. But Armstrong's exploding talent put
him under strain and introduced into the sessions a spirit of
striving tension which was different from the blithe, relaxed
feeling of a perfect New Orleans ensemble.

The recordings in which Johnny Dodds seems to me absolutely at home and in command are those which he made with
his Washboard Band in July 1928. This was not an isolated
session—in the years between 1927 and '29, he made forty-odd
recordings with trios and small bands, including a seven-piece
group with Louis Armstrong and Earl Hines in which Louis,
perhaps because he was under contract elsewhere, played a
subdued role which suited Dodds. But the Washboard Band date
stands out for several reasons. Johnny Dodds, not a strong
harmonist, as we noted in the analysis of 'Potato Head Blues',
was in his element among the simple chord progressions of the
blues. Even here, his approach was not one of great melodic or
harmonic subtlety. His solos and ensemble playing, especially in
the up-tempo numbers, were built upon simple arpeggios,
innocent of the ninth and diminished chords which Louis Armstrong so eagerly exploited in the context of the Hot Five. And
yet, upon this simple basis, Dodds seemed to be able to create
endless variations, each of which had some distinguishing mark
of its own. The Washboard Band session consisted of four blues
numbers, two up-tempo and two slow, each pair showing such
similarity that one might be excused for thinking on first hearing
that it represented two 'takes' of the same piece. But there are key
differences—the two up-tempo numbers are in B flat and F
respectively, while both slow pieces are in C—and the set emerges
as a four-part study of the blues in varying moods. And that is
how I propose to examine it, treating the separate numbers as a
whole rather than invidiously selecting one for special consideration.

The band which Johnny Dodds leads on these records was one
which, with occasional personnel changes, enjoyed a six-year
residence at a club called Kelly's Stables from 1924 onwards.

With the exception of its piano-players—Lil Hardin Armstrong and Charlie Alexander are the two who appear with Dodds on records—the band featured New Orleans men, and its music was strongly representative of the home style. The two brass players, cornetist Natty Dominique and trombonist Honoré Dutrey, come down on records as extraordinarily fitful players, veering between on and off days in an inexplicable way. July 6, 1928 was happily a good day for both of them and, with only occasional lapses by Dutrey, they fulfilled perfectly the uncomplicated roles which the carefree blues session demanded of them. For many years, discographers scratched their heads over the identity of the piano-player, who on this date was manifestly not Lil Armstrong. With or without a cautious question mark, the name of Charlie Alexander is now generally accepted, although his contribution is unlikely to elicit more than mild curiosity from most listeners.

One of the great joys of this session is the well-recorded and splendid bass-playing by Bill Johnson, who has already made an appearance in this book as the banjoist on King Oliver's 'Dippermouth Blues'. I shall have more to say about the contribution of New Orleans to the art of jazz bass-playing when I come to the work of Pops Foster in Luis Russell's Band. All I need do here is draw the listener's attention to the great variety of sounds and rhythms which Johnson employs, sometimes booming away two-in-the-bar with a resonance that suggests that he is using the bow in places, and at other times slapping out a resilient four-beat rhythm with frequent variations. As for Baby Dodds, we are confronted here, as elsewhere, with a problem. Johnny's rumbustious younger brother, often spoken of with some awe by the normally unshockable Louis Armstrong as a formidable hell-raiser in his youth, survived his staid, teetotal brother by a margin of nineteen years (he died in 1959) and so made a significant contribution to the post-war New Orleans Revival. I was one of those fortunate enough to hear him in person playing with Mezz Mezzrow's Band at the first International Jazz Festival at Nice in 1948. His performance there, distinguished by a driving rhythm, feather-light press rolls on the snare-drum and a whole firework display of exploding noises from every corner of the kit, confirmed for me his reputation as one of the great masters of New Orleans

drumming to whom a generation of younger men, including Gene
Krupa and George Wettling, bowed in homage. It has to be said
that I never heard a record which did even a hint of justice to
him, and often have difficulty in convincing friends that he was
not the rather clumsy thunderer that often comes across on disc.
In this session, pounding a washboard with thimble-capped
fingers, he has little chance to do more than show a spritely line
in time-keeping.

'Bull Fiddle Blues' gets off to a shaky start with a trombone
break by Dutrey who fluffs a note at a rhythmically inopportune
moment. But this is not frail, finely-poised music likely to be
thrown by a minor accident, and with joyful disregard, the
ensemble takes up the chorus. From the first, Johnny Dodds
shows who is in charge by establishing the beat with a few notes
hit firmly on the nose. And then he is off, weaving and bobbing in
a sustained manner reminiscent of his early work with King
Oliver. At once, we notice one of the chief characteristics of
Dodds's playing, which is an insistence on driving home the beat
at every stage in his flowing variations. 'My brother was serious,
but he had play days too,' Baby Dodds recalled—and for all the
poignancy of Johnny's blues-playing at all times, there is in these
up-tempo numbers a great sense of exhilaration, too, a joyous
romping which lifts the spirit. Much of it derives from the way in
which, in the opening bars of each chorus especially, Dodds
usurps the trumpet's dominating role and lays down the beat
with a string of dictatorial crotchets.

At times in these performances, this reminder of the beat was
not only stimulating but strictly necessary. When, in accordance
with recording demands, the bass and washboard abandon Charlie
Alexander at the start of his brief piano solo, his urgent desire to
reach the end of it intact plays havoc with the number's steady
rhythm. Likewise, poor Dutrey, handicapped by lung damage
incurred on war service, is often found battling with technical and
time-keeping problems in his up-tempo breaks. But it is no mere
sentimentality to say that these flaws really do not matter. Indeed,
I positively welcome them, if only for the ecstasy of hearing the
ensemble with Johnny Dodds at its head pick the performance up
by the seat of its pants and boot it on its way!

In 'Blue Washboard Stomp', it is Alexander's carbon-copy solo (he seems, from the evidence here, to have been equipped with no more than two ideas for all-purpose use in fast and slow tempos respectively) which gives the impression that this is just another version of the first piece. Apart from the change of key from B flat to F, there are other differences. Natty Dominique, who showed considerable reticence in 'Bull Fiddle Blues' outside of a pleasant solo, asserts himself more strongly. Much of the critical scorn which his playing has attracted over the years derives from the fast and rather uneven vibrato which has been put down to feebleness in the holding of a tone. From the increasing number of recordings of native New Orleans music which have become available since the Revival, we recognise that 'nanny-goat' vibrato as a conscious characteristic of one school of New Orleans playing. It was fundamental to the style of one of the legendary New Orleans men, 'Papa' Mutt Carey, who recorded some fine sides with Kid Ory in the Forties. That it was no mere instability of lip or lung is shown in the ensemble choruses of 'Blue Washboard Stomp', when Dominique uses it deliberately as a rhythmic device, rather like a roll on a drum, to link staccato phrases. In other ways he contributes to the highspots of this blues piece, coming up with some across-the-beat phrasing, in the chorus after the bass breaks, which reminds us of the way old Bunk Johnson played during his brief Indian summer in the Forties. And again, in the very last chorus of all, he holds a sustained note in the upper register which offsets Dodds's restless clarinet figures perfectly, while Bill Johnson's bass pounds out an unexpected drum rhythm.

When it comes to Johnny Dodds's turn in the break choruses which are a feature of 'Blue Washboard Stomp', we have a demonstration of his resourcefulness in varying the simplest of blues choruses. He has already played a solo of similar construction in the first number. On this occasion he gives each break a different character with a legato phrase here, an expressive upward glissando there. Compared with some of his contemporaries—Bechet, for example, or Jimmy Noone—Johnny Dodds did not boast a fast or flashy technique. For one thing, the heavy tone which he cultivated, with its broad vibrato and incisive edge, did not lend itself to rapid runs over the full length of the instrument. Indeed, there are occasions in his recorded work when it seems as if he is loading the long-suffering clarinet with more emotional weight than it can stand. But the ability suddenly to charge the most skittish of breaks with a sudden surge of passion amply compensates for any lack of pyrotechnics.

When we move into the two slower blues pieces in B flat, we find Johnny Dodds in his most intense mood. On clarinet, Sidney Bechet and the British player, the late Sandy Brown, are the only rivals to Dodds in the ability to feed a high-voltage current of sustained passion into a solo built upon long, throbbing notes. At the outset of 'Weary City', an old friend from a previous chapter reappears—namely, an introductory quotation from the 'Holy City'. It serves to establish a mood which I can only describe as one of melancholy dignity in which it is Johnny Dodds and not the reticent Dominique who gives the ensemble its character. It is interesting to note, with Dodds, that the emphasis on the four beats to a bar which gives his up-tempo work such lift is not abandoned in these slower tempos. Nobody except Bessie Smith ever made it quite so clear in the first bar of a blues exactly what tempo was required. The on-the-beat style would be rhythmically stiff and unyielding were it not for the elasticity which is given to each beat by the whole band from Baby Dodds and Bill Johnson upwards. This ability to expand what, on paper, would be written as four crotchets or quarter-notes to the bar into loping, unhurried steps that are rhythmically linked to each other is what, in the Twenties, distinguished the New Orleans style from all others. It saved much music which, as in this Johnny Dodds band, was based on the eight-to-a-bar rhythmic approach, from sounding jerky and square, and it gave to Louis Armstrong the impulse to abandon that rhythm for his own more loping 12/8 style. I can best describe it in non-musical terms by saying that, in their early recordings, the New Orleans bands bounced on a trampoline when others marked time on a barrack-square.

It was the treatment of these two blues pieces, 'Weary City' and 'Bucktown Stomp', that confirmed me in my decision to treat the four numbers as one whole, developing work. (Incidentally, it seems probable to me that the titles became muddled up somewhere along the way, a not unusual occurrence in early recording. 'Bucktown Stomp' is the most inappropriate name for the bluesiest of the four pieces and I suspect that it was at some time confused with 'Bull Fiddle Blues'). When Charlie Alexander has delivered his one slow blues idea and Dutrey and Dominique (the former much happier in this slower tempo) have contributed good solos, it is Johnny Dodds who, consciously or intuitively, develops the theme from one piece to another. 'Weary City' finds him in his most sober mood, lending such a serious air to the proceedings that, when Baby Dodds takes his turn on the tuneless washboard in a series of breaks with piano, trombone and bass, we are disinclined to giggle. The low-register clarinet solo, centred upon the fifth degree of the scale around which it swoops and stalks with a searing melancholy, is a beauty, with an assertive, almost theatrical entrance that contrasts with the shy and unspectacular image of the man himself that has come down to us.

Listening to the two C major blues pieces one after the other, one might think, if one did not know it to be far-fetched, that Johnny Dodds was deliberately holding back in 'Weary City' in order to pull all the stops out for the final 'Bucktown Stomp'. This piece starts with a C major chord which sounds as if it is to be a reprise of the previous number. But no, the chord is a launching pad for a break by Dodds which soars into the high register in a positive shriek of anguish and announces that this is to be Johnny Dodds in the emotive mood which nudges the very limits of the boundary that separates the sublime from the ridiculous. Many clarinet-players in the New Orleans Revival of the Forties and Fifties adopted the Dodds manner in tackling the blues, and all too many of them, aiming for high tragedy, succeeded only in achieving a sort of ludicrous pomposity or, in theatrical terms, pure 'ham'. The danger lies in the elaborate runs in which Dodds seems to take his inspiration not from standard clarinet practice but from the more angular contortions of the blues guitarists. The electric guitar inhabited the realms of science fiction when Dodds recorded his finest solos in the Twenties, so there is something prophetic in the similarity between the introductory break in 'Bucktown Stomp' and the wild, heavily vocalised wailing of a modern blues guitarist like B. B. King.

From the opening break onwards, Dodds is in charge of 'Bucktown Stomp'. He takes the lead in the first chorus as if he had temporarily forgotten that the other front-line men were present, and Natty Dominique has to insinuate himself into the proceedings as best he can. Much is always made of Sidney Bechet's tendency on soprano saxophone to elbow the trumpet out of the dominant role in the front-line. Here and elsewhere, Johnny Dodds was quite capable of doing the same thing, and without the assistance of a soprano saxophone! Through these first two majestic choruses of 'Bucktown' he has the best of both worlds, stating his theme with typical trumpet phrases heavily on the beat *and* filling in with impassioned guitar-style runs. When it comes to his solo, he sings the blues in the same unrestrained way, sustaining until the anguished break at the very end of the piece a mood which is totally consistent and convincing. Indeed, if I may borrow a cliché from contemporary critical jargon, it is the commitment which Johnny shows to all of the numbers in this set of four—and, I should add, to any number that he ever played—which in the end puts the scoffers and the flip imitators to shame.

Johnny Dodds was a blues player at heart. He always worked with small bands heavily slanted towards the blues. During the Thirties, when his New Orleans contemporaries were either retired or reaping the rewards of the new-style swing music, Dodds remained in Chicago, leading his bands in little clubs remote from the attentions of recording companies. In 1938 he was brought to New York for a recording session organised by Lil Armstrong in which his 'Chicago Boys' were mostly hip young New York musicians to whom he gave a salutary lesson in how to play the blues.

It is a strange thing that Jimmy Noone hardly fared any better. With a few adjustments—one or two isolated recording sessions in the Thirties, for instance—the story told in the preceding paragraph applies equally to Noone. Indeed, in one respect he was less fortunate than Dodds whose reputation was well established by prolific recordings in the Twenties in such prestigious surroundings as the bands of King Oliver, Louis Armstrong and Jelly Roll Morton. Jimmy Noone's presence on some Oliver recordings was only fully established quite recently after years of deliberation and head-scratching by discographers. A few records which he made with Louis Armstrong in 1928 cast them as accompanists for Lily Delk Christian whose non-jazz—and come to that, non-musical—singing until recently kept record-collectors at bay. Much the same deterrent effect was exerted by Doc Cook's Dreamland Orchestra, a cumbersome dance-band with which Jimmy Noone worked on and off through the Twenties.

The reason I find it strange that Noone met with as little commercial success as Johnny Dodds is that his clarinet style and his repertoire were both more accessible than those of Dodds. The records which he made with his Apex Club Orchestra in 1928/9 consisted largely of popular songs aimed at a much wider audience than the 'race' market towards which Dodds's blues recordings were directed. And Noone was always careful to stress the melody, often playing it himself in a limpid, seductive way far removed from the jangling angularities of Dodds. It was Noone rather than Dodds who had the greatest impact on the succeeding generation of clarinet men. If we take account of Albert Nicholas's playing with Louis Russell and Louis Armstrong, of Barney Bigard with Ellington and of both Jimmy Dorsey and Benny Goodman with their own celebrated orchestras, it is hard to think of any area of the Swing Era of the Thirties which was untouched by Noone's influence.

If we are bewildered by Noone's failure in the commercial field, it is perhaps less hard to see why jazz enthusiasts over the years have tended to pay him more lip service than genuine heed. Jimmy Noone was a Creole, heavily influenced in his upbringing by the Creole tradition of light music and the role of the clarinet within it. The manifestly self-taught blues styles of Bechet and Dodds were an exception among the first recorded generation of New Orleans clarinettists. The rest of them were taught to treat the clarinet as the versatile instrument that it is, and acquainted themselves with the rapid fingering, fast tongueing, pure-toned aspects of conventional clarinet style. Jimmy Noone epitomised this approach. Quite a large corner of his repertoire over the years was set aside to demonstrate his acquired technique, with the result that the explorer into the territory of Noone recordings has to step fastidiously around some rather quaint and old-fashioned clarinet doodling in 'speciality' vein and the occasional quagmire of syrupy sentimentality.

The recording I have chosen as a Jimmy Noone masterpiece is not widely acknowledged as such. I suppose most jazz collectors would pick 'Apex Blues', a fine blues performance whose succession of riffs have become standard in the traditional jazz repertoire. I have tried instead to find something which typifies the method of ensemble playing which Noone handed down to the likes of Nicholas and Bigard and at the same time shows us something of the instrumental brilliance which, through its impact on Benny Goodman and Jimmy Dorsey, paved the way for the clarinet's dominating role in the Swing Era that was to come.

The clarinettist Mezz Mezzrow, in his book *Really the Blues*, defined these qualities of Noone's with his usual blend of perception and purple prose. 'What Jimmy didn't do with that clarinet of his, weaving in and through and all around those cats like an expert hackie in heavy traffic, just ain't been invented yet ... He played strictly New Orleans style, with a soulful tone instead of the shrill twittering effects you hear today, and he played all over that instrument from top to bottom, hitting every register but the cash one. The little flourishes he came up with "in the windows", fill-ins at the ends of phrases where the other players took a breath, were really amazing. He was always inventing new things, but they were in the New Orleans idiom every time.'

The only point at which I take issue with Mezzrow is in his belief that there was some abstraction called 'New Orleans style' or the 'New Orleans idiom' to which all players had a duty to pay homage. It was the musicians who forged the New Orleans style, and much of what we retrospectively acknowledge today as the very epitome of New Orleans clarinet-playing emanates from recordings made by Jimmy Noone towards the end of the heyday of New Orleans music.

It is one of these recordings, a version of a popular song by Jimmy McHugh called 'Every Evening', which I have selected as my Noone masterpiece. In the light of Mezzrow's comments, it is ironical that the little band from the Apex Club with which

Noone recorded some of his best pieces did not conform to the classic New Orleans line-up of cornet or trumpet, clarinet and trombone. Noone's only partner in the front-line was Joe 'Doc' Poston, a saxophone player from Alexandria, Louisiana who had been a colleague of Noone's in Doc Cook's Dreamland Orchestra. A negligible jazz soloist, Poston nonetheless did all that was expected of him in this little band, which was to provide a straightforward melody line around which Noone could demonstrate his mastery of the art of contrapuntal clarinet. The only other star name in the band was that of the Pittsburgh pianist Earl Hines, who had arrived in Chicago in the mid-Twenties and was, at the time of this recording, on the point of making his mark as one of the greatest and most influential jazz pianists.

'Every Evening' starts deceptively with what sounds like a dance-band arrangement of a typically platitudinous popular song of the period. But in the event the relatively straight statement of the verse serves to heighten the sense of exhilaration when, with the arrival of the main chorus, Jimmy Noone peels off into his more familiar ensemble role, diving and swooping around Poston's stolid alto lead like a swallow harrassing a crow. What raises his work above mere fussy decoration is the rhythmic lift which he gives to the proceedings with ever-changing patterns in which the sudden incursions into the high register are used much in the way that a drummer will use explosive beats to create shifting accents. And of course, the whole performance is enhanced by the most ravishing clarinet tone in all of jazz.

Outside of Jelly Roll Morton's band work and that of the best Harlem stride pianists, jazz piano solos had up until this point been rather diffident, hangdog affairs, clogged with heavy chording and obfuscated by inadequate recording. With every leaping, cocksure solo that Earl Hines contributed in the late Twenties, he seemed to give notice, like a militant shop steward of the Amalgamated Union of Ticklers and Allied Keyboard Operatives, that never again would the pianist be regarded as the work-horse of the jazz band. For many years, jazz historians, wise after the event, attributed what they called Earl Hines's 'trumpet-style' piano-playing to the influence of Louis Armstrong. 'Trumpet-style' is really quite a good description of the way in which Hines produced a strong, unequivocal melody line with the right hand playing strident octaves rather than chords and arabesques. And it is certainly true that, having devised this way of playing, his melodic variations did owe something to Armstrong. But his own explanation for the origin of the style is less romantic: 'I got sick of playing a lot of pretty things and not being heard . . . we had no microphones then, and I figured that if I doubled the right-hand melody line with octaves, then I would be heard as well as the trumpets and clarinets.' Whatever its origin, the device was immediately effective. I shall have more to say about Hines in later consideration of his recording with Louis Armstrong, but the listener to 'Every Evening' will not fail to notice the interesting harmonies with which he transforms the ordinary tune, the rhythmic 'trumpeting' in the right hand, and the way in which the left hand, totally emancipated from its previous oom-chah role, now takes a more important harmonic and rhythmic part than had ever been conceived before.

After the piano solo, there is a typical Noone passage in which, for half a chorus, he has the rest of the band playing the sort of choppy phrases usually supplied to tap-dancers while he performs some tricky runs on the clarinet that are not far removed from tap-dancing in their staccato agility. This nimble work, pointed up with some fast tongueing that makes each note in the tracery distinct, continues to the end of the chorus when the ensemble has returned to normal. And then comes one of Noone's most effective devices, a short glissando up to a piercing high note which leads into the final chorus, followed by stabbing notes in trumpet rather than clarinet style, giving the chorus a thrilling climax which owes nothing to Doc Poston and his stolid reiteration of the tune. Halfway through this chorus, the drummer rolls a fierce crescendo that drops immediately to eight bars of whispering ensemble before flaring into furious life again for the ride-out. This was another Noone device, borrowed and reproduced in a rather less subtle way by the young enthusiasts from the Austin High School who haunted the Apex Club and took in Jimmy Noone's lessons.

Indeed, the jazz of the white Chicagoans, and of the musicians from far and wide who spent time in Chicago, reflected the dual influences of Johnny Dodds and Jimmy Noone in varying strengths for some years to come. The odd thing, in the light of the very simple and straightforward model for New Orleans-style clarinet-playing which Noone presented, is that when young musicians in their twenties all over the world began to recreate New Orleans jazz in the Revival of the late Forties, it was Johnny Dodds's more idiosyncratic and difficult style which they emulated. Bob Helm in San Francisco, Sandy Brown, Wally Fawkes and Cy Laurie in Britain, Claude Luter in France, Pixie Roberts in Australia, all could be heard in their early days emoting tremulously in the Dodds manner. And when more primitive New Orleans jazz superseded old Oliver and Armstrong records as the inspiration, it was the cue for the sound of New Orleans veteran George Lewis to take over. Perhaps this chapter, together with the greater availability in recent times of the complete Noone recordings, will reassert what the young musicians who commuted from Kelly's Stables to the Apex Club and back again will have understood—that Johnny Dodds and Jimmy Noone represented in extreme forms two indivisible facets of New Orleans jazz.

Louis Armstrong and Earl Hines

IT IS DIFFICULT, in the dry process of retrospection and reassessment, to imagine the excitement that must have been in the air in the Chicago of 1927/28. Jazz was everywhere, in literally scores of dives, dance-halls and movie theatres. Crime was everywhere, too, and its impact on the music scene is succinctly encapsulated in two oft-quoted sentences by Chicago drummer George Wettling: 'At the Triangle Club, the boss was shot in the stomach one night, but we kept working. After that he walked sort of bent over.' But the jazz histories which harp on the details of gangsterdom underestimate the musician's capacity for detaching himself from his surroundings. Speakeasies and shady clubs provided the environment in which jazz could flourish, but they had as little effect on the music itself as did the pimps and prostitutes in the red-light district of New Orleans.

In the jazz context, the genuine excitement in Chicago at that time is measured in terms of creativity. Most of the great men from New Orleans were still active in the city. Their young disciples, rallying around the team from Austin High, were in the heady throes of making their first recordings. Furthermore, the finest representatives of the jazz that had been blossoming in New York through the decade—the stars of the Henderson and Whiteman orchestras, the classic blues singers and their accompanying bands—constantly passed through the city on tour or moved in for extended seasons. And over everything, inescapably, the giant shadow of Louis Armstrong, reaching the very height of his creative powers. Bud Freeman tells a story that exemplifies Louis' standing in the city, the power of his presence. 'In the days in Chicago, before Louis became world famous, he spent a great deal of time walking the streets of his neighbourhood on the south side . . . One afternoon, as he strolled along 35th Street, he noticed a small crowd gathered around two street musicians. He stopped and listened and much to his delight, the trumpet-player was playing Louis' improvised chorus of "Struttin' with some Barbecue". At the finish of the number, Louis walked over to the street musicians and said: "Man . . . you're playing that *too slow*!" "How would you know?" they challenged. "I'm Louis Armstrong . . . that's my chorus you're playing!" The next day the street musicians had a sign next to their tin cup. The sign read . . . "PUPILS OF LOUIS ARMSTRONG".'

Louis was not alone on the Olympian heights. The reminiscences of jazzmen who were on the scene are peppered with the names of trumpet-men who were 'as good as Louis at that time'—June Clark and Louis Metcalf, two young lions from New York, and the formidable Jabbo Smith who had the technical ability to match and even surpass Louis in speed and range, if not in the taste and nobility of his invention. None of these claimants to the crown left any evidence on record that they had the measure of Armstrong. Much more important in terms of results was the discovery by Louis of a friend and colleague who was, by 1928, his equal in every respect.

Earl Hines had worked with Louis Armstrong as pianist and musical director at the Sunset Café for some months before he replaced the second Mrs Armstrong in the Hot Five recording band. I find quite credible the story that it was Hines who persuaded the loyal and easy-going Louis to replace the New Orleans men in the Hot Five with musicians who were more attuned to the modern ideas which Louis himself had been largely responsible for propagating. The fact that two of the new men—Jimmy Strong the clarinettist and Fred Robinson on trombone—were lightweights without the authority of Johnny Dodds or Kid Ory is sometimes used by purists to suggest that Hines was a bad influence on Louis in seducing him away from the straight and narrow path of New Orleans jazz. I hope to have shown in the references to Louis in these chapters that in the course of nature

Louis Armstrong had a different rhythmic concept from almost all of his contemporaries. It was not just that he fully realised the 12/8 implications in the relaxed and loping New Orleans beat. Within that rhythm he had a freedom that enabled him to move around, across and over the beat with an instinctive poise that was remarkable. In Earl Hines, he found a colleague who had the same capability. And all considerations of modernity or trendiness apart, it was inevitable that Louis would move away from the carefree atmosphere of the first Hot Five into a musical environment that stretched him more fully.

With the New Orleans drummer Zutty Singleton, two years older than Louis but another forward-looking musician, Louis and Hines made up three swashbuckling musketeers on the Chicago jazz scene. At one point they went into business together, booking premises and attempting to start a club of their own. In view of the close links between Chicago nightlife and the highly organised underworld, it is hardly surprising that their venture was a total failure. But the experience did not appear to do more than temporarily split up the formidable trio. Hines recalled: 'Louis was wild and I was wild, and we were inseparable. He was the most happy-go-lucky guy I ever met. Then Louis and I and Zutty formed our own group, and I don't know what happened but we like to starve to death, making a dollar or a dollar and a half apiece a night, so we drifted apart . . .' But the association continued in the recording studios, where Louis, Hines and Singleton continued to make records under the name of Louis Armstrong's Hot Five which were to inspire a new generation of young jazz musicians who would emerge as trend-setters in the mid-Thirties.

The partnership of Louis Armstrong and Earl Hines is epitomised in their duet recording of 'Weather Bird'. It was not, as is often suggested, the first trumpet and piano duet in a long line of such collaborations that stretch up to the present day. King Oliver and Jelly Roll Morton had made two fine duets back in 1924. But certainly Louis and Earl, in that studio in December 1928, established records for rapport and brilliant daring which have not been broken to this day. We can argue with equal confidence that 'Weather Bird', in presenting two musicians of genius unencumbered by lesser mortals, is the most perfect recording to be made during the entire decade of the Twenties.

Having said this, I am assailed by a reluctance to embark upon an analysis of the piece. The tune itself is one that Louis and King Oliver wrote for Oliver's band back in 1923. As recorded by that band (under the title 'Weather Bird Rag') it is a spritely tune in three-part march format, amply suited in its simple chord structure to the joyful, stomping treatment, full of breaks and driving ensemble, that it receives. The way that Louis and Earl convert it into a bravura performance of enormous complexity has such a feeling of spontaneity and freshness that detailed discussion of it brings to mind Duke Ellington's cautionary dictum about critics: 'They take a flower and say "Isn't that beautiful" . . . then, to show how beautiful it is they pull off the petals, strip the leaves, split the stem and in the end—no flower!'

In *Early Jazz*, Gunther Schuller dissects 'Weather Bird' with a musician's care, including a chart of the latter part of the record when the two musicians abandon the set format of the tune in order to challenge each other more keenly with phrases hurled across an irregular number of bars. I mention this not only to direct the reader to a fine piece of critical analysis but also to warn him, when it comes to listening to the record, that if, as I did for some years, he tries to link the Armstrong/Hines exchanges to the original shape of the tune, he is inviting a brainstorm.

The introduction epitomises swing. The notes are not only timed with split-second accuracy, but each one has a spring and resilience of its own. In the very first chorus we see how Louis and Earl propose to go about things. Louis takes care of the melody, more like a snake than a bird in its curling and twisting lines. Hines clearly has no intention of merely providing 'oom-chah' accompaniment. He realises quite well that, between them, he and his partner have enough innate rhythmic sense to carry the beat without assistance, and he is content therefore to suggest it from time to time, but otherwise to leave it to be implied while he places stabbing chords all around it in the most exhilarating way. Meanwhile, as I noted in the chapter on Jimmy Noone which introduced Hines, he had devised his 'trumpet-style' octave playing in the right hand that enabled him to play forceful melodic lines to match those of any blowing instrument. Using this technique and applying it to the lower half of the keyboard, he is able here to furnish a counter-melody to Armstrong's lead. Whether he was influenced by Armstrong's phraseology or simply thought along the same lines, the result is the nearest one could get, on the days before electrical 'dubbing', to *two* Louis Armstrongs in duet.

The reader will be well practised by now at picking out little gems of construction and invention from an Armstrong performance of this period. 'Weather Bird' is not an easy tune to play, especially on trumpet. Its melody line weaves and dodges in a way that defies supple phrasing, and yet Louis gets around it with the poised agility of a lightweight boxer limbering up. Listen to the fifth and sixth bars of the opening theme, where he gives the awkward phrase a special sinuousness by allowing the three notes at the very end of bar five to vanish practically out of earshot. This device pre-dated by some seventeen years a favourite dodge of the modern 'bebop' musicians led by Charlie Parker and Dizzy Gillespie. Then the practice of barely articulating certain notes in a long and rapid phrase in order to give it rhythmic variation became known as 'ghosting' the notes. Louis does it throughout 'Weather Bird' as though born to the idea.

To get a notion of how Armstrong's instinctive rhythmic ideas are assisted and, no doubt, triggered off by Earl Hines, stop a while at the fourth bar of the secondary theme. Here again there is a bit of melody which, in the original King Oliver version, is a raggy, symmetrical phrase punctuated by short breaks. We know from previous examples that Louis Armstrong, like all the great solo-builders who followed him, had a built-in radar which foresaw and automatically steered away from dully symmetrical phrases. In this instance, he alters the second matching phrase by extending it across that fourth bar with a legato triplet of quarternotes. Simultaneously, Earl Hines suspends the steady left-hand rhythm and substitutes instead one of his octave 'trumpet' phrases, very Louis-ish in its conception right down to the suggestion of a whip-up at the beginning. The result is a stroke of musical wit of which any composer, having laboured over it for days and nights, would feel justifiably proud. That it emerged in the course of a few minutes' spontaneous improvisation is nothing less than a miracle.

But such miracles abound in 'Weather Bird'. Take, for example, the rhythmic gymnastics with which Earl Hines challenges himself when it comes to his turn to play a solo variation on the secondary theme. Anyone who is not quite sure up to now what 'trumpet-style' means apropos Earl's piano-playing will find here a perfect example. He leaps straightaway into a bit of melodic improvisation hammered out in octaves that could have come straight from the trumpet of Louis Armstrong, complete with a vigorous tremolo in the fourth bar that simulates the trumpeter's rapid vibrato or 'shake'. After the halfway mark, however, he abandons this in favour of a percussive, hand-to-hand karate assault on the basic rhythm, throwing the accents to and fro in a cavalier fashion which must have frightened the daylights out of every other pianist within earshot. In a television interview when he was around seventy years of age, Hines spoke of his habit of constantly exploring new harmonic devices to reach a certain point in a familiar tune. He said, in effect, 'I'll never take the same route twice—and when you see me smile, that means I'm lost!' Similarly, he has never outgrown an apparent compulsion to try and trip himself up rhythmically, chopping the beat up in such a way that, many times, the listener is encouraged to believe that he is lost, only to find when the regular rhythm is resumed that he has not missed a fraction of the beat.

This rhythmic challenge, thrown at Louis Armstrong and eagerly taken up, is what eventually elevates 'Weather Bird' to the level of a supreme masterpiece. We get a hint of what is to come when, after Louis Armstrong has played a reprise of the first theme, there is a short interlude or 'bridge' into the third strain. Gunther Schuller sets out this passage in conventional notation. The complex result looks more like a chemical formula than a piece of music. I can testify to the fact that, fifty-odd years later, the bridge remains impossibly difficult to play solo with any degree of conviction. For two musicians to create it spontaneously and successfully at one attempt (there was no second 'take' of 'Weather Bird') leads us once again into the realm of miracle.

From here on, the piece builds with mounting complexity. For the listener who finds the trumpet/piano exchanges hard to follow, it is helpful to know that, once Earl Hines has taken a full 16-bar piano solo on the third theme, the duettists pay little heed to the actual shape of that theme. On paper, they are simply splitting the sixteen bars into two sections in which a two-bar break is followed by six bars of duet. Reading 'ensemble' for 'duet', this is the format that is followed on the original King Oliver recording. But in that performance, notwithstanding its exhilarating drive, there is nothing to confuse or tax the mind—every cadence is in its predictable place, clearly signalled. What Louis and Earl do is to ignore the natural rise and fall of what is, after all, a pretty basic theme and to play instead a catch-me-if-you-can game with fragments of free melody no more than one or two bars in length. The result is that when they return to base each time with a four-bar phrase identical to the ending of the very first theme, that phrase often appears to crop up in the wrong place. In its way, this final section of 'Weather Bird', leading inexorably to the complex coda out of which Louis climbs triumphantly to a high C finish, comes nearer to the ultra-modern conception of 'free improvisation' than anything that was to be recorded in the Thirties or Forties. Only by purging his mind of preconceptions and abandoning it to the music can the listener do full justice to its glories.

Luis Russell

EMILE COUÉ, the French psychotherapist whose advocacy of Auto-Suggestion had as much impact on America immediately after World War I as the music of the Original Dixieland Jazz Band, coined the therapeutic slogan 'Every day, and in every way, I am getting better and better'. As a cure for individual depression and self-doubt, it may well be effective. But when it comes to mankind's outlook in general, no such slogan is necessary. It is an understandable human tendency for each new generation to speak of any kind of development—in education, technology, scientific discovery, the arts—in terms of improvement. Without any semantic justification, the word 'progress', meaning simply 'to move forward', is taken to imply a move *upwards* in the direction of something better or more valuable.

If we are discussing civilisation, in the sense of learning how to live together sensibly and comfortably, the concept of gradual improvement is not altogether absurd. It is possible to picture an ultimate goal, a vague Utopia in which today's wrongs are eventually righted. Bringing it down to its most mundane and materialistic level, we can at least argue that, in having our houses heated by radiators or concealed wiring, we have 'progressed' from mediaeval times when they piled logs in the middle of the living-room floor.

When we apply this interpretation of 'progress' to the arts—and jazz writers have been arch-offenders in this over the years—we are on much more hazardous ground. Progress towards what? 'The Search for Truth' is the nearest that philosophers have come to formulating an artistic goal to which all the creating and exploring and theorising aspires. And it doesn't get us very far. Deprived of even the foggiest notion of what Perfection is, we nonetheless cling to a touching belief that we are moving towards it. One jazz 'history' written in America in the Fifties (its very partisanship in that highly partisan era has happily led to its own relegation to past history, so I have no need to identify it) epitomised this belief. Taking the 'modern jazz' of that time as a criterion in which he could apparently see no blemish, the author treated the work of all the early jazzmen—with the obligatory exception of Louis Armstrong—with massive condescension, splashing words like 'crude' and 'primitive' about and conceding to them little merit other than that they 'paved the way' for the glorious things to come. One might say, in mitigation, that he was over-reacting against the vociferous New Orleans Revival movement which at that time was putting forward the equally insubstantial view that Utopia, in the form of the 'pure' New Orleans style, had already been and gone. The advocates of 'modernism' and 'traditionalism' were—and in some areas still are—both making the same mistake in criticising musicians for the tools that they used, rather than in the light of the use they made of them.

This brief homily has been necessary because, in the course of this survey of some of the jazz masterpieces, a theme has emerged. In talking about it, I am bound, short of tedious circumlocution, to use the words 'progress' and 'advance', and I want to make it clear that these imply no judgement, for or against, on things that simply happened. I made the point, in the chapter on Bix Beiderbecke, that rhythms—and the same goes for the various conjunctions of notes which we call harmonies—do not themselves go in and out of fashion or supersede each other. They just exist, to be used or misused. Let's take the two most striking examples of musicians who were 'ahead of their time'. Louis Armstrong, from the first recording that he made, showed an instinctive feeling for rhythms more complex than those employed by most of his contemporaries. Bix Beiderbecke, a devotee of Debussy and Maurice Ravel, revealed in his solos (on piano especially) a familiarity with the harmonic devices of modern

European music which jazz musicians in general did not acquire for almost a decade. The prophetic aspect of their genius was amazing, to be sure. But it was not this that made their music great. For a long time after each musician was first heard on record, superb jazz was played which owed nothing to their example. Had Bix never lived, it was inevitable that musicians would eventually have made use of the harmonic ideas that already existed in the works of the modern European composers. Louis Armstrong's impact on the rhythmic notions of the time was rather more fundamental, for reasons which I shall come to in a moment. But even so, it was during his lifetime that musicians such as Horace Silver and Herbie Hancock chose to revert, in much of their work, to the once 'corny' eight-to-a-bar rhythm from which Louis departed. And contemporary jazz–rock music has gone on to make a new fashion out of the old-fashioned beat. If we measure musical stature simply in terms of quasi-scientific discovery, then both Louis and Bix were made totally redundant when avant-garde musicians in the Sixties discarded the whole notion of basic harmony and regular metre as having been exhausted. From which cautionary tale we learn that we would be wise to avoid the assertion, so often made, that artists like Louis and Bix were great because they influenced generations, and to stick to the safer premise that they influenced generations because they were great!

The theme that runs through every chapter so far has been the gradual change in the rhythmic approach to jazz improvisation and writing during the Twenties. It may be thought that I have given too much attention to this, and not enough to the melodic-cum-harmonic advances which were made. But if we leave out of account the experiments which Bix Beiderbecke and some of his white associates and disciples made in adapting the sophisticated harmonies of modern European music to jazz—experiments which were not taken up and extended on any large scale until the end of the Thirties—we find that the chordal foundation on which jazz musicians improvised were limited to virtually the same simple harmonic progressions, borrowed from European church and military music, which underpinned New Orleans music. Indeed, it was well into the decade before some very elementary extensions of the basic diatonic system were fully assimilated. I noted, in the chapter on Louis Armstrong's 'Potato Head Blues', that Johnny Dodds was not altogether at home with the harmonies. Specifically, there is a point in the twenty-eighth bar of his solo when, against the D seventh chord of the tune, he plays his break resolutely on the tonic chord of F. Recorded in 1927, this aberration harks back to some of the King Oliver band recordings four years earlier when, in blues that are pitched in B flat, the rhythm section (guided no doubt by the classically-trained Lil Armstrong) started in the eighth bar the now familiar alternative sequence of G seventh, C seventh, F seventh, B flat, while the front-line men pursued the simpler course of B flat, F seventh, B flat. Years later, when the New Orleans Revival brought into the limelight musicians who had never left the city, a similar indifference to harmonies other than the basic blues chords, especially in the sequence which I have just outlined, was noticeable in recordings by, for instance, George Lewis's Band.

But the relatively slow harmonic growth of jazz in the Twenties is not my only reason for putting emphasis on the rhythmic changes. Harmony, in the specific sense of a system of chord 'progressions' on which melody is based, is not an essential ingredient of music. Nowadays, most of us are familiar with the sound of Indian *raga*, which makes no use of that kind of harmony. African drum ensembles, dispensing with both harmony and melody and concentrating instead on rhythm and pitch, achieve a rhythmic complexity far beyond anything that Beethoven could possibly have conceived.

Spokesmen for Western civilisation reach for the word 'primitive' whenever they encounter a music with strong rhythmic foundations. It is a word which cropped up frequently when critics and record reviewers, brought up in a predominantly European culture, first turned their attention to jazz recordings. Their preoccupation with harmonic elegance and the genteel manners of the concert-hall led all but the most perceptive to patronise, if not openly condemn, musicians like Johnny Dodds or Jelly Roll Morton while turning with unfeigned relief to the polite and house-trained music of Red Nichols. The London

Melody Maker, in its infant days in the late Twenties, affirmed, in chorus with many other critical organs, that the records by Red Nichols represented 'the ultimate in "hot" style'. Their record reviewer was not entirely deaf to the charms of Johnny Dodds, conceding, in the introductory remarks about one of his recordings, that 'the nigger has a heart as big as his great woolly head'. To be fair to that paper, it was one of the first to run any kind of regular review of jazz recordings, and within a very few years the fine critic and musician Spike Hughes, writing under the name of 'Mike', was urging its readers to turn away from Nichols and lend an ear to the music of such men as Armstrong, Ellington and the great soloists in Fletcher Henderson's Orchestra.

But the fact remains that, at the outset, critical appraisal of jazz demanded that the basic European rules of harmony should be observed. As late as the Forties and Fifties, the New Orleans Revival focused attention on some unknown elders who had remained, semi-active in music, in the city of New Orleans throughout the lifetime of jazz. Their music was frequently derided, even by those who were amiably disposed towards the traditional forms of jazz, as being 'out of tune' and riddled with 'wrong chords'. I put those terms in quotes not because the allegations are untrue by European standards, but because they are irrelevant by the standards of the musicians concerned. It transpired that the music of, for example, Jelly Roll Morton's Red Hot Peppers at their best did not represent the earliest form of jazz, as many people had believed—especially those who had already labelled it 'primitive'. On the contrary, it appeared to be a comparatively polished culmination of the New Orleans tradition. If we listen to recordings made around the same time by Sam Morgan's Band, still operating in New Orleans, we hear something much more like the music that George Lewis was to introduce about twenty years later. This is music in which the building up of rhythmic impetus and complexity clearly had higher priority than the harmonic conventions.

A perfect example of what I mean was recorded by George Lewis and his band in 1944. The number they chose to play was a ragtime composition by James Scott called 'Climax Rag'—a tune, incidentally, which Morton also tackled in quite a different way in a 1939 session shortly before his death. Like all ragtime pieces, the composition has more than one theme and goes through quite a range of conventional harmonic patterns. The Lewis Band launches into the piece like a cavalry charge getting under way, scattering 'wrong chords' in all directions. Half-way through the record, when the simpler final theme has been safely reached, they have attained a smooth gallop, careering along with a joyful abandon. I once played this record on an old-fashioned portable record-player with the sound turned down to a whisper and my hand resting on the closed lid of the machine. In this situation, what came through to me strongest was the rhythm of the music, transmitted through the lid to my hand. It was an extraordinary experience to feel the complex vibrations at my finger-tips and to realise that, with the melodic and harmonic content almost completely faded out, what was left was something much nearer to an African drum ensemble than a conventional jazz band, an exciting and compelling tapestry of rhythms.

George Lewis and his men led us to see that there was a phase, in the very early days of jazz, when conventional harmony played a minor role. One thing that listeners brought up on the Dixieland music of the Twenties and Thirties noticed when the so-called primitive end of the New Orleans jazz spectrum came to light was that the trumpet, clarinet and trombone players did not always deploy themselves into separate three-part harmonies, but played the melody virtually in unison with a certain amount of that sour but evocative dissonance which one finds in the instrumental folk-music in many areas of the world. And, of course, the very same pattern existed in the development of the blues, which did not reach the formalised harmonic framework of the 'twelve-bar blues' until a fairly sophisticated stage in its evolution.

Once conventional European rules of harmony had been assimilated into jazz, it was inevitable that jazz musicians would begin to explore, as a basis for improvisation, the ramifications which already existed in so-called 'classical music'. In the mid-Thirties, the trumpeter Roy Eldridge deliberately sharpened his facility and speed so that he could 'run changes' like a saxophone player—in other words, base his improvisation on the notes of a rapidly-changing progression of chords. Bebop, the earliest manifestation of modern jazz in the Forties, demanded even greater agility from the soloist, to the extent that, inexorably, the reserves of feasible 'new' harmonies were exhausted. What the advance guard of jazz improvisers have been doing from the late Fifties onwards is to search for a new basis of improvisation once 'running changes' no longer presented a challenge. This is not the place or time to go into them all, but it is sufficient to say that, in advanced forms of jazz in the Seventies, harmony in the sense of chord progressions has become redundant. Indeed, in some extreme instances, linear melody too has been spurned, with identifiable notes being replaced by sounds and harmony giving way to 'texture'.

It is possible, then, to imagine a history of jazz in the foreseeable future which will treat harmonic development as an episode through which the music passed. The concept of rhythm is not so easily shrugged off. Any two notes—or even sounds—that follow each other in time suggest a rhythm. The very movements that are used to produce the sounds—the raising and lowering of a stick or mallet, the action of the fingers on keys or valves, the actual breathing between phrases—contain their own rhythm (anyone who saw Louis Armstrong in action will remember how, holding the fingers of his right hand stiff, he whacked them down on the trumpet valves as if he were tapping a drum). While some avant garde musicians long ago discarded what is generally accepted as melody and harmony in their work, it would be a brave and foolhardy musical revolutionary who harboured ambitions to divest his music of rhythm. The outward symptom of rhythm is that forward-moving impetus which jazz people call 'swing'. It is significant that the devotees of ultra-modern performers who have discarded all the normal rhythmic conventions such as regular tempo, bar-lines and time-signatures still assert that their music 'swings', thereby implying that somewhere at the heart of seeming chaos a rhythmic pulse is beating.

So it can be argued—and I have been arguing it for the past few pages—that the really fundamental changes in jazz over the years, changes that have distinguished one style or epoch from another, have been rhythmic. On this premise we can specify more accurately still the theme which links these jazz masterpiece^s of the Twenties. It is one of musicians slowly coming to term^s with the new rhythmic concept revealed in the work of Bessie Smith, Sidney Bechet and, above all, Louis Armstrong. In almost every recording (Jelly Roll Morton's being a notable exception) there are signs of rhythmic schizophrenia, whether it be Louis conflicting with his colleagues in King Oliver's Band and the Hot Five or Bix overcoming the two-beat straitjacket of Trumbauer's Orchestra. And yet, within a very few years everyone, from the West to the East, was swinging away in the loose-limbed 12/8 manner over a steady, thrusting four-in-a-bar beat. There must, one feels, be a missing link somewhere between the records I have discussed so far and the jazz that was to earn for the Thirties the title of the Swing Era.

Indeed, there was such a link, and it is to be found in the Luis Russell Band in general and in the playing of George 'Pops' Foster in particular. Luis Russell, born in Panama, moved to New Orleans in his teens. In Chicago in the Twenties, he spent several years in the rather cumbersome band which Joe Oliver led after the break-up of the Creole Jazz Band, showing himself on records to be an indifferent pianist whose solos had a disconcerting habit of parting company with the rest of the rhythm section and running uncontrollably downhill. His talents clearly lay in organisation. When Oliver's Band played in New York in 1927, Joe Oliver was offered, and refused, a residency at the new Cotton Club, and the job went, with historic results, to the young Duke Ellington. It was no doubt managerial gaffes such as this that disaffected several of Oliver's ambitious sidemen, including Luis Russell. He left Oliver and, within months had become leader of his own band in New York, gathering together a highly talented team of musicians, several of whom had been with King Oliver. With Ellington and Fletcher Henderson already established in the city, the arrival of trumpeter Henry Red Allen, clarinettist Albert Nicholas, trombonist J. C. Higginbotham and drummer Paul Barbarin to join Russell, not forgetting the brilliant Boston-born altoist Charlie Holmes who was already on hand, led to a formidable concentration of jazz talent in Harlem from 1927 onwards, and one which swiftly transferred the focal point of jazz from

Chicago to New York.

George 'Pops' Foster, who joined Russell in 1929 and whose contribution to the band's style will be discussed in detail later, gave an idea in his autobiography of how the Russell band operated at that time. 'We worked seven days a week and we loved it. We'd rather be working than be at home. It was like it was back in New Orleans. Back then I used to sit around wishing I could go to work. It was a pleasure to work in those days. Russell's band was romping so good in twenty-nine we had everything sewed up around New York. We were playing the same style we played in early New Orleans.'

Anyone scouring the personnel of the band on record sleeve or in a discography might well raise an eyebrow at the last sentence. For by the standards of the day, Luis Russell's Orchestra, with two or three brass, three saxophones and a four-piece rhythm section, was nearer to a full-sized dance band than a small New Orleans-style ensemble. And at first hearing, the recordings themselves confirm this impression. The band not only romped, it roared. Using arrangements for the introductions, statement of the themes, modulations and solo backings, the five or six front-line instruments often played as a single section, moving en bloc in a striking departure from the polyphonic New Orleans pattern. Sometimes, coming nearer to the modified New Orleans style which King Oliver had used once saxophones had invaded his band, two of the saxophones were given a busy, bustling part to read while trumpet, clarinet and trombone improvised loosely around them. And sometimes again it was each man for himself in a mêlée of collective improvisation.

What gave the Russell Band its great feeling of informality and joie de vivre was the manner in which the arrangements were played—and this in turn arose from the musical personalities and backgrounds of the musicians themselves. The trumpeter Henry Allen was clearly and audibly a disciple of Louis Armstrong, achieving much of Armstrong's luxuriant, fur-lined tone. The facet of Louis which Allen took to naturally was the intense, dramatic and sometimes wild playing, full of slurred notes and impassioned 'shakes', with which Louis brought high drama to blues and stomps alike. Where Allen differed from Louis—and

by the time he joined Russell he was very much his own man—
was in the direction in which this high emotional intensity pushed
him. Where Louis would harness it to his strong feeling for
structure to produce majestically-conceived and very explicit
melodies, Allen was given to more oblique utterances, building
up a mood, an impression, with tense bursts of sound rather than
creating a new melody as Louis did. Henry Allen's own masterpiece, 'Feelin' Drowsy', recorded in the same period, is a fine
example of this 'impressionist' approach, one which anticipates,
by thirty years or so, the avant garde musicians who 'painted
pictures' in sound. Allen's emotional temperament happily spilled
over into his ensemble-playing, with the result that he paid more
attention to the spirit than the letter of Luis Russell's arrangements. The relaxed, joyous feeling that illuminates almost every
Luis Russell recording in 1929/30 springs to a high degree from
the loose interpretation which Allen put on the arrangements in
front of him.

The trombonist J. C. Higginbotham was a perfect foil for
Allen, and indeed they struck up a musical partnership which
lasted on and off into the Fifties. If the credit for first giving the
jazz trombone a fluent solo voice belongs to Miff Mole, it has
always seemed to me unjust that Higginbotham's name is rarely
put at the very top of the list of those who geared that mobility
to the fast and furious pace of jazz in the late Twenties. The use
of saxophone sections, albeit small to begin with, to supply a full
set of harmonies to the ensemble relieved the trombone of a great
part of its harmonic role. You will not hear J. C. Higginbotham
pumping out the root harmonies in the manner of the New
Orleans 'tailgate' men. Much of the time he can be heard providing
an independent part at the lower end of the ensemble, its impassioned tones reminiscent of the free harmonising of the bass
singer in a black gospel choir. His solo work was quite unrivalled
in the Twenties for its mobility and ferocious attack. He overcame
the heavy-handedness inherent in the instrument's awkward
mechanism by a lip-control that could produce fast trills and
'slurs', the latter being the technical term for a rapid alternating
between notes a major or minor third apart. It is a rare Higginbotham solo that does not utilise either or both of these effects.

Albert Nicholas, a contemporary of Louis Armstrong's and a boyhood friend of Sidney Bechet, was a Creole (in New Orleans the name was given the French pronunciation, 'Nicola') who inclined naturally to the fluent, technically-agile style epitomised by Jimmy Noone. With a tone which was drier and less seductive than Noone's, Nicholas nonetheless followed Noone's way of weaving and dodging through the ensemble, using the whole range of the instrument and occasionally starting a downward run with a piercing and electrifying high note.

The career of Charlie Holmes epitomises the chance factor in the entertainment business. He was born in Boston where his boyhood friends were Harry Carney and Johnny Hodges. Holmes moved into New York with Harry Carney in 1927, and when Carney almost immediately went into the Ellington Band, Charlie Holmes might well have joined the Duke too, on Carney's recommendation. But when a vacancy did arise in the Ellington Band, it was Johnny Hodges who caught the leader's eye, or ear. Judging from recordings at that time, there was very little to choose between the two alto men, who played in much the same style. Jazz history records fully how Hodges, working in a band which was built around the individual 'voices' of its soloists, flourished with Ellington and became, in effect, the first great master of the alto saxophone in jazz. With Luis Russell, Charlie Holmes contributed some fine solos, comparable to those that Hodges recorded with Ellington. But by the standard of Duke Ellington's own oft-quoted definition of success—'doing the right thing at the right time, in the right place, before the right people'—Charlie Holmes was in the wrong place in Luis Russell's band. The roaring, stomping band of the period under discussion declined, in the 1930s, into a quite ordinary big band whose work was undistinguished by talented arrangements or original compositions. When the band was virtually taken over by Louis Armstrong in the mid-Thirties, the scope for its other soloists, on record at least, dwindled further. Charlie Holmes remained until 1940 and thereafter sank into obscurity and partial retirement from music. Listening to his solos throughout his time with Russell, and especially in the 1929/30 period, it is hard to understand how a career could so sadly misfire.

The other important and influential member of the Luis Russell Band was its bassist, George 'Pops' Foster. Born on a Louisiana plantation in or around 1892, Foster moved into New Orleans at the age of ten, so it is fair to speak of him as one of the distinguished breed of New Orleans bass-players whose talents we have already encountered in the work of Bill Johnson with Johnny Dodds and John Lindsay with Jelly Roll Morton. In *Early Jazz*, Gunther Schuller analyses in some detail the peculiar qualities shown by these string-men from the Crescent City. Some early jazz 'histories', ill-informed and badly researched, gave the false impression that the original bass instrument in jazz was the brass tuba, which at some time in the Twenties was superseded by the double bass. To this oversimplification was added the frivolous and unlikely legend that an unnamed bass-player in a Dixieland Band once broke his bow in the excitement of the moment and there and then invented the plucked-string, or pizzicato style. The facts, borne out by reference to photographs of early New Orleans bands, are that most of those bands from the very first days of jazz used string basses in a sedentary or indoor situation. Marching bands would use the tuba for the obvious reason that it is easier to carry and has a greater volume. To get regular work, most bass-players would naturally 'double' on both in-struments. With the arrival of recording in the Twenties, similar adjustments had to be made. In the primitive days when bands simply huddled round a huge cone-shaped horn, it was no doubt difficult for a string bass to get a note in edgeways. We have seen how two important bands, the King Oliver Creole Band and Louis Armstrong's Hot Five, dispensed with a bass instrument altogether, delegating its role to the pianist, banjoist or, in some Oliver performances, a bass saxophone. Another obvious solution was the tuba, whose incisiveness and audibility compensated, for a while, for the lack of mobility and versatility which eventually rendered it obsolete.

In extolling the superior capacity to 'swing' of the string bass, Gunther Schuller drew overdue attention to the great variety of rhythmic subtlety which bassist John Lindsay contributed to Jelly Roll Morton's recordings. 'We can hear how perfectly he alternated the basic two-beat rhythm (2/2) with the hard-driving

4/4s on one hand and whole-note single beat passages on the other. These changes of pace do not occur at phrase junctures, but are apt to break in at any point in the sixteen and twenty-bar phrases, balancing with and reacting to the soloists and ensembles.' The style was not John Lindsay's alone. We have come across it to great advantage on the Johnny Dodds recordings with Bill Johnson. Students of Duke Ellington's recordings with the great New Orleans bassist Wellman Braud will call to mind many instances of an ensemble or solo passage being given a sudden rhythmic boost when the bassist switches from two to four beats in the bar in response to innate musical instinct. And in Pops Foster's own autobiography as told to Tom Stoddard, Foster recalls that 'in New Orleans we'd have two pick notes in one bar, then you'd go to six bars of bowing, and maybe have one note to pick.'

Pops Foster was no musical theoretician. When I first met him and heard him in the flesh at the 1948 International Jazz Festival at Nice, we had in our British contingent a bass-player of 'modern' inclinations who, though little impressed by Pops Foster's 'old-fashioned' style, felt that he should approach the famous man for some advice. The response he got left him more bewildered than ever. 'When you get tired, stop playing and smile at the girls.' The American bassist Bill Crow, quoted in the Foster autobiography, was once equally dismayed to hear Pops expounding his harmonic theory in a New York club between sets: 'Hell, I just play any old go-to-hell note, as long as it swings!'

When these sage utterances were recorded, Pops Foster was approaching his sixtieth year, and he may have felt that he had handed out enough free advice for one lifetime. Whether or not he ever formulated his musical ideas more concisely, he was certainly a musician who knew what was required in any musical circumstance—and how to deliver it. What was required in the New York-centred jazz of the late Twenties was a coherent rhythm section style to complement the new rhythmic ideas that had stemmed from Louis Armstrong and were rapidly being assimilated into all of jazz—something, in fact, to resolve the rhythmic schizophrenia which was apparent in most of the recordings hitherto discussed. The tuba, short-winded and slow to move, had helped to perpetuate a stolid two-in-a-bar backing when the general movement was in the direction of a steady, surging four-in-a-bar. Soloists, becoming in Armstrong's wake ever more fleet and ambitious, demanded rhythmic support which sustained their fluent and thrusting improvisations. The answer was already to hand, within the armoury of the New Orleans bassists. Their big, resonant notes, endowed with what wine-bibbers call 'length', had, since they first appeared on record in the mid-Twenties, conformed to the relaxed twelve-eight feeling that Louis Armstrong introduced. The rhythmic variety—two beats here, four there, and occasionally just one—that Gunther Schuller noted, contained an element which Pops developed into a speciality. He played a four-beat style and 'when I went to New York playing that way, everybody wanted to do it. Right after that, about 1929 or 1930, they started writing arrangements that way, with a four-to-the-bar bass part.'

Here we are, then, on the threshold of the Thirties, a decade that was shortly to blossom into the Swing Era. Benny Goodman and his Orchestra, streamlining many of the arrangements already recorded by Fletcher Henderson, were soon to spearhead the attack by big band jazz upon a mass audience, a development which led jazz historians, ready for easy answers, to trace the seeds of Swing Music in all its ramifications to the Henderson Band exclusively. But if it is continuity we are after, it would be sounder to start with the rhythmically mature rhythm of the Luis Russell Band, whose pumping, four-in-a-bar beat dominated by the bass is surely a natural forerunner of the Count Basie rhythm section with Walter Page, the Duke Ellington rhythm section with Jimmy Blanton, the Woody Herman Herds with Chubby Jackson and his successors, and indeed those often frenetic but wildly swinging jam-sessions that have been staged under the banner of 'Jazz At The Philharmonic'.

I have chosen 'Panama' from the repertoire of Luis Russell recordings because, from its opening bars, it typifies this rhythmic maturity. It needs to be said at the start that 'Panama', originally a stately dance tune by Will Tyers, consists of four distinct themes, the first of which is dispensed with in this arrangement. It is characteristic of the Russell band's headlong, let's-get-going approach that after a jaunty introduction it goes straight into the final rip-roaring theme with Pops Foster driving it along four-to-a-bar as if time was already running out. Here is the band phrasing en bloc with that passionate abandon which, if it lacked the meticulous precision of the leading white bands of the period, certainly saved the arrangement from the clipped jerkiness which puts a date on so many of the big band performances in the early Thirties. This is particularly applicable as the band moves in similar style into the second theme, which has in this arrangement some choppy and angular phrases which need—and receive—relaxed interpretation to round off the sharper corners. There is a long and, in musicians' terminology, 'round the houses' modulation from E flat to A flat in which, through some wide gaps, we get an uninterrupted sound of Pops Foster's magnificently resilient and sonorous bass tone. In his autobiography, he explained: 'When we used to pick the bass we'd hold on to the bow at the same time, now they have little things called bowcaddies you put the bow in while you pick. I still usually hold on to the bow while I pick unless I'm going to slap the strings too.' We can see why in 'Panama', for within seconds of pumping out those muscular pizzicato 'breaks', Pops is underlining the legato character of the third theme with some rich two-in-a-bar bowing under Henry Allen's solo.

It is difficult to describe in words the furnace-hot thirty-two bars which Allen contributes here. If we take the word 'hot' literally, then all the manifestations of heat are there—a searing tone, steaming energy, phrases that leap like flames and then die off in a wisp of smoke. Throughout the forthcoming Thirties—and indeed on into the era of modern jazz—trumpeter-players in bands far bigger than Luis Russell's were to be called on to rise up (often under the gaze of Hollywood cameras) and generate spontaneous excitement with wild and high-flying solos. Few ever did so as naturally and constructively as Henry 'Red' Allen. His great strength is that he made no forced effort to 'swing'. Indeed, he sometimes seems deceptively to be striving in the very opposite direction, stringing a phrase lazily across the beat in a manner very typical of several New Orleans trumpet-men—Louis Armstrong to some degree, Lee Collins very markedly. This very controlled pacing of a solo, in however scorching a tempo, rendered Red Allen's work invariably passionate and exciting but never hysterical.

In 'Panama', the superb J. C. Higginbotham follows hot (in every sense) on Henry Allen's heels. When one thinks of the limited role which the trombone had played in jazz for most of the Twenties—the inflexibility of its tone, the awkwardness of its action and its inability to do more than grunt and stutter at fast tempos, then one can only marvel at the strides which a single generation of trombonists starting with Jimmy Harrison and Jack Teagarden and spreading to Higginbotham, Benny Morton and Claude Jones, made in the space of a few years. Here, Higginbotham's solo abounds with his familiar trade marks—the agile phrasing, ferocious 'shakes' and whooping incursions into the high register. Later, between two ensemble choruses, he comes up with another, a burst of machine-gun quavers that tumble chromatically in a sort of rhumba rhythm with accents on the first, fourth and seventh quaver.

If the trombone can be said at this stage to have been fully emancipated from its brass band role, then the tenor saxophone, only recently given an authoritative voice by Coleman Hawkins, had yet to come of age in similar fashion. Greely Walton was by no means an inferior player by the standards of the day, but the hollow, rather puddingy tone and flat, unexpressive phrasing fixes his solo in an era when the instrument was still on the threshold of its full flowering. After him, the ensemble takes over again, flaring up after the trombone break into what is usually the climactic, or in jazz terminology, 'ride-out' chorus of the tune. Such was the informality of recording in those days that we cannot be absolutely sure that the band did not intend to end there, but received a signal that there was more time in hand. Certainly there is a brief moment of indecision at the end of the chorus, in which the redoubtable Pops Foster holds things up virtually single-handed. And from this point until the end of the record, there is no more formal arrangement—things simply career onwards in what was later to become the characteristic jam-session style.

Whatever the truth of the matter, we end up with more treats in store. First, Albert Nicholas leaps in with a bustling clarinet solo couched very much in the manner of his idol Jimmy Noone but with more spiky asperity in the tone. Then Charlie Holmes takes over to show that any reservations which we may have about the tenor saxophone in this period does not apply to the alto. There are still vestiges of the 'running' clarinet style in his playing, but the phrasing has great swing and buoyancy and the tone and vibrato have shed all trace of the cloying sentimentality which the instrument had always assumed in its dance-band environment. In this period and for many years to come, solos by Charlie Holmes invariably provided unmitigated pleasure.

One aspect of this alto solo is worth discussion, and that is the spontaneous backing which the rest of the front-line, dominated by Henry Allen, play behind Holmes. Riffs, that is to say short phrases or figures repeated over and over with minimal alteration to accommodate changing harmonies, have been a feature of jazz for years. And not only of jazz. Anyone who ever heard Negro church music—often called 'gospel' music—will be familiar with the interplay between preacher and congregation or lead singer and choir. We have already come across it apropos the ring-shouts. It is the familiar 'call and response' characteristic of much black American music, being reflected in the rhythmic worksongs of the railroad and chain gangs and the relationship between early blues singers and their accompaniment. The formula is always the same, striking a contrast between the free voice of the leader and the repetitive backing from chorus or band. In the contrapuntal music of New Orleans the 'call and response' pattern was not marked, although there are traces of it in the King Oliver Band's work when Oliver, as in 'Dippermouth Blues', got to work on one of his declamatory 'wah-wah' muted cornet sermons over the ensemble. When bands began to get bigger, the enlarged front-lines were unsuitable for the New Orleans style of collective improvisation, for the simple reason that, under the pressure of an instrumental traffic-jam, the contrapuntal lines became an unholy mess. Written arrangements were an obvious solution, and where they were not available, simple formulae were devised which could easily be committed to memory and were known as 'head arrangements'. Somewhere along the line, the 'call and response' pattern, already familiar in the black churches, was brought into service as a simple way of deploying the instrumental resources. Recorded jazz abounds in examples of this formula, in which the soloist or vocalist assumes the role of the leading voice while the rest of the ensemble plays a repeated phrase or riff in response. In some of the early Count Basie Band recordings in the late Thirties, it was sometimes one section of the orchestra—the trombones, say, or the saxophones—which chanted a 'call' while the rest responded.

On the basis of very limited research I would hesitate to assert that the use of the 'call and response' formula in band jazz began with the Luis Russell Band. But I can think of no previous recorded performances in which it had been so marked. Church influence seems to have been strong in the Russell band. Several of their recorded titles reflect it—'On Revival Day', for instance, and 'Feelin' the Spirit'—and in a piece called 'Saratoga Shout', there is the first reference on record to the now ubiquitous hymn, 'When the Saints Go Marching In' (which, surprisingly, did not appear on jazz records under its own title until the same Luis Russell band, under Louis Armstrong, recorded it in 1936). When, in 'Panama', the band is finally left to its own devices, one of those devices is an exact reproduction of the modus operandi of a black church choir. While Charlie Holmes says his piece, Henry Allen leads a 'choir' behind him, chanting a three-note phrase which only changes minimally to follow the harmonies of the tune.

The essence of an effective response or riff is its monotony—which is perhaps why British and Continental jazz musicians have never been at home in this type of playing. Long before the repetition has achieved the hypnotic effect which is its main purpose, they become embarrassed and changed to something else. Luis Russell's men suffer from no such inhibition. When Charlie Holmes has finished his solo, he takes over the same riff with the remaining saxophone and the trombone while, in a curious but exciting blend of traditions, Henry Allen rides out in true New Orleans street parade style with Albert Nicholas's clarinet running rings around him and piercing the ensemble with dazzling high notes. They end with one of the extended endings so much beloved by the King Oliver Band, with Paul Barbarin's joyous tom-tom beats reminding us that his drumming, chiefly on the snares in true New Orleans style, has up to this point been the soul of rectitude and discretion. 'We'd rather be working than at home,' said Pops Foster. And listening to 'Panama', who could doubt it?

Select Bibliography

Albertson, Chris. *Bessie*. Stein & Day, 1972

Armstrong, Louis. *Satchmo: My Life in New Orleans*. Prentice-Hall, 1954

Bechet, Sidney. *Treat it Gentle*. Hill & Wang, 1960

Blesh, Rudi. *Shining Trumpets*. Da Capo Press, 1945

Blesh, Rudi, and Harriet Janis. *They All Played Ragtime*. Alfred Knopf, 1950

Brunn, H.O. *The Story of the Original Dixieland Jazz Band*. Louisiana State University Press, 1960

Chilton, John. *Who's Who in Jazz*. Chilton Book Co., 1970

Condon, Eddie. *We Called It Music*. Henry Holt and Co., 1947; Greenwood, 1948

Ellington, Duke. *Music Is My Mistress*. Da Capo Press, 1976

Feather, Leonard. *Encyclopedia of Jazz*. Horizon Press, 1960

Foster, Pops, as told to Tom Stoddard. *Pops Foster: The Autobiography of a New Orleans Jazzman*. University of California Press, 1971

Freeman, Bud. *You Don't Look Like a Musician*. Balamp Publishing, 1974

Handy, W.C. *Father of the Blues*. Macmillan, 1970

Hentoff, Nat, and Nat Shapiro. *Hear Me Talkin' To Ya*. Peter Smith, 1955

Jones, Max, and John Chilton. *Louis: The Louis Armstrong Story 1900-1971*. Studio Vista, 1971

Lomax, Alan, *Mister Jelly Roll*. Duel, Sloan and Pierce, 1950

Mezzrow, Milton and Bernard Wolfe. *Really the Blues*. Doubleday, 1972

Oliver, Paul. *The Story of the Blues*. Chilton, 1969

Rust, Brian. *Jazz Records 1897 to 1942 A-Z*. International Publications Service, 1969-70

Schuller, Gunther. *Early Jazz: Its Roots and Musical Development*. Oxford University Press, 1968

Smith, Willie "The Lion," with George Hoefer. *Music on My Mind*. Doubleday, 1964

Sudhalter, Richard, and Philip Evans. *Bix: Man and Legend*. Schirmer Books, 1975

Williams, Martin (ed.). *Jazz Panorama*. Macmillan, 1958

Discography

'Tiger Rag' *The Original Dixieland Jazz Band*
Nick LaRocca, cornet; Eddie Edwards, trombone; Larry Shields, clarinet; Henry Ragas, piano; Tony Starbaro, drums.   Any version, circa 1917–1919
'Carolina Shout' *James P. Johnson*, piano solo. October 18, 1921
'Dippermouth Blues' *King Oliver's Creole Jazz Band*
King Oliver, Louis Armstrong, cornets; Johnny Dodds, clarinet; Honoré Dutrey, trombone; Lil Hardin, piano; Bill Johnson, banjo and 'vocal'; Baby Dodds, drums.
April 6, 1923
'Wild Cat Blues' *Clarence Williams's Blues Five*
Tom Morris, cornet; John Masefield or Mayfield, trombone; Sidney Bechet, soprano saxophone; Clarence Williams, piano; Buddy Christian, banjo.   July 30, 1923
'St Louis Blues' *Bessie Smith, accompanied by*
Louis Armstrong, cornet; Fred Longshaw, harmonium.
January 14, 1925
'Nobody knows you when you're down and out' *Bessie Smith, accompanied by*
Ed Allen, cornet; Garvin Bushell, alto sax; Arville Harris, tenor sax; Clarence Williams, piano; Cyrus St Clair, tuba.
May 15, 1929
'The Original Jelly Roll Blues' *Jelly Roll Morton's Red Hot Peppers*
George Mitchell, cornet; Omer Simeon, clarinet; Kid Ory, trombone; Jelly Roll Morton, piano; Johnny St Cyr, banjo; John Lindsay, bass; Andrew Hilaire, drums.
December 16, 1926

'The Stampede' *Fletcher Henderson and his Dixie Stompers*
Russell Smith, trumpet; Rex Stewart, Joe Smith, cornets; Buster Bailey, clarinet, saxophone; Benny Morton, trombone; Coleman Hawkins, tenor saxophone, clarinet; Don Redman, alto sax, clarinet; Fletcher Henderson, piano; Charlie Dixon, banjo; Ralph Escudero, tuba; Kaiser Marshall, drums.   April 4, 1926

'Potato Head Blues' *Louis Armstrong's Hot Seven*
Louis Armstrong, trumpet; Johnny Dodds, clarinet; John Thomas, trombone; Lil Hardin Armstrong, piano; Johnny St Cyr, banjo; Pete Briggs, tuba; Baby Dodds, drums.
May 10, 1927

'Singin' the Blues' *Frankie Trumbauer's Orchestra*
Bix Beiderbecke, cornet; Bill Rank, trombone; Jimmy Dorsey, clarinet; Frankie Trumbauer, C melody sax; Itzy Riskin, piano; Eddie Lang, guitar; Chauncey Morehouse, drums.   February 4, 1927

'Black and Tan Fantasy' *Duke Ellington and his Orchestra*
Bubber Miley, cornet; Louis Metcalf, trumpet; Joe 'Tricky Sam' Nanton, trombone; Otto Hardwicke, alto sax; Harry Carney, baritone sax; Rudy Jackson, clarinet, tenor sax; Duke Ellington, piano; Fred Guy, banjo; Wellman Braud, bass; Sonny Greer, drums.
October 6, 1927

'Nobody's Sweetheart Now' *McKenzie and Condon's Chicagoans*
Jimmy McPartland, cornet; Frank Teschmacher, clarinet; Bud Freeman, tenor sax; Joe Sullivan, piano; Eddie Condon, banjo; Jim Lannigan, bass; Gene Krupa, drums.
December 8, 1927

'Bull Fiddle Blues' 'Blue Washboard Stomp' 'Weary City Blues' 'Bucktown Stomp' *Johnny Dodds's Washboard Band*
Natty Dominique, cornet; Honoré Dutrey, trombone; Johnny Dodds, clarinet; Charlie Alexander, piano; Bill Johnson, bass; Baby Dodds, drums.   July 6, 1928

'Every Evening' *Jimmy Noone's Apex Club Orchestra*
Jimmy Noone, clarinet; Joe 'Doc' Poston, alto; Earl Hines, piano; Bud Scott, banjo; Johnny Wells, drums.
May 16, 1928

'Weather Bird' *Louis Armstrong*, trumpet and *Earl Hines*, piano
December 5, 1928

'Panama' *Luis Russell and his Orchestra*

Henry Allen, trumpet; J. C. Higginbotham, trombone; Albert Nicholas, clarinet and saxophone; Charlie Holmes, alto sax; Greely Walton, tenor sax; Luis Russell, piano; Will Johnson, banjo; George 'Pops' Foster, bass; Paul Barbarin, drums.   September 5, 1930

Index